The ICT Handbook for Primary Teachers

D1647400

The ICT Handbook for Primary Teachers will help all those involved in primary education, whether in training, teaching or leadership roles, to develop the ICT knowledge, understanding and skills required to enhance children's learning in the classroom. This new edition reflects the changes to the curriculum from 2014. It includes a new section on the Computing curriculum and an overview of the reorganisation of those online agencies that serve to support ICT.

Covering theory and practice this essential handbook explores and outlines the usefulness of a wide range of up-to-date ICT resources in a range of primary contexts, and advice is offered on assessing whether ICT is preferable to other approaches for 'enhancing learning'.

With reference to supplementary online resources, providing activities, multimedia resources and further reading, the book covers: the requirements of the new Computing curriculum, the place for ICT in enhancing teaching and learning across the curriculum, using ICT in core curriculum subjects and in cross-curricular contexts, different models of e-learning (interactive whiteboards, tablet PCs, mobile devices, the Internet etc.), how ICT can be used to help pupils with special educational needs and using ICT for planning, delivery, assessment and recording.

This book is an indispensible guide to ICT for students on PGCE, BEd and undergraduate teaching courses, along with practising teachers, SENCOs, ICT coordinators and school leaders.

David Hall is a tutor and course author with the education department of Derby University where he specialises in digital education, and leadership and management. He runs the website www.primaryict.org.uk and offers publications and training courses to schools in ICT.

The ICT Handbook for Primary Teachers

A guide for students and professionals

Second edition

David Hall

Routledge
Taylor & Francis Group

LONDON AND NEW YORK

Second edition published 2015
by Routledge
2 Park Square, Milton Park, Abingdon, Oxon OX14 4RN

and by Routledge
711 Third Avenue, New York, NY 10017

Routledge is an imprint of the Taylor & Francis Group, an informa business

© 2015 David Hall

The right of David Hall to be identified as author of this work has been asserted by him in accordance with sections 77 and 78 of the Copyright, Designs and Patents Act 1988.

All rights reserved. No part of this book may be reprinted or reproduced or utilised in any form or by any electronic, mechanical, or other means, now known or hereafter invented, including photocopying and recording, or in any information storage or retrieval system, without permission in writing from the publishers.

Trademark notice: Product or corporate names may be trademarks or registered trademarks, and are used only for identification and explanation without intent to infringe.

First edition published 2010 by Routledge

British Library Cataloguing in Publication Data
A catalogue record for this book is available from the British Library

Library of Congress Cataloging-in-Publication Data
A catalog record for this book has been requested

ISBN: 978-1-138-85367-6 (hbk)
ISBN: 978-1-138-85370-6 (pbk)
ISBN: 978-1-315-72264-1 (ebk)

Typeset in Bembo by
HWA Text and Data Management, London
Printed by Ashford Colour Press Ltd, Gosport, Hants.

Contents

Illustrations

Figures

Tables

Acknowledgements

The author would like to thank all the people who contributed to the content of this book, including Tameside Authority for providing a case study on the use of Audacity and Movie Maker to support a Y4 child with MLD and ADHD in language development.

Feedback

As the reader of this book, *you* are the most important critic and commentator. Your opinion is extremely valuable no matter what it happens to be. In order to continually improve this book in future revisions, please let the author know what you have found interesting and how the content can be improved.

Send an email to: office@primaryict.org.uk.

Permissions and copyright notices

All rights in the names, trademarks, and logos of the Mozilla Foundation, including without limitation, Mozilla®, mozilla.org®, Firefox®, as well as the Mozilla logo, Firefox logo, and the red lizard logo are owned exclusively by the Mozilla Foundation. Copyright 2005–2009 Mozilla. All Rights Reserved.

Moodle is a registered trademark of the Moodle Trust.

Microsoft product screen shot(s) reprinted with permission from Microsoft Corporation.

Screen Tinter Lite © Professor David Thomson, www.thomson-software-solutions.com

Illustration from Understanding Religion reproduced with permission of Immersive Education: www.immersiveeducation.com.

Introduction

1

Introduction

Aim of the book

Technology is a key factor in everyday life and opportunities for its use in children's education and wider social development should be widely embraced.

ICT has the unique capacity and potential for developing and enlivening all domains of learning and has a significant role in helping to support learning and teaching and in managing both the curriculum and the school as a whole. Despite recent changes to the curriculum, ICT should remain a high priority.

This book will help you to develop the ICT knowledge, understanding and skills required to enhance the teaching and learning of children and the administration and management of primary schools (and the foundation stage).

A promotion of the use of technology within learning environments can only be successful if practitioners in the field have a clear idea of its benefits and are confident in its use. These are the issues which this book aims to address. The book is informed by contemporary issues, best practice in schools and the latest government initiatives.

By the end of the book you will be better positioned to:

- deliver the latest Computing/ICT/Digital Literacy curriculum;
- recognise the many ways in which ICT can enhance teaching and learning across the primary and foundation curriculum;
- incorporate a range of ICT resources (software, hardware and the Internet) into children's learning activities;
- identify a number of approaches ('models') to digital learning;
- appreciate the diversity of available ICT resources and assistive technology that can be used to support children with special educational needs (SEN);
- provide opportunities for extended learning using a learning platform and mobile devices;
- make effective use of ICT in the planning, delivery, assessment and recording of learning;
- effectively manage and lead the improvement of a school's ICT capability (and achieve the Naace ICT Mark).

Who is this book for?

The book is built around the notion that successful implementation of ICT in a school depends upon the identification, management and operation of a number of key processes. It also maintains that success depends not only on good leadership but also on the involvement of all stakeholders – teachers, teaching assistants, pupils, subject heads, technicians, SENCO, ICT coordinators and the head/deputy head teacher.

There is something in the book for all practitioners in primary schools and the early years foundation stage. It is also suitable for trainee teachers on primary PGCE, BEd and SCITT programmes, students of Education, ICT, Early Years and Early Childhood Studies degrees and local authority ICT advisers.

What does the book cover?

The development of ICT in UK schools

Offers a short, historical perspective on the use of ICT in schools since the early 1970s in terms of the resources deployed and associated developments in the school curriculum.

ICT in the National Curriculum

Examines the current national curriculum for computing/ICT/digital literacy in terms of the knowledge, skills and understanding which should be gained in primary school. This chapter presents some initial ideas for ICT activities and resources, relating them to the National Curriculum.

Using ICT to enhance literacy, numeracy and science

Two chapters that deal with the many ways in which ICT resources, used in carefully planned activities, can enhance children's learning in the core National Curriculum subjects. Emphasis is placed on the achievement of desired learning outcomes rather than simply the motivational effect of technology. The reader will be invited to participate in a variety of activities (via the author's website), carefully reflecting on each. The aim is to ascertain when and why ICT-based activities might be comparable, or indeed preferable, to conventional approaches.

ICT in non-core subjects

Follows on from the core subjects and, aside from considering the importance of ICT in each discrete subject, it introduces the notion of a cross-curricular approach to teaching, learning and assessing. In this chapter the emphasis switches toward the 'reader as researcher' and promotes an exploratory approach to the discovery of appropriate ICT 'tools' to use in other areas of the curriculum.

Models of digital learning

This chapter outlines a number of approaches to the delivery of learning. These 'models' of digital learning include interactive whiteboards, the Internet and World Wide Web, mobile learning (including tablet PCs and educational apps), learning platforms, computer-mediated communication, podcasting and vidcasting, video conferencing, computer games, subscription websites, play-based learning, visualisers and document cameras and computer configurations.

ICT and special educational needs

Investigates strategies for using ICT to support learners with a wide range of learning needs including: communication and interaction; cognition and learning; behavioural, emotional and social difficulties; sensory, physical and medical; physical disabilities; English as an additional language (EAL); and gifted and talented (G&T).

ICT management and leadership

Leadership is a crucial component in the effective application of ICT in schools. This chapter provides knowledge and skills for those with educational management roles and ICT responsibilities. It will help them to make informed decisions about the purchasing and implementation of ICT resources and activities and will consider a range of methods which will help in using ICT effectively in strategic planning, management, and leadership at all levels.

ICT resources

Outlines a process for identifying, selecting and managing software, hardware and web-based resources (including individual and aggregate purchasing). It also addresses the need to properly evaluate ICT resources before using them with children and before committing to buy. A range of possible suppliers is identified and, in addition, the potential for using open source software is explored.

How does this book compare to others?

There are of course other books on the topic of ICT but this edition of the *ICT Handbook for Primary Teachers* has the wider focus and detailed approach that make it an 'essential' read for every teacher from initial teacher training and beyond. It is a well illustrated publication which offers:

- a broad yet detailed coverage of all the important Computing and ICT issues;
- an unusual balance between practical advice and academic rigour;
- access to lots of resources in electronic format;
- listings of important publications and suppliers.

Supplementary materials

The book is supported with a number of activities, some of which require supplementary materials. These are available from the Primary ICT website at primaryict.org.uk/icthandbookv2.htm.

 Activity

The activities in the book, which include sample ICT resources, readings, presentations, videos, and audio excerpts, are highlighted by this laptop icon.
The activities are optional but offer you the opportunity to explore some of the issues in more detail.

Hyperlinks

Throughout the book you will find a number of hyperlinks to useful websites. Whilst the future stability of these links cannot be guaranteed, it is better that they are included rather than omitted. You can usually find your way to the intended information via the root of the site if the full path doesn't work.

A final thought before you begin the book

Imagine that the head of your primary school has provided you with a sum of money to spend on ICT and Computing equipment which is to be used to support the whole curriculum. The amount is limited and you certainly can't afford everything that you would like.

What would you purchase and what justification could you provide? Would you consider free software? How would you go about teaching ICT/Computing? How might you embed ICT it into the curriculum?

You might like to consider these questions whilst reading the book and, by the end, you should have most of the answers. Read on …

The development of ICT in UK schools

A brief history of computing in schools

As long ago as the early 1970s, educational researchers could appreciate that the system of didactic teaching was about to undergo a transformation. The notion that most learning is the result of teaching was, even then, an illusion. The reasons for this are many but the advent and steady development of technology has certainly played a major part.

Many teachers once feared that there was a danger of the machine replacing them in the classroom. It is hardly surprising that they were ambivalent about these devices; but the mood is ever-changing and the current model of computing in schools is one of the computer and other ICT resources as tools, rather than as teaching systems, enhancing learning rather than leading it.

The first computer terminals appeared in schools in 1970 in the guise of mini-computers. However, these were very much the preserve of administrators. By 1982 most primary schools had at least one primitive computer for the purpose of educating children (usually the BBC B model). During that decade, computing began to permeate into the curriculum in some schools under the heading of Curriculum Science.

Personal computers (PCs), in the desktop format with which we are now familiar, were available in the mid-1980s though they were prohibitively costly (£2000–£3000 each), suffered from a lack of available software and ran using pre-Windows operating systems which were not particularly user-friendly.

When the National Curriculum was introduced in 1988, technology was included as a subject in its own right. It wasn't until the mid-1990s however that the subject made any real impact and 1994/95 marked an important milestone – the introduction of the Windows 95 operating system and the formation of the World Wide Web Consortium (W3C). It was around this time that the PC was marketed to the public and began its real journey as an educational tool both in school and at home.

In 1997 the cost of computing was already falling steadily and the projection was that it would continue to do so. The prospect of realising the potential benefits of information and communication technology (ICT) became a reality and the government announced plans to encourage its widespread use by equipping schools with modern ICT facilities, creating a National Grid for Learning (NGfL) and providing organised training for teachers.

In 1998, the British Educational Communications and Technology Agency (Becta) was formed as an agency of the Department for Education and Skills (DfES). It was the government's lead partner in the strategic development and delivery of its e-strategy for schools. Becta was one of a number of key agencies that provided information and advice on ICT.

At the turn of the twenty-first century, ICT became a National Curriculum subject both as a discrete topic and as a means of supporting and enhancing learning across all subjects (including the newly introduced national literacy and numeracy strategies). The government also established Regional Broadband Consortia (RBC) which were consortia of local authorities that procured cost-effective broadband connectivity for schools in England. There were 10 RBCs covering the 150 local authorities. All of the RBCs were interconnected via the SuperJANET backbone and were collectively known as the National Education Network.

The first decade of the twenty-first century witnessed significant development in all aspects of ICT. The range of available resources increased exponentially whilst the incurred costs fell commensurately. Realistic funding provided the opportunity for the government to realise its aims; equipping schools with networked computing and Internet connectivity, training staff and providing many initiatives and projects to help schools to become 'e-enabled'. The government invested almost £6billion in schools' ICT between 1997 and 2010. Progress looked set to continue.

Where are we now (Spring 2015)?

Today, in many schools, the computer and many other ICT resources can be found in abundance. They are providing learners, teachers, administrators and management with an effective set of tools to improve the preparation and delivery of the curriculum, to enhance learning processes, to enable and empower pupils, to extend learning beyond the classroom, to reach disaffected learners, to enable communication between stakeholders and to manage information.

However, the climate changed considerably following a change of government in May 2010. The UK entered into a period of austerity with severe cuts to many public sector services and the demise of some. ICT provision in schools suffered the same fate and the momentum gained over the previous decade suddenly began to slow down.

It may have been reasonable to reduce costs and to abolish or consolidate existing services. Sadly however the action taken was sudden and somewhat unexpected. Agencies such as Becta, the Qualifications and Curriculum Authority, the DfES Standards website, the National Curriculum Online and Teachernet disappeared overnight along with repositories such as the Teacher Resource Exchange and Teacher's TV. The Department for Children, Schools and Families (DCSF) reverted back to the Department for Education (DfE), subsuming other agencies and archiving much of the existing information and resources. Whilst the intent may have been honourable, the actions of the DfE appeared to be overly hasty. Some of the existing information and resources have become difficult, if not impossible to locate.

The four years from May 2010 to January 2014 were filled with uncertainty about the shape of the proposed national curriculum and, in particular, the continuance of ICT as a subject in schools. The picture has now become clear with the publication of the new Computing curriculum and the creation of identifiable agencies and networks.

Perhaps the most significant changes with regard to ICT are:

- the curriculum is now located in the Department for Education area of the GOV.UK website (gov.uk/government/organisations/department-for-education);

- broadband provision and other services are now provided by the NEN – The Education Network (nen.gov.uk);

- the administration of the ICT Mark returned to NAACE, its founding organisation (naace.co.uk);

- the main source of ICT resources is TES Connect.

On a positive note, those schools and teachers that felt undue pressure to utilise ICT and to conform to government requirements (such as implementing learning platforms) might breathe a sigh of relief. The new curriculum frees them up to deliver ICT as they deem fit for their own pupils. The downside however is the requirement to provide a new Computing curriculum. If this appears daunting then this book is here to help.

Looking ahead

Primary schools on the whole have developed their ICT provision well over a number of years and are making effective use of a range of technologies which are capable of bringing about improvement to all aspects of the school. These include learning, teaching, assessment, administration, leadership, information management, communication, pupil attainment, extended learning and working practice.

In an age of austerity it is perhaps now time to consolidate and to consider how to make the most of existing technology whilst planning future expenditure wisely. In other words, achieving more with less and sharing resources and repositories of re-usable learning objects with other schools.

The Internet as a source of information and a means of communication and interaction has expanded exponentially and, as a result, there is naturally an increased emphasis on keeping children safe online.

Summary

Computers and other ICT resources have become established as generic tools for learning and teaching across the entire curriculum. Many teachers now accept ICT as an integral part of their professional life and understand how to use it effectively both in lessons and in their general working practice.

Despite changes to the curriculum, technology will continue to play an important role in schools and the new Computing curriculum will provide a challenge for everyone involved in children's education.

The second edition of the *ICT Handbook for Primary Teachers* aims to help teachers prepare for the challenges ahead.

ICT in the National Curriculum

Introduction

In January 2008, the government commissioned Sir Jim Rose to undertake an independent review of the primary curriculum. His final report (Rose, 2009) was published in 2009 and his recommendations were due to be implemented in September 2011.

However, in May 2010, when the new coalition government came to power, the Secretary of State for Education, Michael Gove, announced that the Rose recommendations would not be implemented and, following a period of consultation, a replacement national curriculum came into force in September 2014.

With regard to ICT, two changes were made:

1. A new Computing curriculum was introduced (which also includes elements of ICT/Digital Literacy).

2. The pre-2014 ICT curriculum was disapplied but schools are free to develop their own curricula for ICT that best meet the needs of their pupils, or to continue to follow the pre-2014 programmes of study if they so choose.

To cater for these changes, this edition of the book covers both the new Computing curriculum and the pre-2014 ICT curriculum (for those schools that choose to use all or part of it). The book also covers the use of ICT in enhancing teaching and learning across the new national curriculum as a whole.

Why computing?

A high-quality computing education equips pupils to use computational thinking and creativity to understand and change the world. Computing has deep links with mathematics, science and design and technology, and provides insights into both natural and artificial systems. The core of computing is computer science, in which pupils are taught the principles of information and computation, how digital systems work and how to put this knowledge to use through programming. Building on this knowledge and understanding, pupils are equipped to use information technology to create programs, systems and a range of content. Computing also ensures that pupils become digitally literate – able to use, and express themselves and develop their ideas through information and communication technology – at a level suitable for the future workplace and as active participants in a digital world.

National Curriculum (2014)

It's easy to think of Computing as a complex, high level subject for university undergraduates embarking on a software engineering or gaming design degree.

However, the principles of Computing and, in particular, programming, involve a number of basic competencies which can (and should) be introduced at an early age. These include:

- Creativity (writing a program can be like composing music or designing a house).
- Following instructions/writing instructions (including taking turns).
- Clarity of expression (instructions don't work unless they are precise).
- Problem solving (programs have clear objectives).
- Clear logical thinking and reasoning.
- Analysis and synthesis.
- A range of mathematical concepts such as spatial awareness and estimation.

In fact the basic competences of programming can begin at the Foundation stage – with programmable toys.

Why ICT/digital literacy?

Information and communication technology (ICT) and digital literacy prepare pupils to participate in a rapidly changing world in which work and other activities are increasingly transformed by access to varied and developing technology.

Pupils can use digital tools to find, explore, analyse, exchange and present information responsibly, creatively and with discrimination. They can learn how to employ ICT to enable rapid access to ideas and experiences from a wide range of people, communities and cultures.

Increased capability in the use of ICT promotes initiative and independent learning, with pupils being able to make informed judgements about when and where to use ICT to best effect, and to consider its implications for home and work both now and in the future.

The importance of ICT is widely recognised, not necessarily as a subject to be taught independently, but as a means of enhancing learning and teaching in all subjects across the curriculum. The information and guidance in this book will apply whether schools adopt their own ICT curricula or continue to follow the previous programmes of study.

Accessing the curriculum

In addition to printed versions, the Computing curriculum (from 2014) is available online from the GOV.UK website at gov.uk/government/collections/national-curriculum. The site provides links to the TES Connect website for access to free computing resources at community.tes.co.uk/national_curriculum_2014/b/computing/default.aspx and to a number of short films about the new curriculum on the GOV.UK website at gov.uk/government/publications/national-curriculum-video-interviews-for-schools.

Incidentally, the old curriculum (pre-2014) is archived at webarchive.nationalarchives.gov.uk/ 20131202172639/http://www.education.gov.uk/schools/teachingandlearning/curriculum/primary.

The primary computing curriculum

Aims

The national curriculum for computing aims to ensure that all pupils:

- can understand and apply the fundamental principles and concepts of computer science, including abstraction, logic, algorithms and data representation;
- can analyse problems in computational terms, and have repeated practical experience of writing computer programs in order to solve such problems;

- can evaluate and apply information technology, including new or unfamiliar technologies, analytically to solve problems;

- are responsible, competent, confident and creative users of information and communication technology.

Subject content

Key Stage 1 pupils should be taught to:

- understand what algorithms are; how they are implemented as programs on digital devices; and that programs execute by following precise and unambiguous instructions;

- create and debug simple programs;

- use logical reasoning to predict the behaviour of simple programs;

- use technology purposefully to create, organise, store, manipulate and retrieve digital content;

- recognise common uses of information technology beyond school;

- use technology safely and respectfully, keeping personal information private; identify where to go for help and support when they have concerns about content or contact on the Internet or other online technologies.

Key Stage 2 pupils should be taught to:

- design, write and debug programs that accomplish specific goals, including controlling or simulating physical systems;

- solve problems by decomposing them into smaller parts;

- use sequence, selection, and repetition in programs;

- work with variables and various forms of input and output;

- use logical reasoning to explain how some simple algorithms work and to detect and correct errors in algorithms and programs;

- understand computer networks including the Internet; how they can provide multiple services, such as the world wide web; and the opportunities they offer for communication and collaboration;

- use search technologies effectively, appreciate how results are selected and ranked, and be discerning in evaluating digital content;

- select, use and combine a variety of software (including Internet services) on a range of digital devices to design and create a range of programs, systems and content that accomplish given goals, including collecting, analysing, evaluating and presenting data and information;

- use technology safely, respectfully and responsibly; recognise acceptable/unacceptable behaviour; identify a range of ways to report concerns about content and contact.

Attainment targets

By the end of each key stage, pupils are expected to know, apply and understand the matters, skills and processes specified in the relevant programme of study.

You'll find a copy of the 2014 Computing curriculum on the Primary ICT website at primaryict.org.uk/ icthandbookv2.htm.

The Computing Curriculum will be covered in detail in Part 2.

The old (pre-2014) primary ICT curriculum

This section outlines the requirements of the old ICT curriculum (pre-2014) for the benefit of those schools that choose to use all or part of it (as an extension to the Computing curriculum).

Subject content

Key Stage 1 pupils should be taught to:

■ explore ICT and learn to use it confidently and with purpose to achieve specific outcomes;

■ start to use ICT to develop their ideas and record their creative work;

■ become familiar with hardware and software.

Key Stage 2 pupils should be taught to:

■ use a wider range of ICT tools and information sources to support their work in other subjects;

■ develop their research skills and decide what information is appropriate for their work;

■ begin to question the plausibility and quality of information;

■ learn how to amend their work and present it in a way that suits its audience.

In both stages this is achieved by four elements of knowledge, skills and understanding:

1. Finding things out from a variety of sources, selecting and synthesising the information to meet their needs and developing an ability to question its accuracy, bias and plausibility.

2. Developing their ideas using ICT tools to amend and refine their work and enhance its quality and accuracy.

3. Exchanging and sharing information, both directly and through electronic media.

4. Reviewing, modifying and evaluating their work, reflecting critically on its quality, as it progresses.

The complexity of each of these four aspects increases with each key stage.

Attainment targets

Competence in ICT is assessed using attainment targets (levels 1 to 8 and exceptional performance).

■ Children work within levels 1–3 at Key Stage 1 (and should attain at least level 2 by the end of the key stage).

■ Children work within levels 2–5 at Key Stage 2 (and should attain at least level 4 by the end of the key stage).

 Activity

If you would like to familiarise yourself with the pre-2014 ICT curriculum you'll find a copy on the Primary ICT website at primaryict.org.uk/icthandbookv2.htm.

You might examine the knowledge, skills and understanding (KSU) for Key Stage 1 and Key Stage 2 to see how they compare. They each have the same four aspects though the level of complexity increases at Key Stage 2. For example, Key Stage 1 children will gather information from a variety of sources which have been identified by the teacher, whereas Key Stage 2 children will be expected to decide for themselves where they might find the information they need.

Activity

Think about the types of activity (and resources) that children might carry out in order to satisfy the knowledge skills and understanding.

For example, in what way might Year 2 children gather and store information, alter the information they have gathered, and present this information effectively. There are lots of possible activities and you'll come across plenty in this book. One example would be for the teacher to prepare a short piece from a familiar story (e.g. Goldilocks) as a text file in MSWord, with errors in it. Children would access the file from the school learning platform and save it into their own workspace. They would then correct the passage (less able children might be given an error-free version in print form for comparison). Finally, they would add their own name, save it and print out the finished story. This activity could follow on from reading the story from a book or a talking story on CD-ROM or the Internet.

 Activity

Return to the Primary ICT website and examine the attainment targets in the pre-2014 ICT curriculum. How would you modify the previous activity such that it would be suitable for a child working toward attainment level 4?

You could start by highlighting the essential differences between attainment levels 2 and 4 (Key Stage 1 and Key Stage 2). Children might find a passage of a story themselves (perhaps from the Internet). The text could be formatted using a variety of features (include a picture perhaps). Finally, the work could be shared with others in the school learning platform or social network.

As you will discover in this book, ICT is about much more than just computers.

Schemes of work

The archived DCSF Standards website provides schemes of work for all subjects (available at time of writing – Spring 2015).

They may provide you with some useful ideas or whole activities. You may find that some schemes of work are, to some extent, dated because they don't entirely reflect advances in technology. However, they are a good starting point for developing lesson plans.

 Activity

Visit the archived DCSF Standards website and examine the ICT schemes of work for years 1 to 6. (webarchive.nationalarchives.gov.uk/20090608182316/standards.dfes.gov.uk/schemes3).

Make a note of the principles involved, the resources used and the types of activity in which children might be engaged. Are children in your school engaged in such activities? Are you familiar with these principles and resources yourself? It may be that you are not entirely comfortable with retrieving, storing, manipulating and presenting information yourself. You may not have experienced some of the software in the schemes of work (e.g. presentation software, spreadsheet and database). Whilst this may appear daunting, there is no need to feel overly concerned. You (and your pupils) need only be familiar with the basic features of these packages.

The Foundation Stage ICT curriculum

The Statutory Framework for the Early Years Foundation Stage (birth to 5) was updated in September 2014.

 Activity

Link to the Primary ICT website at primaryict.org.uk/icthandbookv2.htm and consult the statutory framework for the Early Years (2014). Determine what the recommendations are for the use of ICT in the foundation stage.

You should find that the framework emphasises the importance of technology in Understanding the World (UTW) and in Expressive Arts and Design (EAD). It expects that children will recognise that a range of technology is used in places such as homes and schools and that children can select and use technology for a particular purpose.

ICT is not restricted to UTW and EAD. It can easily be applied to all areas of learning. You will find some useful documents relating to the early years on the National Archives website at webarchive.nationalarchives. gov.uk/20110809091832/http://teachingandlearningresources.org.uk/early-years.

If you have a reception class, then most of the principles which relate to Key Stage 1 and Key Stage 2 will also hold for the Foundation Stage. You need not adopt the same structured approach as may be required for the National Curriculum but you can nevertheless plan suitable activities which use ICT to enhance learning. Many of these will be play-based in nature.

ICT relating to the National Curriculum and Foundation Stage will be covered in detail in Section 3.

ICT resources

The Primary and Foundation Stages are encouraged to use a wide range of resources. The range includes: lower-case keyboards, infant mice, large monitors for whole-class activities, colour printers, speakers, headphones, microphones, scanners, digital cameras (with movie facility), digital microscopes, overlay keyboards, talking word processors (with a word bank facility), paint programs, data-handling packages, presentation programs, drag-and-drop software, a range of CD-ROMs, floor robots, remote control toys, video recorders, radios, tape recorders, CD players, DVD players, video cameras, music keyboards, photocopiers, laminators, calculators, toy and real telephones, mobile phones, cookers, microwaves, fridges, toasters, toy cash registers, swipe cards, typewriters and other play equipment that model ICT appliances.

This list is far from exhaustive but does highlight the fact that ICT is about much more than computers and software. You might think of it in terms of the equation: $\mathbf{ICT} \neq \mathbf{PC}$.

 Activity

Link to the Primary ICT website at primaryict.org.uk/icthandbookv2.htm and watch the Primary ICT video and/or the Foundation ICT video (depending on your preference).

The computing curriculum

Computing curriculum (computer science)

Introduction

This chapter covers the requirements of the computer science elements of the computing national curriculum. ICT/Digital Literacy elements are outlined in Chapter 5.

The use of ICT across the curriculum is covered in much greater detail in Part 3.

After outlining the benefits of computer science you will be introduced to a number of programming activities for children of all ages. It will begin with programmable toys for young children and move on to simple programming languages such as Logo and Scratch for Key Stage 1/Key Stage 2.

The content here is not complex. It is designed to be fun and motivating as well as educational.

All of the software applications used in this chapter are free or available as free trials.

Aims of the computer science curriculum

The computer science elements of the national curriculum for computing aim to ensure that all pupils:

- can understand and apply the fundamental principles and concepts of computer science, including abstraction, logic, algorithms and data representation;
- can analyse problems in computational terms, and have repeated practical experience of writing computer programs in order to solve such problems.

Subject content

Key Stage 1

Pupils should be taught to:

- understand what algorithms are; how they are implemented as programs on digital devices; and that programs execute by following precise and unambiguous instructions;
- create and debug simple programs;
- use logical reasoning to predict the behaviour of simple programs.

Key Stage 2

Pupils should be taught to:

- design, write and debug programs that accomplish specific goals, including controlling or simulating physical systems; solve problems by decomposing them into smaller parts;
- use sequence, selection, and repetition in programs; work with variables and various forms of input and output;

■ use logical reasoning to explain how some simple algorithms work and to detect and correct errors in algorithms and programs.

Activity

If you are inquisitive, you will find a copy of the 'Computing Curriculum' and the 'Subject knowledge requirements for Computer Science Teaching' on the Primary ICT website at primaryict.org.uk/ icthandbookv2.htm (ch3 and ch4).

What is programming?

Writing programs is a lot like writing down the steps it takes to do something.

For example, you might ask your pupils to write out a specific sequence of steps on how to make a peanut butter sandwich. Then, working in pairs, each pupil follows their partner's instructions exactly to see what the outcome is.

It sounds simple (and it is) but you may be surprised how the outcomes for each pupil can differ (for example, trying to put peanut butter onto a knife without taking the lid off the jar is quite a challenge!).

 Activity

Try out the peanut butter activity (or something similar) with your own pupils.
Aside from this being a fun, motivating activity it will undoubtedly generate a variety of outcomes. From these you might get the children to identify the pitfalls involved in writing instructions and how important certain aspects are.

There are hundreds of similar activities such as making a cup of tea, brushing your teeth, posting a letter and so on. As you can see, these activities are not restricted to computer science, they can (and should) be designed to cover all aspects of the primary curriculum.

Why children should program

Everybody should learn to program because it teaches you to think …

Steve Jobs

The next section explores a number of avenues for all pupils and begins at the Foundation stage with programmable toys.

Programming languages and programmable toys

a. Programmable toys

Programmable toys simply respond to instructions given by their owner. Toys will have a limited number of instructions that they can understand.

Imagine that you have a robot dog named DogBot. You only know of seven words that DogBot understands: GO, FORWARD, BACKWARD, TURN, LEFT, RIGHT and FEET.

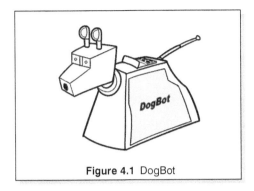

Figure 4.1 DogBot

DogBot also understands numbers. When you say
"GO FORWARD 3 FEET" DogBot moves forward three feet.
When you say "TURN LEFT," DogBot turns 90° to his left.
If you say "MAKE ME A SANDWICH," DogBot doesn't do anything. Why? Because none of the words in the instruction "MAKE ME A SANDWICH" are part of DogBot's language – he only understands numbers and the words GO, FORWARD, BACKWARD, TURN, LEFT, RIGHT and FEET.

Now, let's say that DogBot is in the living room by the front door. You want him to go to the bedroom but you don't want to pick him up and carry him because he's too heavy. You can't say "DOGBOT! GO TO THE BEDROOM!" because he doesn't understand these words. However, if you can give DogBot the right directions to the bedroom you can get him to go there himself. So you tell him how to get there with these directions:

- GO FORWARD 10 FEET
- TURN LEFT
- GO FORWARD 3 FEET
- TURN RIGHT
- GO FORWARD 4 FEET
- TURN RIGHT
- GO FORWARD 11 FEET

And here's the result.

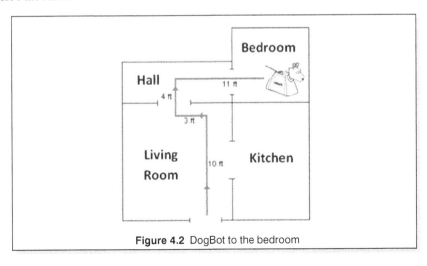

Figure 4.2 DogBot to the bedroom

The above set of instructions is a **program** comprising instructions (commands) that the programming application (DogBot) understands.

Activity

Try the DogBot activity with your own pupils.

You might use your classroom or playground as the house, positioning desks or cones to create the rooms. Pupils can play the role of DogBot.

Begin by having them follow pre-prepared instructions. Have pupils observe each other to get a feel for the distance they travel for each step taken.

Then split the class into pairs (or small groups). Each pair is given a different start point and finish point for DogBot. They are to write a set of instructions that will take DogBot from start to finish (estimating the number of steps to take).

The pairs can collaborate during the design process. The pairs then try out their instructions (tell them that if they are about to bump into anything they must stop).

If the instructions don't work get them to determine why and then modify* the instructions accordingly (emphasise the need to be precise).

The objective here is to achieve the goal with the least number of re-writes.

You can rotate the groups and, with luck, they will get better over time.

The degree of difficulty should match the age and ability of your pupils. Build in some harder challenges for those who progress quickly.

* Correcting instructions that don't work or modifying them to make them work better is an important part of the process. However, there's no need to get hung up about correct computing language (e.g. de-bugging, algorithm, etc.) until the latter stages of Key Stage 2.

DogBot is of course fictitious but there are several real programmable toys/robots available on the market such as the Bee-Bot, Ladybird and iBug.

Once you have experience of programmable toys it is likely that you could see them as potentially useful in other early learning goals and across the whole curriculum at Key Stage 1 and Key Stage 2.

Bee-Bot

Bee-Bots are extremely useful in mathematics for activities involving estimation, angles and direction, shape, spatial awareness, instructions, control and investigation. In addition to number work, robots facilitate group work, design and technology, and road safety. There are also several software versions which will allow you to simulate the actions of the robots on-screen. Examples include: TextEase Turtle, Tizzy's First Tools (Move) and Bee-Bot Simulation.

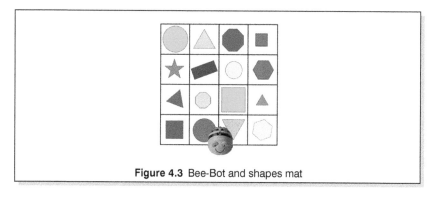

Figure 4.3 Bee-Bot and shapes mat

You will of course need access to floor robots in order to try them out. If your school owns a floor robot there are many activities you can carry out such as travelling around the room, knocking down skittles, finding treasure and exploring a maze. Activities can also be linked to other areas of the curriculum.

 Activity

Try the Bee-Bot activities on the Primary ICT website at primaryict.org.uk/icthandbookv2.htm. You may find some of these can be used with your own pupils.

If you don't have any floor robots then we recommend that you get yourself a Bee-Bot (or two!). Meanwhile, why not have a go with a software version?

 Activity

Download the Bee-Bot 14 day trial demo software from: focuseducational.com/html/bee-bot-international-free-trial.php.
Experiment with the software and the Bee-Bot

There's also a free App available from iTunes.

 Activity

There are plenty of sample activities to be found on the Internet.
You will find a useful video on You Tube at youtube.com/watch?v=zGyLBzKR_VA.
Now you might design a simple activity for your pupils (or get them to design one).

You should of course consider the capabilities of your pupils – are they able to specify instructions or simply follow them?

When specifying instructions, consider the competencies already mentioned. For example, you might use an alphabet mat and ask your pupils to write down the steps required for the Bee-Bot to reach the letter 'A' or to spell out a simple word by visiting letters in the correct sequence.

Example – to spell 'CAT':
  Forward 2 squares
  Turn right
  Forward 3 squares
  Turn left
  Forward 1 square
  Turn left
  Forward 1 square
  Turn left
  Forward 2 squares

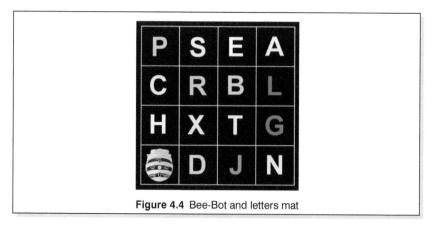

Figure 4.4 Bee-Bot and letters mat

They might do this in pairs (like the peanut butter sandwich example) with partners trying out the instructions to see how well they work. If solutions don't work then the next step might be for pupils to re-examine the steps to decide where they went wrong.

Children as young as 3 or 4 can perform this activity. Is it programming? Yes – it's specifying a set of sequential instructions – and that's what a program is! In this case the instructions are in plain English – but that still counts.

b. LOGO (Turtle)

Logo is a programming language used in education. It was created in 1967 by Seymour Papert and today it is mainly associated with turtle graphics (e.g. TextEase Turtle and Tizzy's First Tools [Move]).

> Seymour Papert is a mathematician, computer scientist and educator. He is one of the pioneers of artificial intelligence, as well as the inventor of the Logo programming language.
>
> At Massachusetts Institute of Technology (MIT), Papert was the developer of an original and highly influential theory on learning called constructionism, built upon the work of Jean Piaget. He is widely considered the most brilliant and successful of Piaget's protégés.
>
> Papert used Piaget's work in his development of the Logo programming language. He created Logo as a tool to improve the way that children think and solve problems. A small robot called the "Logo Turtle" was developed and children used it to solve problems.

In its simplest form, Logo performs directional commands which drive an onscreen object (usually a turtle) using angles and directions. For example:

```
FORWARD 100
LEFT 90
FORWARD 100
LEFT 90
FORWARD 100
LEFT 90
FORWARD 100
LEFT 90
```

 Activity

What do you think the above instructions achieve?

The on-screen object (turtle) will move forward 100 units and turn 90° left. This sequence is repeated 4 times. The net result is that the turtle traces out a square.

The instructions can be abbreviated to FD 100 LT 90 FD 100 LT 90 FD 100 LT 90 FD 100 LT 90 (the spaces are important).

The distance travelled by 1 unit is determined by the software and can usually only be found by trial and error. Some logo applications have levels. The lowest level (for younger children) will have a restricted set of commands. Higher levels may allow the object to move backwards and turn through angles other than 90°.

 Activity

Can you list the logo instructions to trace out:
a. An equilateral triangle
b. A hexagon
c. A circle?
Just use a pencil and paper.

You'll find the answers in Appendix 1.
So far you haven't used a computer. Nor do you necessarily need to!

- You can use pen and paper.

- You can use the children themselves – get them to pace out the instructions on the floor.

- You can use a floor robot.

However, since you are learning a little programming then let's find ourselves some suitable software applications.

1. A Turtle application with keypad control.

2. A specific Logo application.

You can cover these in any order though younger children will probably need to start by using a turtle with keypad control.

Turtle applications

Turtle software applications provide an onscreen simulation of a floor robot and are used to give similar instructions to those used for Bee-Bots etc. The turtle (or other selected object) can be controlled by keypads or by typed commands.

Examples include 2Go (by 2Simple), Tizzy's First Tools (Move) and Terrapin Logo, popular commercial software applications used by many schools.

2Simple also offer a trial version of turtle software via their Purple Mash website.

 Activity

Visit 2Simple's Purple Mash website at http://www.2simple.com/purple-mash and click on the 30 Day trial. Sign up for the trial.
Access 2Go (via the Creative Tools menu).
Try out the Turtle using the keypad.

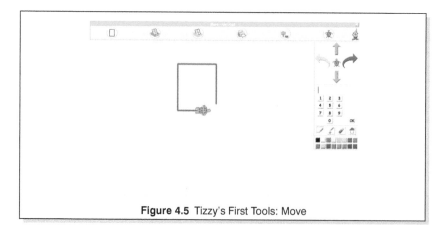

Figure 4.5 Tizzy's First Tools: Move

FMSLogo

FMSLogo is one of a number of free Logo programming environments. It allows you to control an object on the screen using the type of instructions that you have already written in preceding activities. The on-screen object is a small triangle but it is referred to as a turtle.

The purpose of Logo is to teach people (children and adults) how to program. It is modelled after a popular and powerful language called LISP. Logo fills a gap that most traditional languages do not. That is, it gives immediate feedback. Immediate feedback makes it fun and easier to learn programming.

You should begin by downloading and installing a copy.

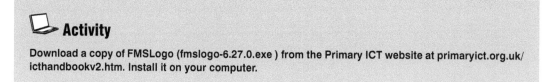

Activity

Download a copy of FMSLogo (fmslogo-6.27.0.exe) from the Primary ICT website at primaryict.org.uk/icthandbookv2.htm. Install it on your computer.

Now run FMSLogo. You should be presented with the following screen:

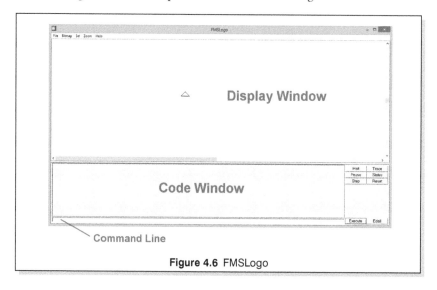

Figure 4.6 FMSLogo

The Help menu offers a comprehensive tutorial though the program is quite intuitive.

 Activity

Let's begin with a few simple activities.
1. Type the following into the Command Line and click Execute (or press Return):
   fd 100 rt 90 fd 100 rt 90 fd 100 rt 90 fd 100 rt 90
   * Ensure you enter the spaces, they are an important part of the Logo syntax.
2. Your code will appear in the Code Window, the code will be executed and the turtle should draw a square of side length 100 units.
3. Using the **Set** menu, experiment with Pen Size and Pen Colour.
4. Try creating other shapes such as a triangle, rectangle and hexagon.

Loops

It can be tedious typing in long strings of commands so let's simplify things by using loops. Loops are created using the **Repeat** command.

 Activity

Square revisited
1. Click **Reset** to clear the screen.
2. Type the following on the Command Line and then Execute:
   repeat 4 [fd 100 rt 90]

Hopefully your commands inside the square brackets were repeated 4 times to create a square.

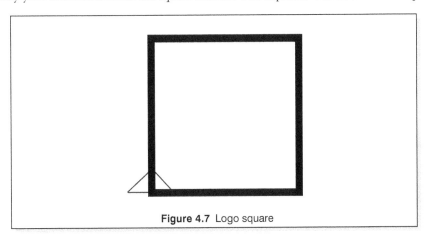

Figure 4.7 Logo square

Activity

Repeated square
Type the following on the Command Line:
repeat 36 [repeat 4 [fd 100 rt 90] rt 10]
Before you Execute, try to work out what it does.

If the purpose of the code isn't obvious you can break it down into chunks:

1. Create a square using **repeat 4 [fd 100 rt 90]**
2. Turn the turtle through 10° using **rt 10**
3. Repeat the first two steps 36 times using **repeat 36 []**

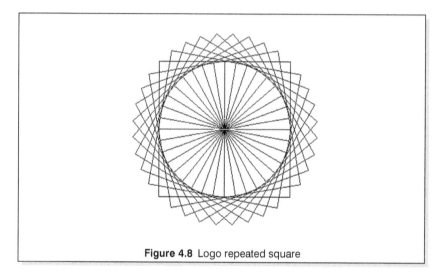

Figure 4.8 Logo repeated square

The result is much more elaborate than the square and begins to indicate the power of computer programming.

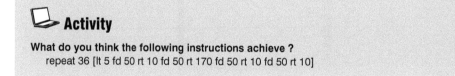 **Activity**

What do you think the following instructions achieve ?
repeat 36 [lt 5 fd 50 rt 10 fd 50 rt 170 fd 50 rt 10 fd 50 rt 10]

You'll find the answer in Appendix 1.

Before you immerse yourself in more programming exercises it's worthwhile reflecting on how this benefits your pupils:

■ There can be no doubt that these activities are fun and motivating.

■ Producing shapes and other designs is very creative.

■ Asking pupils to write instructions that will produce a desired result (e.g. square, triangle, their own name) encourages logical thinking, problem solving and precision.

■ Testing the instructions and remedying errors encourages reasoning and practises the iterative design cycle which is a recurring theme throughout education and life.

■ Asking pupils to interpret pre-written instructions promotes analysis.

Note: The activities have not been allocated to specific age groups. They are progressive and you, as the teacher, should determine how and when they are best undertaken.

Procedures

A procedure allows you to group a set of instructions and give it a name. That way you can use it again just by typing in the procedure name rather than the whole list of instructions.

 Activity

Try this with the square:
Reset your Display Window.
Click the Edall button to open the Edit Window.
Type in the following:
    to square
    repeat 4 [fd 100 rt 90]
    end
Click File/Save and Exit.
Now type **square** onto the Command Line and Execute.

Note: If you close FMSLogo your procedure will be lost. However, if you save your session you can reopen it later and use any procedures you've already created. Do this now – save your session as session1.lgo

What you have done so far is to start with some very basic commands and build upon them by learning the repeat command and how to write a procedure. Even a complex program can be split into a sequence of basic steps. For this reason, simple languages like Logo are capable of complex and powerful outcomes.

 Activity

Advanced Logo – a working clock
    Visit the Primary ICT website at primaryict.org.uk/icthandbookv2.htm. Download the file CLOCK.LGO and open it. Choose Yes to run the clock example.

Not bad for simple turtle software!

You would of course need to learn a few more Logo commands and get some serious practice before you could achieve this yourself.

If you open the editor (click Edall) you will see the procedures used in this example. You may be surprised how relatively few instructions there are.

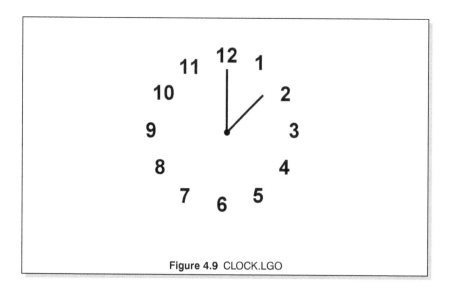

Figure 4.9 CLOCK.LGO

 Activity

Other commands

You can now experiment further (or perhaps take the tutorial provided on the FMSLogo Help Menu). In doing so, can you find the Logo commands that will perform each of the following?

1. Clear the screen
2. Change the pen colour
3. Lift the pen up
4. Put the pen down

You'll find the answer in Appendix 1.

Finally you will find a number of Logo challenges in Appendix 2. You might try these yourself and then with your pupils. There are many variations on each challenge – perhaps you (or your pupils) can devise some?

c. Scratch

Commercial turtle applications (e.g. TextEase Turtle) and free Logo applications (e.g. FMSLogo) use the same programming language – Logo. Whilst it can be fun and beneficial to program using a set of instructions it can also be somewhat limiting. It takes a lot of experience and a good deal of time to produce a visually stimulating product.

For this reason there are many applications which allow the user to produce results quickly using pre-prepared code and objects. This is often achieved using drag and drop.

Examples include office programs such as MS PowerPoint and MS Excel, authoring tools such as Mediator and Opus and so on.

Scratch is a new programming language that makes it easy to create your own interactive stories, games, and animations – and share your creations with others on the web. Scratch is developed by the Lifelong Kindergarten research group at the MIT Media Lab (llk.media.mit.edu) and is specifically aimed at children's education so that they learn important mathematical and computational ideas whilst also learning to think creatively, reason systematically and work collaboratively.

Figure 4.10 Scratch logo

 Activity

Download and install Scratch from info.scratch.mit.edu/Scratch_1.4_Download.
Try out the activity in the 'Scratch – Getting Started' document on the Primary ICT website at primaryict.org.uk/icthandbookv2.htm. What do you think ?
You may feel that it is more suitable than Logo for some of your children. I'm sure you'll agree too that it does have its limitations!

If you'd like to explore this application further, and create learning activities for your own pupils, you'll find that there's much more on offer on the Scratch website (scratch.mit.edu and scratch.mit.edu/starter_projects). There are also several books available on Scratch programming.

d. Flow charts

Flow charts are easy-to-understand diagrams showing how steps in a process fit together. This makes them useful tools for communicating how processes work and for clearly documenting how something is done. Furthermore, the act of mapping a process out in flow chart format helps to clarify the understanding of the process and helps to identify where the process can be improved.

Flow charts are also a visual way to depict a set of program instructions (sometimes called an algorithm). Some would argue that it is easier to understand a program in flowchart form and that the creation of a flowchart is a useful intermediary step in the design of a program. Once the flowchart is complete a set of instructions can be written using the chart as a guide.

Competent programmers will most likely skip the flowcharting stage though children will benefit from the visual learning experience.

Flowcharts can easily be drawn by hand and there are also several flowcharting applications for children. They usually come as part of a control package such as the Economatics Control Station (and Universal Logicator Software) and 2controlNXT. These work in conjunction with physical output devices and can control of a variety of miniature systems such as traffic lights and motors.

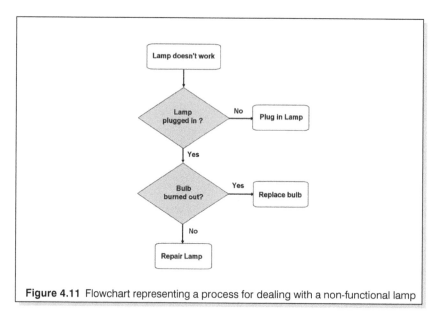

Figure 4.11 Flowchart representing a process for dealing with a non-functional lamp

Figure 4.12 is a simple flowchart from the 2controlNXT application. You should recognise this flowchart as the square tracing program you tried earlier. The chart is constructed by dragging and dropping elements from a bank. The most common elements are:

Rectangles indicating processes.

Diamonds indicating decisions.

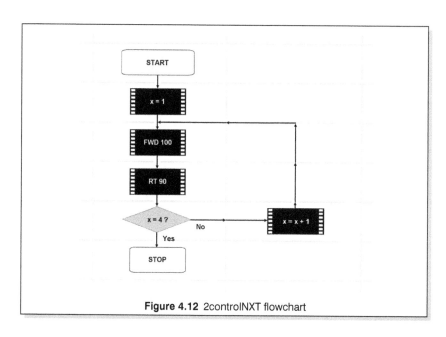

Figure 4.12 2controlNXT flowchart

Activity

Try this out on your pupils.
1. Have them place the following instructions (for making toast) into the correct order.

Remove toast from toaster	Wait 2 minutes
Start	Put bread into toaster
Stop	Push down handle

2. They should then convert the result into a flowchart.
3. Finally, they should add a 'decision' to check (at regular intervals) whether the toast is ready.

You'll find the solution in Appendix 1.

e. Small Basic (Key Stage 2/Key Stage 3)

With the advent of home computers in the early 1980s the first programming language to become available to the general public was BASIC (Beginners All-Purpose Symbolic Instruction Code). Since that time BASIC has been mainly superceded by more powerful languages such as C++ and Java. However, Microsoft Office and some other applications use a version called Visual Basic (VBA). A little knowledge of VBA can be very helpful at times.

A number of simpler Basic applications have been developed for beginners and younger pupils. One such application is Small Basic. You can try out Small Basic with your pupils though it should be aimed at Year 6, Key Stage 3 and gifted pupils.

Activity

Download and install Small Basic.
Download the guide *Microsoft Small Basic: An introduction to Programming*. (Copies on Primary ICT website at primaryict.org.uk/icthandbookv2.htm.)

Follow the guide – *Microsoft Small Basic: An introduction to Programming* – to get started.

The application is intuitive to use and has a simple toolbar so it shouldn't present any major problems.

Some of the code can appear strange at first because it follows the syntax used by Visual Basic. For example, to write the text 'Hello World' you need to use

TextWindow.Write("Hello World").

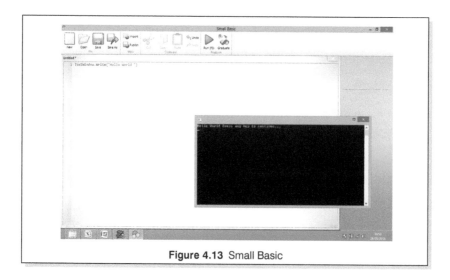

Figure 4.13 Small Basic

You can work your way through the whole guide or cherry pick the bits you find most useful. You might concentrate on numbers, variables, conditional statements and loops.

*CAUTION: The **GoTo** statement is peculiar to Basic and does not sit comfortably in a sequential programming environment. You are strongly advised not to use it.*

f. JavaScript

Those schools that engage Key Stage 2 pupils in simple web design might want to dabble with Javascript. Javascript is perhaps the most widely used language and, of course, is used in billions of web pages around the world.

Aside from being a powerful language it requires only a plain text editor to write the code (e.g. Windows Notepad) and a browser to display it (e.g. Internet Explorer, Firefox, Chrome etc).

Many would-be web designers use Dreamweaver as a design package but professional designers use just a text editor. A good choice of editor is Notepad++ available to download free from notepad-plus-plus. org. It betters the basic windows notepad because it provides line numbering, colour coding and a number of other features.

Teaching you JavaScript is outside the scope of this book. Instead we refer you to an online teaching environment called Happy Fun Coding. This site provides tutorials (by way of a series of videos) and a coding page where you can type in your instructions and see the results immediately on the same page.

 Activity

Visit Happy Fun Coding at happyfuncoding.com.
 The site will not open in Internet Explorer. Instead you must use Firefox or Chrome. If you don't have either of these browsers they are free to download from the Internet.
 Run through the tutorials on the Tutorials tab. You will soon get an appreciation of whether Javascript is for you (and your pupils).

g. Dedicated computing hardware

Rather than installing software onto your PC you might opt for a hardware solution. The company FUZE (fuze.co.uk) provides a number of hardware solutions for computing. One example is the FUZE Maximite which connects to a monitor and 'boots' straight into the BASIC programming environment in seconds. It also comes with a comprehensive electronics kit allowing pupils to participate in computer programming and hobby electronics.

Figure 4.14 FUZE hardware (images supplied by FUZE Technologies Ltd fuze.co.uk)

h. Other software and hardware

Finally, here's a listing of other programming applications and associated hardware that you may wish to explore yourself. Some are free and some commercial.

Table 4.1 Programming software and hardware

Name	Link/Description
Alice (free)	alice.org Alice is an innovative 3D programming environment that makes it easy to create an animation for telling a story, playing an interactive game, or a video to share on the web. Alice is a teaching tool for introductory computing. It uses 3D graphics and a drag-and-drop interface to facilitate a more engaging, less frustrating first programming experience.
Terrapin Logo	terrapinlogo.com Terrapin Logo is the latest version of the Logo computer language from Terrapin Software. Terrapin Logo includes all the features that make Logo a powerful and fun learning environment along with many exciting new ones that extend Logo's capability and make it easier to use.
TextEase Studio CT	rm.com TextEase Studio CT is an integrated set of nine core software tools accessible through one easy-to-use interface. The tools include the TextEase Turtle mentioned in this chapter.
Lego Mindstorm (and other peripherals)	education.lego.com/en-gb/products A range of products covering key curriculum areas.

Name	Link/Description
Phrogram	phrogram.com Phrogram is a programming language and environment designed to introduce how to write, test and debug code. With Phrogram, you can learn how to create your own programs and explore the world of real programming.
Kodu	research.microsoft.com/en-us/projects/kodu Kodu is a new visual programming language made specifically for creating games. It is designed to be accessible for children and enjoyable for anyone. The programming environment runs on the Xbox, allowing rapid design iteration using only a game controller for input.
Codecademy (free)	codecademy.com Codecademy is an easy way to learn how to code. It is interactive, fun, and children can do it with their friends.
Just BASIC (free)	justbasic.com Just BASIC is a programming language for the Windows operating system. It is completely free and it is suitable for creating all kinds of applications for business, industry, education and entertainment. It is easy to learn and it has been extended with structured programming facilities and with easy-to-use GUI commands so you can create your own Windows programs without needing to learn about the Windows operating system.
Simple (free)	simplecodeworks.com A fun and exciting way to create your own computer programs.
Kids Ruby (free)	kidsruby.com Kids Ruby makes it fun and easy to learn how to program.
MicroWorlds EX	microworlds.com MicroWorlds EX is an environment in which students can explore and test their ideas as they create science simulations, mathematical experiments, interactive multimedia stories and whatever they can imagine!
Scratch sensor board	info.scratch.mit.edu/Sensor_Boards A small printed circuit board used in conjunction with Scratch programming.
Raspberry Pi	raspberrypi.org The Raspberry Pi is a credit-card sized computer that plugs into a TV and a keyboard. It's a capable little PC which can be used for many of the things that a desktop PC does, like spreadsheets, word-processing and games. It also plays high-definition video. Its designers would like to see it being used by kids all over the world to learn programming.
Crystal ICT	shop.sherston.com An easy-to-use comprehensive online solution for teaching the new Computing curriculum.

Name	Link/Description
Espresso Coding	espresso.co.uk Launched in October 2013 and designed to help primary teachers to deliver the coding aspects outlined in the 2014 Computing curriculum. 78 step-by-step lessons and tablet-friendly activities, 100s of short, helpful video guides and a bespoke website where apps can be published and shared by schools.
Education City Computing	educationcity.com A new computing module for the Education City subscription website.
2DIY	2simple.com/2diy Creates interactive Flash resources, activities, games, puzzles and quizzes. Teachers and primary school pupils can create cross-curricular personalised resources and use them on whiteboards, websites and even on learning platforms.
Makey Makey	makeymakey.com MaKey MaKey is an invention kit for the 21st century. It allows you to turn everyday objects into touch pads and combine them with the Internet. It's a simple invention kit for beginners and experts doing art, engineering, and everything in between.
Switched On Computing	risingstars-uk.com Written for the new curriculum, Switched on Computing offers creative units using the latest software in a format that is designed for teachers of all levels of experience to pick up and use.

Game design

Game design is an excellent vehicle for pupils to consolidate their learning of Computing. In particular, it involves them in creativity, problem solving, clear logical thinking and reasoning, analysis and a range of mathematical concepts. What's more, it's fun and extremely motivating.

Here are a few ideas:

1. **Scratch** (covered earlier in the chapter) is the perfect introduction to programming for younger primary school children. Children in Key Stage 2 (and perhaps Key Stage 1) can learn how to program a simple animation or video game. Rather than writing out lines of code, children learn the fundamentals of programming using the easy-to-understand drag-and-drop method.

2. **Kodu**, created by Microsoft, is an icon-based graphical programming language designed specifically for pupils allowing them to create personalised and unique video games. Kodu allows pupils to design, program and present their own video games while learning about debugging, algorithms and parameters.

3. **GameMaker Studio** by YoYo Games allows novices to design cross-platform games and create fully functional prototypes in just a few hours.

4. **Stage Cast Creator** is an easy-to-learn, easy-to-use software tool for making games and simulations without using a programming language.

5. **Alice** is a 3D programming environment that makes it easy to create an animation for telling a story, playing an interactive game, or a video to share on the web. Alice is a freely available teaching tool designed to be a student's first exposure to object-oriented programming.

6. **Neverwinter Nights** is a Dungeons and Dragons style 3D role-playing game which comes with a free toolset for creating games using the game engine.

Computer networks

Introduction

As part of the curriculum, pupils are required to create, organise, store, manipulate and retrieve digital content. Whilst these procedures can sometimes be carried out entirely on a standalone computer, they often rely on devices that are component parts of a network. A basic knowledge of networks is therefore very useful. The following sections should therefore be considered as the minimum offering for Key Stage 2 pupils.

What is a computer network?

A computer network is simply a collection of computer equipment (devices) that are connected with cables, optical fibres, or wireless links so that the various separate devices can communicate with one another. Networks allow us to share information and resources between devices and across large distances.

Local area network (LAN)

A LAN is usually localised to a building (or group of buildings that make up a school, business or other organisation). It typically comprises two or more computers, printers, scanners and a server linked together via a hub or switch. It may have a connection to the Internet.

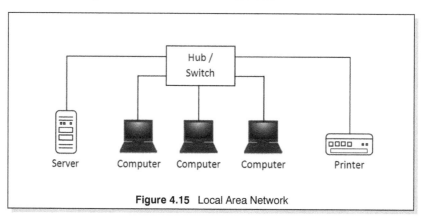

Figure 4.15 Local Area Network

Wide area network (WAN)

A WAN extends beyond a single locality and can cover any geographical area. It typically comprises two or more LANs connected together via a router or gateway and either dedicated links (cables, satellite etc.) or via the Internet.

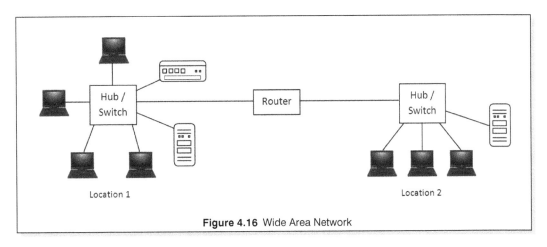

Figure 4.16 Wide Area Network

One example of a WAN is the network that connects all schools and other educational institutes together (and to the Internet). Its name is **SuperJANET**.

 Activity

If you would like to know more about the history behind SuperJANET, visit the NEN at: nen.gov.uk/ aboutus/6/the-history-of-nen.html.

The Internet

The Internet is the interconnection of computers and computer networks across the globe. The Internet is therefore the collection of computers and networks and the cables and other media that connect them all together.

The World Wide Web (www)

The World Wide Web is a massive collection of digital pages. The pages are grouped into websites written mainly using Hyper Text Markup Language (HTML). The Web is viewed by using free software called Web Browsers such as Internet Explorer, Mozilla Firefox and Google Chrome.

By connecting people around the world and passing data from senders to recipients, the Internet and World Wide Web have created many opportunities. These include information (such as web pages and other documents), communication (such as email, video conferencing, blogs and social networks) and collaboration (such as wikis and forums).

Server

A dedicated machine (almost always switched on) that performs one or more of the following actions: controls a network; stores data, email and web pages; houses the software applications used by a network.

Router

Routers guide data from the source to the correct destination using **I.P. Addresses**.

Data and information

Signals must be digitised in order for them to travel over networks and to be stored in computer memory devices. Digitised words, numbers, dates, images, sounds etc., in their raw format, are called **data**.

Information is data that has been processed and presented in such a way as to be meaningful to the person who receives it (e.g. printed documents, web pages and emails).

Data is passed between devices on a network by splitting it into small **packets**. For efficiency, each packet may take a different route from source to destination. At the destination, the packets are re-assembled into their original format.

Activity

You can simulate the sending of data across a network using numbered post-it notes that act as data packets. Your pupils can act as computers and routers.

- Choose 2 pupils at opposite corners of the classroom to act as sending and receiving computers.
- The sender writes a message and transcribes portions of it onto several post-it notes.
- The post-it notes are numbered such that the message can be re-assembled in the correct sequence.
- The sender may pass a post-it note to any pupil (router) within their reach.
- The routers may also pass a post-it note to any pupil (router) within their reach.
- The aim is to get the message to the receiver by the quickest available route.
- Routers must hold on to a post-it note for 10 seconds before passing it on.
- Routers can only hold one post-it note at a time.
- The receiver re-assembles the message once the post-it notes have all been received.

You might ask the following questions:

- How would the receiver know when all the post-it notes have been received?

- What should happen if the receiver doesn't receive all the post-it notes?

You might deliberately introduce problems and question the class about how the problems could be remedied. For example: put one or more routers out of action (temporarily or permanently); lose one or more post-it notes; make the information on one of the post-it notes illegible.

Putting it all together

Thus far we've looked at ideas that can help fulfil the requirements of the Computer Science elements of the Computing curriculum. You will of course need to develop a programme of study with schemes of work that give a clear list of the content that should be covered in each key stage (to which you might like to add further elements of your own).

For illustration purposes, an outline of the programme might look like Table 4.2:

Table 4.2 Programme for computing (computer science)

Foundation	■	Following instructions
Year 1	■	Writing, testing and modifying sequences of instructions
	■	Solving simple problems with Bee-Bots
Year 2	■	On-screen Turtle activities (using beginner level keypad control)
Year 3	■	On-screen Turtle activities (using higher level keypad control and simple Logo commands)
	■	Scripted animations (using Scratch)
Year 4	■	Flow charts and algorithms
	■	Solving problems with Logo (FMSLogo programming with loops, decisions and procedures)
Year 5	■	Controlling external devices (e.g. Economatics: Universal Logicator and Control Station or 2controlNXT)
	■	High level languages (introducing BASIC)
Year 6	■	Simple HTML and JavaScript
	■	Exploring a simple computer (activities with Raspberry Pi)
	■	Computer Networks
	■	Game Design

This programme is just a suggestion. The important thing, whatever you decide to do, is to ensure you have covered the key elements:

Key Stage 1: precise and unambiguous instructions; algorithms; programs; debugging; predicting program behaviour.

Key Stage 2: solve problems by decomposing them into smaller parts; use logical reasoning; design and debug programs (incorporating sequence, selection and repetition in programs); control input and output devices/systems (physical or simulated); computer networks.

Note: The programme doesn't include ICT aspects of the Computing curriculum. These are covered in Chapter 5.

 Activity

For further ideas you might visit:
1. **Computing at School (computingatschool.org.uk)**, an independent working group providing guidance to all those involved in Computing education in schools.
2. **The Barefoot Computing Project (barefootcas.org.uk)**, whose aim is to help primary school teachers get ready for the computer science element of the new computing curriculum.
3. **Code Club (codeclub.org.uk)**, a nationwide network of volunteer-led after school coding clubs for children aged 9–11.

5

Computing curriculum (ICT and digital literacy)

Introduction

This chapter examines the ICT/digital literacy components of the computing curriculum. It serves only as an outline since ICT is covered in greater detail in Section 3.

Key Stage 1

Creating, organising, storing, manipulating and retrieving digital content

Digital content takes many forms including text, numerical data, images, sound, animation and video.

Creating, manipulating and organising digital content will therefore require the familiar tasks of word-processing, emailing, spreadsheet calculations, creating graphs and charts, presenting, publishing, creating and editing images, creating and editing sound and video and so on.

Storing and retrieving digital content will require a knowledge of storage media, storage capacity and storage structures on computers, networks, external and removable devices and in the Cloud.

At Key Stage 1 the teacher should select the sources of information to be used (or present pupils with pre-gathered data) and select the applications to be used to process data.

These tasks are best performed by embedding them into the wider curriculum – across all subjects and at all levels. This will be covered in Section 3.

Common uses of information technology beyond school

Pupils should be asked to consider the relevance and importance of digital technologies that surround them in their everyday lives at home, at school and in their environment.

The possibilities are almost endless and might include: digital alarm clocks; microwaves; digital TV; computers; tablets; phones; digital games; GPS; management information systems; the Internet and World Wide Web; washing machines; traffic lights; online shopping; cash registers; in car systems and e-books.

Safe use of technology

At Key Stage 1, pupils should be aware of the main risks associated with the Internet and understand the dangers associated with sharing certain types of personal information online. Equally, they should know that it is their responsibility to treat others with respect and to appreciate their right to privacy.

In the event that they might inadvertently access inappropriate content on the web or encounter unwelcome contact or bullying, they need to know how to report a worry, and they should be encouraged to talk to teachers or parents about their concerns.

Pupils must have a clear understanding of what to do if they have concerns about inappropriate online behaviour (such as unwelcome contact or cyberbullying). Pupils should also know that they can talk directly and confidentially to ChildLine about such matters.

Teachers must follow their school's child protection policy which may include informing the Child Exploitation and Online Protection Centre (CEOP – ceop.police.uk). Further information for teachers on e-safety is available on CEOP's Thinkuknow site (thinkuknow.co.uk).

Key stage 2

Search technologies

Pupils should be aware of a range of search methods including search engines, directories, portals, and key websites.

They should become familiar with the common search engines (Google, Yahoo etc.) and be taught how to use them effectively in order to get the results they want. Searching should rely on specifying the appropriate keywords and key phrases.

Pupils should apply simple criteria to evaluate the credibility and relevance of their results (rather than simply accepting them at face value). They should be aware that the information on sites such as Wikipedia are not always accurate (or even true).

Children should also know what to do should they come across inappropriate content.

 Activity

For information on search techniques you might try:

- How to search on Google: support.google.com/websearch/answer/134479?hl=en.
- Common Sense Media: commonsensemedia.org/blog/teach-your-kids-the-secrets-of-smart-web-searching.
- Kidsmart: kidsmart.org.uk/safesearching.

Select and use ICT resources to collect, analyse, evaluate and present data and information

This follows on from Key Stage 1. The essential differences are that Key Stage 2 pupils:

- will tend to collect data themselves (rather than be presented with it);
- will locate appropriate sources of information and content;
- will select the applications used to process digital content;
- will use applications with increasing independence;
- will use a range of devices rather than just a computer (e.g. mobile devices);
- will use combinations of software applications rather than single packages (e.g. edit an image in Photoshop and use it in a MS PowerPoint presentation);
- will use ICT to enhance wider projects rather than for single tasks.

Safe use of technology

Safe and responsible use of technology at Key Stage 2 builds on skills learned in Key Stage 1. As well as requiring pupils to keep themselves safe and to treat others with respect there is an increased emphasis on responsible use of technology.

Pupils need to consider how their online actions impact other people. They need to be aware of their legal and ethical responsibilities, such as intellectual property rights, keeping passwords and personal data secure, and observing the terms and conditions for web services they use.

Pupils should also develop some awareness of their digital footprint: the data automatically generated when they use the Internet and other communication services, and how this is, or could be, used.

Pupils should be aware of, and abide by, the school's acceptable use policy, as well as the requirements of any other services they use. Encourage pupils to think twice, and to check terms and conditions, before signing up for Internet-based services.

As in Key Stage 1, pupils should report any concerns to a parent or teacher. They should also be aware that they can talk directly to the police, report their concern to CEOP or talk in confidence to counsellors at ChildLine.

Berry (2013)

 Activity

The organisation Computing at School (CAS) has published a document called 'Computing in the national curriculum: A guide for primary teachers'. You'll find a copy on the Primary ICT website at primaryict.org.uk/icthandbookv2.htm.

★ Recent research shows that pupils with special needs are twice as likely to suffer bullying. They are often told just to 'keep their heads down' and 'try to fit in'. However, this may not be a wholly effective solution and additional care should be taken in order to keep these pupils safe.

Putting it all together

This chapter has outlined the requirements of the ICT elements of the Computing curriculum. The best advice for its implementation is to embed these elements into appropriate subjects across the curriculum rather than attempting to deliver them as discreet components. For this reason a sample programme/scheme of work is not provided here.

Further detail on all the elements of ICT, and much more, can be found in Part 3.

Using ICT to enhance teaching and learning

6

Using ICT to enhance English

Introduction

The chapters in Part III will introduce ideas for using ICT effectively in learning and teaching within and across all National Curriculum subjects. References to the requirements for teaching the National Curriculum are taken from the GOV.UK website at gov.uk/government/collections/national-curriculum. We begin with English. There are plenty of activities in this chapter to whet your appetite.

ICT or not ICT?

Before you introduce technology into the learning or teaching of any lesson, in any subject, it is essential that you consider whether or not ICT should be used at all. Don't just use it for the sake of it, ask yourself the following questions. Does ICT:

- facilitate teaching or learning that could not be achieved by traditional methods (e.g. the interactivity provided by an interactive whiteboard, the ease of editing and formatting work using a word processor or the ability to record and recall learning events using a digital camera);
- make it easier, quicker or more enjoyable to accomplish a task;
- improve the quality of work;
- provide a welcome alternative approach to learning;
- enable learners;
- provide motivation;
- satisfy elements of the Computing or ICT curriculum;
- help to achieve the desired learning outcome(s) of the lesson.

Providing that ICT is not the predominant method, it is not overused and it is used effectively then a positive response to any of the above may be a good reason to include it.

The list above is by no means exhaustive; there are other criteria which you might like to consider. For each of the sample activities in this book you can decide for yourself whether ICT is used appropriately.

Whilst there is much evidence of the potential effectiveness of ICT as a tool for learning, not everyone subscribes to this notion. There are those who rightly raise pedagogical, technical or health and safety concerns about ICT. In the end, only you can decide.

Foundation Stage communication and language and literacy

Detail of the curriculum for English for the EYFS is available online at: www.gov.uk

Communication and language is a prime area of the EYFS. Development involves giving children opportunities to experience a rich language environment; to develop their confidence and skills in expressing themselves; and to speak and listen in a range of situations. This involves:

- Listening and attention: children listen attentively in a range of situations. They listen to stories, accurately anticipating key events and respond to what they hear with relevant comments, questions or actions. They give their attention to what others say and respond appropriately, whilst engaged in another activity.

- Understanding: children follow instructions involving several ideas or actions. They answer 'how' and 'why' questions about their experiences and in response to stories or events.

- Speaking: children express themselves effectively, showing awareness of listeners' needs. They use past, present and future forms accurately when talking about events that have happened or are to happen in the future. They develop their own narratives and explanations by connecting ideas or events.

Literacy development involves encouraging children to link sounds and letters and to begin to read and write. Children must be given access to a wide range of reading materials (books, poems, and other written materials) to ignite their interest. This involves:

- Reading: children read and understand simple sentences. They use phonic knowledge to decode regular words and read them aloud accurately. They also read some common irregular words. They demonstrate understanding when talking with others about what they have read.

- Writing: children use their phonic knowledge to write words in ways which match their spoken sounds. They also write some irregular common words. They write simple sentences which can be read by themselves and others. Some words are spelt correctly and others are phonetically plausible.

DfE (2014b)

English National Curriculum

Schools are expected to follow the old programme of study for English (including testing) until September 2015 when the new curriculum then takes force. This chapter covers the key elements of both old and new but with a particular emphasis on the new.

Detail of the curriculum for English for Primary is available online at:

1. The old National Curriculum for English: webarchive.nationalarchives.gov.uk/20131202172639/ http://www.education.gov.uk/schools/teachingandlearning/curriculum/primary.

2. The new National Curriculum for English: www.gov.uk/government/collections/national-curriculum.

English (old and new) is organised under the language skills of speaking (and listening), reading and writing. The new curriculum provides greater detail and is more prescriptive in parts. It also places much more emphasis on spelling, vocabulary, grammar and punctuation.

Speaking

The spoken language is important in pupils' development across the whole curriculum. It underpins the development of reading and writing and is vital for developing their vocabulary and grammar.

Pupils should be taught to:

- listen and respond appropriately to adults and their peers;
- ask relevant questions to extend their understanding and knowledge;
- use relevant strategies to build their vocabulary;
- articulate and justify answers, arguments and opinions;
- give well-structured descriptions, explanations and narratives for different purposes, including for expressing feelings;
- maintain attention and participate actively in collaborative conversations, staying on topic and initiating and responding to comments;
- use spoken language to develop understanding through speculating, hypothesising, imagining and exploring ideas;
- speak audibly and fluently with an increasing command of standard English;
- participate in discussions, presentations, performances, role play, improvisations and debates;
- gain, maintain and monitor the interest of the listener(s);
- consider and evaluate different viewpoints, attending to and building on the contributions of others.

Reading

Reading at Key Stages 1 and 2 consists of two dimensions:

- Word reading.
- Comprehension (both listening and reading).

Skilled word reading involves both the speedy working out of the pronunciation of unfamiliar printed words (decoding) and the speedy recognition of familiar printed words. Phonics should be emphasised in the early teaching of reading to beginners when they start school.

Good comprehension draws from linguistic knowledge (in particular of vocabulary and grammar) and on knowledge of the world. Comprehension skills develop high-quality discussion and from reading and discussing a range of stories, poems and non-fiction. All pupils must be encouraged to read widely across both fiction and non-fiction.

It is essential that, by the end of their primary education, all pupils are able to read fluently, and with confidence, in any subject in their forthcoming secondary education.

Writing

Writing at Key Stages 1 and 2 includes two components:

- Transcription (spelling and handwriting).
- Composition (articulating ideas and structuring them in speech and writing).

In addition, pupils should be taught how to plan, revise and evaluate their writing.

Writing down ideas fluently depends on effective transcription. That is, on spelling quickly and accurately through knowing the relationship between sounds and letters (phonics) and understanding the morphology (word structure) and orthography (spelling structure) of words.

Effective composition involves forming, articulating and communicating ideas, and then organising them coherently for a reader. This requires clarity, awareness of the audience, purpose and context, and an increasingly wide knowledge of vocabulary and grammar. Writing also depends on fluent, legible and, eventually, speedy handwriting.

Spelling, vocabulary, grammar and punctuation

Teachers should take the opportunity to enhance pupils' vocabulary as part of their reading and writing. Throughout the programmes of study, teachers should teach pupils the vocabulary they need to discuss their reading, writing and spoken language. It is important that pupils learn the correct grammatical terms in English and that these terms are integrated within teaching.

Using ICT in English

The following sections provide ideas for using ICT to help achieve the statutory requirements of the English curriculum.

Talking stories

Talking stories utilise colourful pictures, animation and sound to stimulate the senses – words are highlighted as they are spoken. They are often interactive, allowing parts of the picture to be touched or clicked in order to provide further animation and sounds. A wide variety are available. For example:

Table 6.1 Talking stories

CD-ROM	Website
Oxford Reading Tree: Talking Stories	British Council Short Stories: learnenglishkids.britishcouncil.
Talking Big Book CD-ROMs	org/en/short-stories
Wolf Hill Talking Story CD-ROMS	KizClub: kizclub.com/stories.htm
2Simple Talking Stories	Clifford Interactive Stories: teacher.scholastic.com/clifford1
LinguaTALK English	Cbeebies Stories: www.bbc.co.uk/cbeebies/stories
	YouTube: Search for children's stories

In primary schools and nurseries, talking stories are often projected onto a large screen which enables teacher-led group activities in reading and speaking. With the aid of an interactive whiteboard (IWB), the activities can become even more interactive. *There is more information on the IWB in Chapter 9.*

Designing your own talking stories

It is possible to create your own talking stories. You might use MS PowerPoint and use the built-in sound recorder to incorporate voice-overs for your chosen text. A more advanced option would be to use authoring software such as Mediator 9 (by MatchWare) or Opus Pro (by digitalworkshop). There are also bespoke products such as Pictello (by AssistiveWare), a simple way to create visual stories and talking books on an iPad, iPhone or iPod touch and M is for Me (by Yellow Door) for the creation of an interactive class alphabet.

Talking Books

There are a number of actual, physical, talking books on the market. Good examples are LeapReader (by Leap Frog) and Talking Book (from TTS). The former are accompanied by a touch pen which is used to sound out words letter by letter, read sentences in lively character voices and play fun games that build comprehension.

 Activity

Link to the Cbeebies website (www.bbc.co.uk/cbeebies/stories) and explore some of the stories. Decide whether these have educational value. You may find that some are better than others. It depends of course on what we mean by educational value. It helps if they are fun and motivating but it is important that they contribute to the achievement of some desired learning outcomes.

 Activity

Now explore the Internet and see if you can find any other useful sites with talking stories. You may also come across examples of CD-ROMs. There are many sites to be found and you might begin compiling a list (a start has been made for you in Appendix 3). However, you should always fully evaluate websites (and other ICT resources) before using them with children. You will be offered some advice about evaluating resources in Chapter 12 and Appendix 5.

Audio recording

Audio recording is ideal for the development of speaking and listening skills. There are many fun and exciting ways to encourage children to speak without them feeling embarrassed or intimidated.

- Most computers and mobile devices have a built-in recording capability.
- MS PowerPoint records voice to accompany presentations.
- There are many commercial sound recorders/systems including Micro-Speak Digital Voice Recorder (by Talking Products), Talking Tins Voice Recorder (by Talking Products), Planet Portable Vocal Booth (by Planet PC), StoryPhones and Rainbow Easi-Speaks.

Podcasting

The term podcast is derived from 'iPod broadcast'. Podcasting is now a popular activity in many primary schools (including whole school podcasting).

A podcast is an audio recording of an event which is made available as one or more episodes, each contained in an audio file (usually mp3, mp4 or wav). It can be played on a PC, Tablet, Smartphone, mp3 player and other mobile devices.

It's a great way for children to share their work with a wider audience (perhaps over the Internet). It allows schools to promote what they do and to celebrate pupil's achievements. In doing so, pupils develop their speaking and listening skills by recording stories, conducting interviews and so on. Podcasting also develops ICT skills.

Some schools have embarked on wider projects, creating a whole series of podcast 'episodes' and making them available for others to download from the school website (sometimes using RSS feeds).

Teachers are also getting in on the act by recording learning content for use outside school. This can be particularly beneficial for those that have missed lessons or for revision purposes.

Software

Podcasting software includes the commercially available Podium (by RM) and Audacity (free Open Source).

 Activity

Link to the Primary ICT site at primaryict.org.uk/icthandbookv2.htm and listen to the three podcasts. In what ways do you think podcasts can benefit the teaching of English (and other subjects)?

There are many potential benefits for both teachers and pupils including: the convenience of listening anywhere, anytime; useful for children who miss lessons (e.g. due to illness); a new approach to homework (e.g. audio notes to reinforce learning); concentration on speaking and listening skills; and an opportunity for children to exploit their creative talents. You will find more on podcasting (and vidcasting) in Chapter 9.

Phonics

To attain skill in word reading, children need to work out the pronunciation of unfamiliar words (decoding) and recognise familiar words. They should understanding that letters and groups of letters (phonemes) represent the sounds in spoken words (graphemes). Phonics should therefore be emphasised in the early teaching of reading to beginners.

In Foundation Stage Literacy, children read and understand simple sentences by using phonic knowledge to decode regular words and read them aloud accurately.

In Year 1, teachers should build on work from the Foundation Stage. They should ensure that pupils continue to learn new grapheme-phoneme correspondences (GPCs) and revise and consolidate those learnt earlier. In Year 2 and beyond, pupils continue to apply phonic knowledge and skills as the route to decode words until automatic decoding has become embedded and reading is fluent.

A number of ICT packages have been developed for this purpose. These include:

- **Phonics Software** (by Talking Products) – Learn letters and corresponding sounds by building different words.

- **Talking Phonics 1 and 2** (by Mantra Lingua) – Packed with sounds, songs and games, all designed to support practitioners and parents in their understanding and delivery of early phonics.

- **Clicker Phonics** (by Crick) – a complete phonics programme that provides a firm foundation for reading and writing, taking children from the first steps of discriminating environmental sounds right up to systematic synthetic phonics.

- **Jolly Phonics** (by Jolly Learning) – a comprehensive set of phonics classroom resources and software.

- **Story Phonics** (by Letterland International) – story-based software allowing children to listen to sounds, build words on-screen, blend and segment words and share animated versions of the stories.

- **LetterSounds™ 1 and 2** (by ReadingDoctor) – a scientifically based teaching tool which teaches the links between the letters of the alphabet and the speech sounds they represent.

- **Big Cat Phonics** (by Collins) – 72 fully decodable phonic readers, with an equal split of fiction and non-fiction.

- **Learn to Read** (by Starfall) – starfall.com/n/level-a/learn-to-read/play.htm.

■ **Phase 1 Phonics** (by Smart Learning) – smart-learning.co.uk/phase-1-phonics.html.

■ **Dog and Cat Letters and Sounds** (by busythings) – busythings.co.uk.

You may find that, however good the phonics program, it doesn't entirely fit the bill for one reason or another. In this case you may wish to develop some supplementary resources yourself. In the following activity you will examine a self-made activity which has been created in MS PowerPoint.

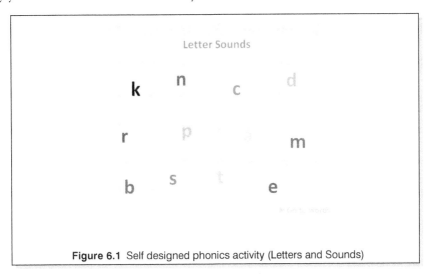

Figure 6.1 Self designed phonics activity (Letters and Sounds)

Activity

Link to the Primary ICT site and try out the CVC Slide Show – Letters and Sounds.
It allows children to practise letter sounds and then introduces a number of Consonant-Vowel-Consonant (CVC) words incorporating the practised letters. If you think the CVC slide show is a useful resource you will find more on the TES Connect website. You may wish to explore these resources (tes.co.uk/teaching-resources). You can adapt them to suit your own learning objectives or you might like to create your own PowerPoint resources from scratch.

Activity

Link to the Primary ICT site where you'll find a Primary Phonics Guide created by Moortown Primary School.
You may want to create a similar resource yourself.

Using word processors to write

Software can be categorised as 'content rich' or 'content free'. Talking Story CD-ROMs are an example of the former – the content already exists (and most likely can't be modified). Content rich packages have the advantage of offering pre-existing, high-quality materials which potentially save teachers a great deal of work. They do however suffer from several disadvantages – they most often don't give you 'exactly' what you want, they only go part way toward achieving your desired learning goals, they can provide the wrong sort of motivation and, of course, they come at a cost.

Content free packages, as the name implies, are blank canvases inside which children can use their creative talents in a variety of ways. They can also be used by teachers to create simple activities for children to follow. These packages often exist as part of a larger suite of programs, sometimes known as 'software toolkits'.

A word processor is a prime example of a content free package. Children will use word processors as one method of presenting their work but they can also be used for a number of useful literacy activities such as creating and editing text (perhaps using prepared word banks), converting text from one form to another (e.g. a narrative to a play), cloze exercises, and labelling and classifying.

MS Word is an obvious choice because it is freely available in all schools and is very much the standard word processor. However, young children will benefit from a child-friendly package such as TextEase CT, Clicker 6 or the 2Simple range. Many word processors for the Primary and Foundation Stages now incorporate a talking facility to aid spelling development (but beware of synthetic voices and American accents).

The sun is in the skie

and the sea is very cold.

We made sand castles

on the beach.

Figure 6.2 Using word processors to write

The choice of word processing activities should match the curriculum and might include: writing about oneself, writing a letter, writing a story or rhyme, writing about a character in a story etc.

Children can also practise computer skills such as mouse control, keyboard skills, formatting and manipulating text, and saving and printing work.

It may prove useful to begin writing by introducing a paper keyboard with upper-case characters and getting children to colour the important function keys (Spacebar, Shift, Delete, Backspace and Enter) and writing the lower-case letters alongside each upper case equivalent.

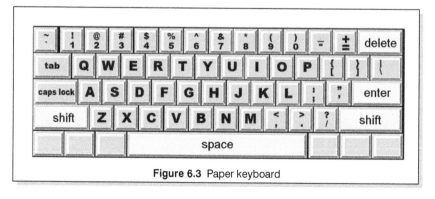

Figure 6.3 Paper keyboard

Activity

Download the paper keyboard (paper_keyboard.doc) and paper keyboard ideas (keyboard_ideas.doc) from the Primary ICT site and try out some activities for yourself.

There are many other useful activities that you can devise using a paper keyboard. Perhaps you can think of some.

 Activity

Another useful activity is editing text. Here, children recognise that ICT lets them correct and improve their work – either as they are working or at a later date. They can also practise formatting.

Use MS Word to create the following text (with deliberate errors) and present to children as an on-screen activity.

Using a printed, error-free version, children can make the necessary corrections to the on-screen version, saving and printing their work if required (don't allow spell-checkers at this stage). More able children can do this without the printed copy.

The Gingerbread Boy

One day a litle old wuman made a boy out of jinger bread and the boy came to life and ran away and evryone chast him. A sli fox saw him by the river and the fox trikked the boy into climing up onto his back. Hafway acros the river the fox tost the boy into the air and opened his jaws and SNAP the jinger bread boy was gon.

Children are taught to present text to different audiences for different purposes. It is possible to change a piece of text designed for one audience to make it suitable for another. For example, a short story involving two or three characters is written as a 'narrative'. This can be changed to a presentation by transferring it to a set of slides or to a 'play' with speaking parts for each of the characters.

Table 6.2 Contextualising text

Narrative	Play	
The teacher entered the classroom and said, "Good morning children." The class didn't respond except for a quiet voice in the corner who replied, "Good morning Miss Johnson." It was Sharon.	**Teacher:**	"Good morning children."
	Sharon:	"Good morning Miss Johnson."

The activity fits in well with the requirement for all pupils to participate in and gain knowledge, skills and understanding associated with the artistic practice of drama.

Finally, here are a number of possible writing activities you can offer your class:

- Begin a story, children write the end.
- Read a short story and children draw a picture about it.
- Children practise writing their name.

- Children add labels to a picture.
- Children join letters to the correct picture.
- Children reply to an email from Goldilocks.
- Children build a story using a word/picture bank that you have created.
- Children match picture and word cards that you have created and laminated.

Handwriting

The curriculum requires pupils to write clearly, accurately and coherently. There is a specific emphasis on handwriting and pupils are taught to sit correctly at a table, holding a pencil comfortably and correctly, form lower-case letters in the correct direction, starting and finishing in the right place, form capital letters and form digits.

ICT is no substitute for handwriting with pencil and paper but, in an age of tablet computers and interactive whiteboards there are certainly plenty of opportunities to encourage handwriting in a fun and stimulating way.

Most tablets and smart phones have built-in note taking capability and indeed there are a number of bespoke graphics tablets designed specifically for drawing and writing.

Better still, you could use educational software such as 2Handwrite (by 2Simple) which demonstrates the process of letter formation, handwriting joins and spelling patterns using an interactive whiteboard and tablet PCs. You can also use software like Startwrite 6 (by Startwrite) to create customised handwriting practice sheets for pupils.

Spelling, vocabulary, grammar and pronunciation

The new curriculum includes statutory elements and features that should be included in the teaching of spelling, vocabulary, grammar and pronunciation

Aside from the spelling, grammar and thesaurus features of word processing packages, there is a huge range of software available on these topics including:

Spelling

- Ultimate Spelling (by Ultimate Spelling).
- Spelling Made Simple (by Spelling Made Simple).
- Spelling Blaster (by Knowledge Adventure).
- School Zone Spelling (by School Zone).
- Spell Track (by Sherston).
- SpellQuizzer (by SpellQuizzer).
- Show Me Spelling (by Spectronics).

Vocabulary

- Ultimate Vocabulary (by Ultimate Vocabulary).
- Vocabulary Super Stretch (by Merit).
- Vocaboly (by Vocaboly).
- Word-Pal (by Word-Pal).

Grammar

- Free Grammar Checker (by Ginger).

- Grammarly (by Grammarly).

- CorrectEnglish (by CorrectEnglish).

- Grammar Expert Plus (by Wintertree).

- Editor (by Serenity Software).

- RightWriter (by RightWriter).

- ClearEdits (by (ClearWriter).

Pronunciation

- Perfect Pronunciation (by Antimoon).

- Pronunciation Power (by ESL.net).

- BBC Learning English: Pronunciation tips (by BBC).

- Pronunciation King (by Clump Software).

Dictionaries and encyclopaedias

There are several dictionary and encyclopaedia packages on CD-ROM and on the Internet. Some of the many examples are:

Table 6.3 Dictionaries and encyclopaedias

On CD-ROM	*Internet*
The Oxford English Dictionary	dictionary.com
Longman Children's Picture Dictionary	yourdictionary.com
My First CD-ROM: Dictionary	pdictionary.com
Webster's New World Children's Dictionary	wordsmyth.net
Britannica Kids	bigiqkids.com/spellingwords/onlinedictionary.shtml
Dorling Kindersley Children's Dictionary	en.wikipedia.org

The Internet offerings now tend to take precedence because they are free, much more comprehensive and continually updated.

Cloze exercises

Several software packages (e.g. Cloze Pro and 2Simple Developing Tray) provide cloze exercises. Children fill in the gaps in the text produced by the program. This tests knowledge of language use and reading comprehension. Words may be chosen from a bank and the word chosen for each gap will be the most appropriate one that fits the sentence and paragraph in both grammar and meaning.

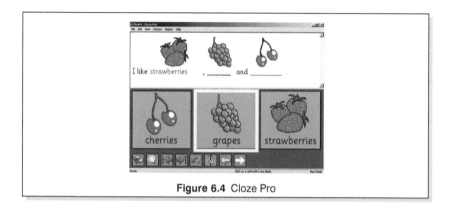

Figure 6.4 Cloze Pro

💻 Activity

Use MS Word to create the following cloze passage. The word bank is optional.
To do this use MS Word's 'Forms' toolbar (Office 2003) or the Protect Document, Restrict Formatting and Editing feature (Office 2007/2010).

<u>My Cat</u>

My _ _ _ is called Molly. She is black. She has got a long _ _ _ _ that she swishes when she is cross. She uses her _ _ _ _ _ _ to wash herself. When she's hungry she makes a _ _ _ _ sound.

Cat meow tongue tail

You might also try **Paragraph PAL Clozemaker**, a free software package enabling the creation of cloze exercises (parapal-online.co.uk).

Labelling and classifying

Labelling and classifying are useful activities that help children learn that information can be used to describe objects. They learn to use simple criteria to divide groups of objects into sub sets and to identify objects by key words.

Software packages exist for this purpose but it is often best for the teacher to design an activity using a simple word processing or graphics package (e.g. MS Word, TextEase, Publisher or 2Simple Science Simulation). This can include posters and collages.

💻 Activity

There are lots of free activities on the Crickweb website. Here's a link to some labelling and classifying activities that you may wish to try: crickweb.co.uk/ks1literacy.html.

Activity

Parapal Hotspots is a free labelling software package that allows you to take any jpeg image and add interactive regions so that pupils can learn new terms and then test themselves.

You can download this package (plus a range of other software) free from the ParaPal website at parapal-online.co.uk.

 Activity

The activity below has been created in MS Word. It makes use of the Forms toolbar and uses drop-down boxes to offer word choice to children.

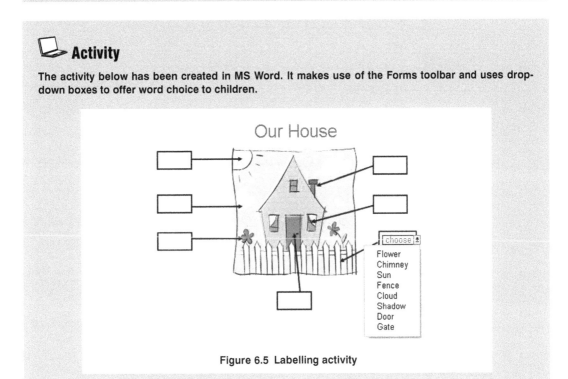

Figure 6.5 Labelling activity

Can you create something similar?

Communicating

ICT surely comes into its own when used for communicating. Children can:

- present their work (e.g. create a slide show using presentation software such as MS PowerPoint or TextEase Presenter);

- publish information (e.g. design a poster using desktop publishing software such as MS Publisher or TextEase);

- use the Internet for a variety of purposes including email, blogging and social networking – we will look at these in more detail in a later section.

Paper-based activities

The computer can be used to produce a number of activities in paper format (e.g. printed and laminated word and picture sets, colouring sheets, number puzzles etc.). These not only provide an alternative method for those who learn better off-line but they also provide a good contingency plan just in case your ICT equipment decides to fail you! You can also find many prepared activities on the Internet (see the list of websites in Appendix 3).

Digital cameras

There are many hardware devices, aside from a PC and its peripherals, which can support literacy (e.g. speaking and writing toys, listening centres and electronic dictionaries). Perhaps the most versatile is the digital camera. They are easy and fun to use and, armed with a camera, children will have the opportunity to use their imagination and be creative and innovative.

They are capable of capturing and permanently storing images of children's own learning experiences which allows for consolidation and reflection at any time in the future. Images can be presented in a variety of ways including wall displays, presentations, teacher-created activities, written work (especially stories), web pages, blogs, and printed and laminated activities. Images of actual objects are an excellent way to create resources and to aid language and number work.

There are great benefits in being able to capture images from the child's actual environment to aid language recognition, to create a link between the text and the concept, and to help rerun specific teaching experiences.

Digital cameras are relatively cheap and are also available in robust, child-friendly versions for as little as £20 (e.g. the Digital Blue collection of still and moving cameras and the Tuff Cam 2 by TTS). Not to mention the built-in cameras on mobile phones and tablet PCs.

Note: Some schools are particularly cautious about taking photos of their children. If you are going to use pictures of children, be sure that you don't infringe your school policy and you have permission from a parent or guardian.

 Activity

Link to the Primary ICT site at primaryict.org.uk/icthandbookv2.htm and watch the Literacy Video.

- Is the digital camera an effective resource here?
- Could you achieve the same learning outcomes without it?
- Is it motivating for children – does it enable them?
- What are the advantages of using a digital camera?
- What are the disadvantages?

Hopefully your identified advantages will outweigh the disadvantages. The teacher and children in the video have certainly used a camera effectively and in a motivating way. The ability to gather pictorial information and recall it whenever it is needed provides for a speedy and clear point of discussion. Cameras are relatively cheap and simple to use. Indeed, as with many other ICT resources, you can allow children to explore and experiment rather than providing formal tuition on the camera.

 Activity

On the Primary ICT site at primaryict.org.uk/icthandbookv2.htm you'll find 100 things to do with a digital camera.

Software toolkits

The most effective (and cost-effective) way to develop a child's ICT capability is by using a good 'software toolkit' (a suite of software packages, mostly content free).

Typical toolkits will include: word processor, spreadsheet, database (including branching database), graphics package, desktop publishing, turtle (LOGO), presentation software, Internet browser and email editor.

Toolkits allow teachers to devise activities (for use on-screen or off) and allow children to use their creative talents in a variety of ways.

Examples include: MS Word, TextEase Studio CT, Tizzy's First Tools, 2Simple, and BlackCat SuperTools.

 Activity

If you haven't already done so you can sign up for a 30 Day trial of 2Simple's Purple Mash from their website at 2simple.com/purple-mash.
There are numerous applications available for you to trial.

Content rich software

There's a whole host of content rich software packages on the market. Some are excellent and others are not. No particular recommendations here – you can explore some of the retailers' websites yourself (e.g. Sherston, Semerc, Blackcat, Cricksoft, Widgit and more – see Appendix 4).

It's important that you evaluate software before using it with children and before committing to purchase. This is covered in Chapter 12 and Appendix 5.

Digital pens

There are two types of digital pen currently on the market.

1. **Digital Pens** (and digital paper) allow conventional writing and drawings to be captured and uploaded to a computer. They incorporate a miniature video camera which captures the pen strokes and, when uploaded, reproduces them faithfully on-screen. Some pens also provide audio capture which is time-aligned with the text. They provide a handy way to capture notes and sketches when away from the computer and pupils can create their own illustrations rather than depend on clipart. Examples include: Livescribe smartpen (by Svensk TalTeknologi AB) and Reading Pen (by Scanning Pens).

2. **Reading Pens** read out loud by capturing words from associated books and worksheets and convert them into voice. Examples include: PENpal and the EAL Starter Kit (by Mantra Lingua).

Apps

As the development of Smartphones and other mobile devices continues to advance at a pace, so does the design of software applications for the Apple, Android and Windows operating systems. This extends the capability for schools to extend learning beyond the classroom.

Some of the many 'apps' on the market are Spellpop, Android Flashcards, Android Wordbank, 2Do It Yourself, AppWriter, CaturaTalk, EduDroid, The Three Little Pigs, Little Red Riding Hood, Goldilocks and the Three Bears and The Gingerbread Man.

Apps are covered in more detail in Chapter 9.

7

Using ICT to enhance mathematics and science

Introduction

Mathematics and science have been deliberately combined in this chapter because many of the available ICT resources and types of activity are common to both.

Foundation Stage mathematics

Detail of the curriculum for mathematics for the EYFS is available online at: gov.uk/government/publications/early-years-foundation-stage-framework--2.

Mathematics is not a prime area but it is a means by which three prime areas are strengthened and applied. Development involves providing children with opportunities to develop and improve their skills in counting, understanding and using numbers, calculating simple addition and subtraction problems; and to describe shapes, spaces and measures.

- Numbers: children count reliably with numbers from 1 to 20, place them in order and say which number is one more or one less than a given number. Using quantities and objects, they add and subtract two single-digit numbers and count on or back to find the answer. They solve problems, including doubling, halving and sharing.

- Shape, space and measures: children use everyday language to talk about size, weight, capacity, position, distance, time and money to compare quantities and objects and to solve problems. They recognise, create and describe patterns. They explore characteristics of everyday objects and shapes and use mathematical language to describe them.

DfE (2014b)

Mathematics and science National Curriculum

Schools are expected to follow the old programme of study for maths and science (including testing) until September 2015 when the new curriculum then takes force. This chapter covers the content of both old and new.

Detail of the curriculum for mathematics for primary is available online at:

1. The old National Curriculum for maths and science: webarchive.nationalarchives.gov.uk/20131202172639/http://www.education.gov.uk/schools/teachingandlearning/curriculum/primary.

2. The new National Curriculum for maths and science: gov.uk/government/collections/national-curriculum.

Mathematics (old and new) requires pupils to:

- reason mathematically by following a line of enquiry, conjecturing relationships and generalisations, and developing an argument, justification or proof using mathematical language;
- solve problems by applying their mathematics to a variety of routine and non-routine problems with increasing sophistication, including breaking down problems into a series of simpler steps and persevering in seeking solutions.

This will necessarily include the study of place value; counting; calculating (using the four number operations); fractions; ratio and proportion; algebra; position and direction; reasoning; exploring shape (2D and 3D); angles; taking measurements; creating diagrams and charts; and presenting results.

Science (old and new) requires pupils to:

- develop scientific knowledge and conceptual understanding through the specific disciplines of biology, chemistry and physics;
- develop understanding of the nature, processes and methods of science through different types of science enquiries that help them to answer scientific questions about the world around them;
- become equipped with the scientific knowledge required to understand the uses and implications of science, today and for the future.

This will require children asking simple questions; observing; using simple equipment; performing simple tests; identifying and classifying and gathering and recording data to help in answering questions. It will necessarily include the study of animals, plants and organisms; everyday materials and their properties; rocks; weather; physical phenomena related to electricity; force and motion; light and sound; energy resources and energy transfer; earth and space; and physical quantities.

ICT in mathematics and science

ICT in mathematics and in science is good for a great many things.
Picture…

- a lesson about the Sun brought to life by an Internet link displayed on a large screen that shows the fiery ball rotating, fountains of fire spurting from the inferno below;
- a fun, collaborative activity using floor robots that allows children to learn by doing and to visualise the results through the actions of colourful, familiar toys;
- how much easier it is to follow a photosynthesis investigation when the results are displayed in real time from a data-logger on the [interactive] whiteboard for comment, annotation and examination;
- taking a digital microscope and laptop outside with a group of nursery children to take a movie of woodlice in their natural habitat to be shown back in the playroom alongside the children's work and ideas.

The advent of durable, simple to use ICT equipment makes all this reality.

ICT resources and activities for maths and science

An imaginary project?

There are many ways in which ICT can be used to support your lessons, but is the following project taking things a little too far?

Activity

Look at the following project:

The teacher launches a science experiment and provides background information using an **interactive whiteboard** and **SMART Notebook**. Some **images** and **data** from previous work are used to refresh the topic. The **notebook file** is saved and uploaded onto the school's **learning platform** so that pupils can access it from home. Pupils undertake the experiment using **data-logging** equipment and take **digital photos** and a **video** as work progresses. On completion, pupils discuss the results with another school using **web cams** and **video conferencing software**.

Pupils go home and reflect on their experiment, sharing and exchanging ideas with other pupils via a threaded **discussion board**. They write up the experiment using **word processing** software, incorporating **images** and references from the **Internet** and from **CD-ROMs** on the school **Intranet**. A summary is uploaded to their personal **e-portfolio** or **weblog**. They also carry out an analysis of the results and incorporate graphs with the help of a **spreadsheet**.

The completed report is submitted to the teacher using the **digital drop box** on the school's **virtual learning environment** (**VLE**). The teacher marks the work **electronically** and sends individual feedback via the drop box.

This is a comprehensive project incorporating a number of resources. Do you think this is realistic or simply imaginary?

Most activities don't incorporate such an extensive range of ICT resources even though it is quite possible. Perhaps this is an exaggeration by one of those teachers who we may class as an 'enthusiast'.

We aren't all enthusiasts and we don't necessarily have the time or the inclination to mimic an activity such as this. However, we should consider making appropriate use of some ICT resources in our Maths and Science lessons.

 Activity

Imagine you are delivering a maths or science lesson. What are the general salient features of ICT resources which might influence you to include them in your activities?

There are of course many features including uniqueness, speed, accuracy, capacity, automaticity, interactivity, dexterity, capability, quality, communication, multimedia, enjoyment, motivation … and more!

Floor robots

Programmable floor robots are extremely useful in mathematics for activities involving estimation, angles and direction, shape, spatial awareness, instructions, and control and investigation. In addition to number work, robots facilitate group work, design and technology, and, of course, programming (see Chapter 4).

There are now many lightweight, low power, rechargeable models on the market including the Bee-Bot, Pro-Bot, Ladybird and iBug.

Bee-Bot

Perhaps the most popular robot is the Bee-Bot.

This well established and extremely versatile resource is used widely, not only in mathematics, science and computing but also in English and other subjects.

There are also a number of supporting resources including a range of mats and activity CD-ROMs.

Figure 7.1 Bee-Bot

 Activity

If you'd like some Bee-Bot activity ideas, try the following:
1. Bee-Bot Guide: primaryict.org.uk/icthandbookv2.htm (ch7).
2. Bee-Bot Activities: primaryict.org.uk/icthandbookv2.htm (ch4).
3. Bee-Bot Lessons: scoop.it/t/bee-bot-lessons-and-ideas.
4. Bee-Bot Treasure Island Activities: primaryict.org.uk/icthandbookv2.htm (ch7).
5. A range of activities from TES Connect: tes.co.uk/teaching-resources/primary-40069/ks1-ict-41488/ controlling-and-modelling-41489/floor-turtle-41491.
You will of course need access to a Bee-Bot in order to try them out.

Bee-Bot software version

There are also several software applications that will allow you to simulate the actions of robots on-screen. The Bee-Bot software, called Focus on Bee-Bot, is currently available as a 14-day trial version from focuseducational.com/html/bee-bot-international-free-trial.php.

For an overview of the software try youtube.com/watch?v=8UTv9hzyV-k.

Bee-Bot app

If your classroom has tablet PCs or other mobile devices then you could use the Bee-Bot App (tts-group. co.uk). Using keypad functionality it mimics the actions of the Bee-Bot floor robot. There is also a free App available from iTunes.

Digital microscopes

The microscope is an invaluable tool in science but conventional apparatus lacks versatility and can often make an activity dull.

This is where the digital microscope comes into its own. Simple to use, portable, robust and inexpensive, digital microscopes have a variety of purposeful uses. Magnified items can be displayed on-screen and, when projected onto a large screen (or interactive whiteboard), they enhance a lesson because they can be viewed by the whole class. Images (still or moving) can be permanently captured and then used to support written work.

Good examples of digital microscopes are the QX7 (by Digital Blue) and the Easi-Scope (by TTS).

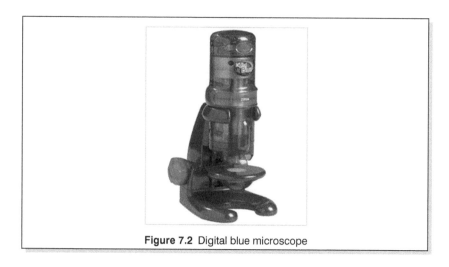

Figure 7.2 Digital blue microscope

 Activity

Link to the Primary ICT site at primaryict.org.uk/icthandbookv2.htm and watch the first part of the Digital Microscope Video.

> **How might you use a digital microscope in your own teaching?**
> There are many experiments you can conduct from exploring 'minibeasts' to examining your own hair.
> On the Primary ICT site you'll also find:

1. **The Teachers SMART Guide to the Digital Microscope.**
2. A list of curriculum related **Digital Microscope Opportunities**.

Digital cameras

The digital camera was introduced in the previous chapter. However, it is such an important resource that it is included again in this section.

You might begin by teaching the whole class how to take pictures with a camera though many children will prefer to work it out for themselves.

Once children are familiar with its operation, there are lots of ideas for using a digital camera in Mathematics. For example, children find groups of objects in the school or classroom which correspond with a given number (e.g. 3 buttons on a coat, 5 crayons, 2 books). The pictures can be imported into MS PowerPoint (or printed out) to create a number book.

There are many cameras on the market and most claim to be robust enough for use by children. These cameras offer an astounding range of features for little money. Examples include the Tuff Cam (by TTS) and the Flip (available from Digital Blue).

* Many old favourites such as the Digital Blue and Flip are now harder to source (or indeed obsolete) as the technology advances and the competition stiffens.

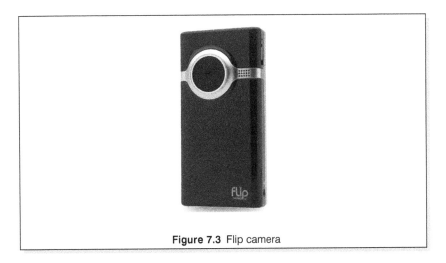

Figure 7.3 Flip camera

 Activity

For ideas on using the digital camera in Maths and Science, link to the Primary ICT site at primaryict. org.uk/icthandbookv2.htm where you'll find the document 'Digital Cameras in Maths'.

Activity

Link to the Primary ICT site at primaryict.org.uk/icthandbookv2.htm and try out the Number Book activity. The book has been created using a digital camera and MS PowerPoint. Is this better than a book off the shelf?

The book is interactive and is supported with voice-overs (created by the children). It could be developed to include other multimedia. Children will take pride in something that they have created themselves. They can reflect on their actual experiences and relate the contents of the book directly to objects in the school or classroom.

Unlike printed materials, the finished product can easily be made available to the whole school via the learning platform and displayed on Interactive Whiteboards for whole class work.

Control

Computer control allows children to create and manipulate models of real life situations. They do this by programming a sequence of events which will take place over a period of time. For example, they can control a set of traffic lights, operate a burglar alarm system, control a plant irrigation system or move a vehicle forwards and backwards. In general, any system which includes output devices (such as lamps, motors, buzzers and bells) and input devices (such as sensors for light, sound or temperature) can be controlled.

Programming can be child-friendly and will use relatively simple instructions or flowcharts. Children can be taught:

■ how to create, test, improve and refine sequences of instructions to make things happen and to monitor events and respond to them (for example, monitoring changes in temperature, detecting light levels and turning on a light);

■ how mechanisms can be used to make things move in different ways, using a range of equipment including an ICT control program.

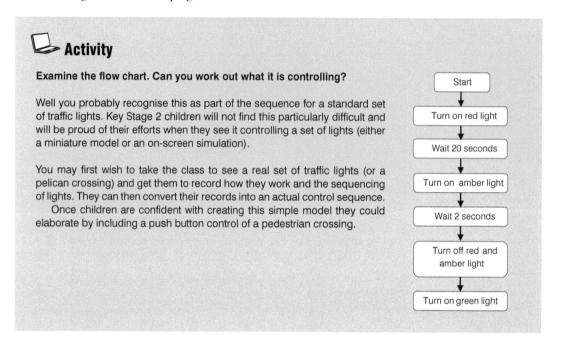

Activity

Examine the flow chart. Can you work out what it is controlling?

Well you probably recognise this as part of the sequence for a standard set of traffic lights. Key Stage 2 children will not find this particularly difficult and will be proud of their efforts when they see it controlling a set of lights (either a miniature model or an on-screen simulation).

You may first wish to take the class to see a real set of traffic lights (or a pelican crossing) and get them to record how they work and the sequencing of lights. They can then convert their records into an actual control sequence.
Once children are confident with creating this simple model they could elaborate by including a push button control of a pedestrian crossing.

There are a number of control kits available including Lego Mindstorms hardware (and icon-based programming interface), Economatics Control Station (and Universal Logicator Software) and 2ControlNXT.

You can download a demo of the Economatics Control Station (and Logicator software) from their website at economatics-education.co.uk/cms/trialandupdates.

Data-logging

Data-logging is the collection of readings from sensors over a period of time. There are many types of sensor but most primary schools keep it simple and use sensors for measuring temperature, light and sound (most data-logging devices will have these three sensors built in).

Data collected can be displayed as charts and graphs or on a continually updated number display.

The sensors may be used as part of scientific experiments which require the gathering of data and they are often used in conjunction with control equipment to control simple systems such as the temperature in a fish tank.

Data-logging equipment will normally be connected to a PC whilst data collection is taking place. However, when information needs to be collected over a long period of time (e.g. weather data), the equipment can be used remotely and the data transferred to a PC later.

Typical data-logging activities include:

■ monitoring the temperature in the classroom;

■ measuring traffic noise outside the school;

■ testing heat insulation and cooling effects (e.g. melting ice);

■ keeping weather records.

You can choose from a wide range of equipment such as LogIt Explorer and Log-Box.

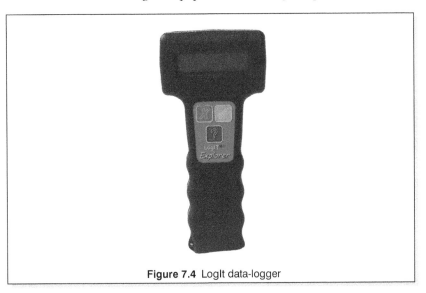

Figure 7.4 LogIt data-logger

Activity

Link to the Primary ICT site at primaryict.org.uk/icthandbookv2.htm and access the files DataLoggingInfo and DataLoggingActivities. The QCA references are now outdated but, nevertheless, these documents should present you with some useful data-logging ideas.

These are simple yet comprehensive activities which fit in well with the National Curriculum objectives for science. You can do some of these activities without data-logging equipment (e.g. you can use a thermometer to measure temperature) but loggers are relatively inexpensive and can be left alone for periods of time, taking readings without manual intervention.

Simulation

Simulations allow children to safely explore concepts which would be difficult or perhaps impossible without ICT. Pupils can experience processes which may be too slow, too fast, too dangerous or too expensive to do in school. For example, learning about electricity, exploring space travel and changes in the populations of micro-organisms in different conditions.

Activity

Link to the BBC website (bbc.co.uk/schools/scienceclips/ages/5_6/light_dark.shtml) and try the Light and Dark simulation (for Years 1 and 2). How does this compare to the real thing?

There is, of course, no substitute for real life situations. However, an experiment such as this would be difficult to set up in school and might prove to be quite dangerous too! In addition, free simulations such as this are easily repeatable.

Simulation packages include: LiveWire; Bright Spark; Junior Simulation Insight; 2Simple Science; and BBC Science Clips (bbc.co.uk/schools/scienceclips).

Content rich software

Content rich software is professionally made and pupils benefit from its interactivity and effective use of multimedia. It is 'ready to use' and may save you the burden of preparing ICT resources yourself. It does however come at a price and you may spend some time finding cost-effective products that satisfy the objectives of the curriculum.

You might explore some of the many retailer websites for ideas – see Appendix 4.

It's important that you evaluate the software before using it with children and before committing to purchase. More on evaluation in Chapter 12 and Appendix 5.

Content free software

There are many content rich software titles on the market, some better than others. But it is often the case that, however good the packages, they don't entirely meet your needs. They may not be specific enough for the intended learning outcomes, they may be too complicated or they may not provide for differentiated learning.

If this is the case then you should consider developing simple activities yourself using content free software such as MS Office, SMART Notebook and TextEase.

Designing activities can of course place great demands on your time and, before starting to create a new project, you might try out some of the existing resources which can be downloaded freely from the Internet. In most cases you are at liberty to adapt them to suit your own needs and this may be better than starting from scratch.

 Activity

Link to the following websites and try out some of the free resources.

- Primary Resources: primaryresources.co.uk
- Numeracy World: numeracyworld.com
- TES Connect: tes.co.uk/primary-teaching-resources
- Primary Games: primarygames.co.uk
- BBC Schools: bbc.co.uk/schools
- Cbeebies: bbc.co.uk/cbeebies
- Science Teaching Ideas: teachingideas.co.uk/science/contents.htm
- Channel 4 Learning: channel4learning.com
- Crickweb: crickweb.co.uk
- Primary Interactive: primaryinteractive.co.uk

There are many other sources of activities to be found on the Internet. Try searching (using Google or Yahoo) to see what you can find. It also pays to search for 'Primary Schools' and 'Grids for Learning' as these are good sources too.

Spreadsheets

Spreadsheets are an essential element of the primary curriculum. Children should be able to enter data (numbers and text), use simple rules and formulae to calculate totals, and create associated graphs and charts. They should be able to apply spreadsheets to simple mathematical and scientific models, answering 'what if …?' questions.

The very thought of spreadsheets fill some of us with trepidation! However, we need to be able to support our pupils and it need not be a major issue if you keep it simple.

Here's an example of some excellent spreadsheet work from Year 5 pupils in a primary school. The pupils had to organise a café, working out the difference between the buying and the selling price of typical items.

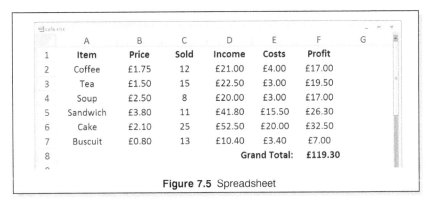

	A	B	C	D	E	F	G
1	Item	Price	Sold	Income	Costs	Profit	
2	Coffee	£1.75	12	£21.00	£4.00	£17.00	
3	Tea	£1.50	15	£22.50	£3.00	£19.50	
4	Soup	£2.50	8	£20.00	£3.00	£17.00	
5	Sandwich	£3.80	11	£41.80	£15.50	£26.30	
6	Cake	£2.10	25	£52.50	£20.00	£32.50	
7	Buscuit	£0.80	13	£10.40	£3.40	£7.00	
8					Grand Total:	£119.30	

Figure 7.5 Spreadsheet

Is this complicated? Well no, it's just arithmetic performed using an advanced calculator! Of course the spreadsheet is capable of much more, including the creation of graphs and charts.

Spreadsheets: benefits for children

Spreadsheet software can support children's learning in the primary school curriculum by:

- helping the child to develop reasoning skills as he or she makes hypotheses and carries out research to test them;
- enabling the child to search for and investigate mathematical patterns and relationships;
- providing tools that the child can use to synthesize and analyse large amounts of information;
- facilitating the development of higher-order thinking skills by modelling 'what-if' processes. For example, 'if we double the price of our most popular school shop item, how much would this increase our overall profit for the school shop?';
- enabling the child to see data in a visual format, thereby facilitating their understanding;
- providing a means for the child to discuss and record the processes and results of his or her work;
- enabling the child to keep records of his or her work or that of groups or sports teams.

Spreadsheets: teacher uses

Teachers can use spreadsheet software to:

- create and maintain records of children's scores, for example, to perform calculations such as computing average marks or comparing marks with those of other classes and other years;
- prepare templates with grid layouts to speed up and simplify worksheet preparation;

- prepare class timetables;

- adapt timetables for individual children, for example children attending learning support classes and special needs;

- create a spreadsheet to collate a record of the costs of classroom materials, and other resources;

- maintain records of children's books and other classroom items.

Examples of spreadsheet packages include 2Simple Infant Video Toolkit, 2Calculate, RM Starting Graph, TextEase and MS Excel.

 Activity

Link to the Primary Resources site at primaryresources.co.uk/ict/ict2.htm where you'll find several resources for introducing spreadsheets in primary school.

Databases

Database software can be used to store, manipulate and retrieve data in the form of text, sound and graphics. A database is an electronic version of a manual filing system and facilitates tasks that would be difficult and more time-consuming if performed manually.

Spreadsheets are capable of performing a number of database tasks though database software itself is much more capable and powerful.

It is perhaps best to introduce the concept of database by first comparing computer-based versions with paper-based systems (e.g. index cards, a phone book, a product catalogue, a library catalogue, a dictionary etc.). Children can then be introduced to the files, records and fields which make up an electronic database. They will use the database to enter and sort data, carry out simple searches, answer simple questions and produce bar charts.

Database: benefits for children

Database software can support children's learning in the primary school curriculum by:

- promoting the use of questioning and analytical skills as the child collects and organises information;

- facilitating the child's ability to organise and analyse groups of information or data;

- enabling the child to analyse a single domain of study (e.g. animal types) using complex queries;

- allowing the child to search the database for information in several fields;

- supporting the child's understanding of information in a new way using visual representations of data;

- helping the child to make the transition from concrete to abstract understanding as they move from graphing with physical objects to creating two-dimensional displays of information.

Database: teacher uses

Database software provides support for teachers in maintaining records of curriculum content for teaching and learning, and also children's records. Teachers can also use database software to:

- plan schemes of work;

- create and maintain lists of contact information for children and their parents and guardians;

- store information and records of children's work and class records;

- keep records of class specific teaching materials and resources and their location;
- keep records of school and/or class library books.

Flat file databases

Standard database packages, such as MS Access, appear as 'flat' two-dimensional tables.

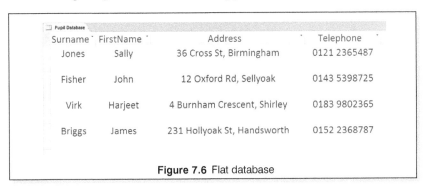

Figure 7.6 Flat database

However, the database in Figure 7.7 may have more appeal to younger children because it is simple to use and can include images too.

Children can apply database applications to handle and present information in other areas of the curriculum such as geography, science, design and technology and history. They can also be used to produce graphs, charts and pictograms.

Examples of database and charting packages are: Tizzy's First Tools (Chart); 2Investigate, TextEase Studio CT and 2Simple Infant Video Toolkit. For activities on minibeasts try Learners' Library: Minibeasts.

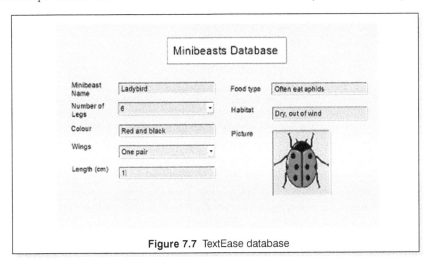

Figure 7.7 TextEase database

Branching databases

Another useful application is the branching database. These are used for children to learn to sort and classify information by using 'yes/no' questions to separate a set of objects into two sub-sets. For example, they can apply this concept to classify plants and animals in science.

The database in Figure 7.8 tests a child's ability to recognise the order of numbers in the range 1 to 10. The child is given a number on a flash card and the speaking database software asks a series of yes/no questions in order to identify the number.

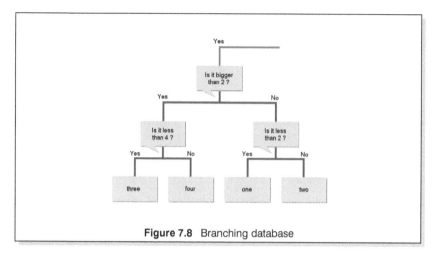

Figure 7.8 Branching database

Examples of database packages include: Tizzy's First Tools (Decide); 2Investigate; TextEase Studio CT; FlexiTREE and MS Access.

 Activity

Link to the Primary ICT site and access the Minibeasts Activities pdf.
 How might you use flat and branching database software to enhance these activities?
 The **Minibeast Key** activity would benefit from a branching database and the **Differences in Minibeasts** activity could use a flat database to record and subsequently manipulate data on the insects.

Calculators

There would appear to be a lack of agreement about the consequences of calculator use in the primary classroom.

Some would profess that it reduces number facility and enables children to 'cheat at sums'. Indeed, the question has been raised by MPs as to whether children's confidence in Maths could be improved if Britain were to take a lesson from better performing nations and restrict calculator use.

Others recognise the potential of calculators in that they have an inbuilt structure of the place value system, the use of signs and symbols and mathematical ideas such as decimal notation and negative numbers.

The jury may still be out, however, as with any ICT resource, the calculator will only ever be used by those who value it as a learning tool. If you are unsure, and want to decide for yourself, then try out some of the activities on the Primary ICT website.

 Activity

Link to the Primary ICT site and try out the Calculator Activities. How do you feel about primary school children using the calculator?

8

Using ICT in other subjects

Introduction

Having covered the core subjects you may now have some ideas of how ICT can be used to support and enhance children's learning. This chapter examines each of the other subjects in somewhat less detail but, nevertheless, offers a number of useful ideas and links.

ICT is such a vast subject area that it is often difficult to know where to start when deliberating over its possible use in any particular subject. Whatever your approach, you should try to avoid the tendency to choose ICT resources and then decide where they might fit into the curriculum. Your strategy ought to be quite the reverse – first identify the learning objectives and outcomes and then choose ICT resources which will help to achieve those objectives.

Some activities will include ICT resources (if deemed appropriate) and some will not. Remember, it's no different to choosing resources in general. Along with books, pencils and paper, paints and crayons, blackboards, flip charts and role play equipment, ICT is just another option to consider.

National Curriculum

The national curriculum for all subjects can be found on the GOV.UK website at gov.uk/government/collections/national-curriculum.

Art and design

The national curriculum for art and design aims to ensure that all pupils:

- produce creative work, exploring their ideas and recording their experiences;
- become proficient in drawing, painting, sculpture and other art, craft and design techniques;
- evaluate and analyse creative works using the language of art, craft and design;
- know about great artists, craft makers and designers, and understand the historical and cultural development of their art forms.

At Key Stage 1 pupils should be taught:

- to use a range of materials creatively to design and make products;
- to use drawing, painting and sculpture to develop and share their ideas, experiences and imagination;
- to develop a wide range of art and design techniques in using colour, pattern, texture, line, shape, form and space;

■ about the work of a range of artists, craft makers and designers, describing the differences and similarities between different practices and disciplines, and making links to their own work.

At Key Stage 2 pupils should be taught to develop their techniques, including their control and their use of materials, with creativity, experimentation and an increasing awareness of different kinds of art, craft and design. Pupils should be taught:

■ to create sketch books to record their observations and use them to review and revisit ideas;

■ to improve their mastery of art and design techniques, including drawing, painting and sculpture with a range of materials [for example, pencil, charcoal, paint, clay];

■ about great artists, architects and designers in history.

ICT in art

ICT has much to offer including: reducing the costs of resources; speeding up processes; allowing experimentation and risk taking without penalty; introducing new media; helping to combine the sensory experiences of sound, images and movement; offering new ways to present and communicate work; and providing ready access to a wealth of information on the Internet.

It can also help pupils to:

■ gain access to the works of a range of artists, craftspeople and designers through the Internet or CD-ROM;

■ find tools to help them select, organise and present information;

■ explore and develop their ideas, for example by using digital microscopes to examine textures, or using image editing software;

■ make choices about their work, for example using a digital camera to take several pictures before deciding which to keep to use in their art work and which to discard;

■ take risks and demonstrate creativity, for example by combining sensory experiences, through the use of digital video or animation techniques incorporating sound effects;

■ develop confidence and work independently, for example by enabling them to create a satisfying product of which they can be proud;

■ present information in a range of ways, for example by creating a slideshow of work to display at a parents' evening or school assembly, or by creating an online gallery;

■ improve efficiency, for example work in progress can be retrieved and modified;

■ enhance interactive teaching and learning styles, for example by using an interactive whiteboard.

Word processors and content free packages

Most word processors and content free packages include features for the creation of simple drawings and shapes (e.g. MS Word, TextEase, Publisher, PowerPoint and the Smart Notebook). They also allow images to be inserted including clipart and pictures that children have taken themselves using a digital camera.

Here, shapes and freehand drawing from MS Word's drawing toolbar have been used by Key Stage 1 pupils. They are exploring shape and colour to create 'my cat'.

Whilst satisfying some of the knowledge requirements of art and design, they are also able to practise many useful ICT skills including mouse control, copy and paste, and grouping.

Figure 8.1 My Cat – a drawing using a content free package

Activity

Link to the Primary ICT site at primaryict.org.uk/icthandbookv2.htm and access the My Cat activity. Can you piece together a cat using the drawing tools ?

MS Word is not the ideal art package but you can produce quite sophisticated drawings if you put your mind to it.

Paint and drawing packages

There are plenty of painting and drawing packages to choose from and most are quite simple to use. You might try 2Paint A Picture, TextEase Paint, Noddy's Paint It, Pretty Things, Dazzle, Revelation Natural Art, AspexDraw, Adobe Photoshop and Microsoft Paint (free with Windows).

Apps for art

Most of the available apps will probably suit older children. Here are a few ideas:

- **For iPad** – Adobe Ideas (free), Quark DesignPad (free), Paper by FiftyThree (free), iDraw, Tayasui Sketches, ASKetch, Inspire Pro, Art Set, Inkist, Layers, Bamboo Paper, Draft, SketchBook Ink, ArtRage, ArtStudio, Auryn Ink, Brushes, Zen Brush, Sketch Club, Sumopaint and FontBook.

- **For Android** – Adobe Photoshop Touch, Infinite Painter, Autodesk SketchBook Pro, Fresco Paint Pro Sketcher Pro, Infinite Desig, SketchBook Express, myPantone, Paperless and Fontly.

- There's also an Art Guide App provided by ArtFund, a national fundraising charity (details under Websites).

Stylus paintbrush

Touchscreen devices operate by the touch of your finger or a dedicated stylus. The latter may be a stylus pen or a stylus paintbrush designed specifically to allow a deft touch to on-screen art creation.

No, it's not the same as traditional painting and drawing but it does add a new 'flavour' to the topic and does suit the digital native. Of the many to choose from you could try Nomad FLeX Brush, Sensu, GoSmart Stylus or TruGlide Pro.

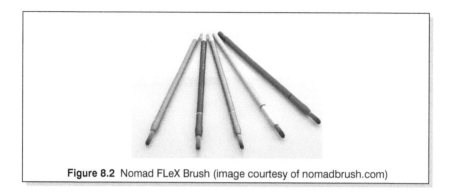

Figure 8.2 Nomad FLeX Brush (image courtesy of nomadbrush.com)

 Activity

Link to the Primary ICT site at primaryict.org.uk/icthandbookv2.htm and try out the two MS Paint activities: Using Paint 1 and Using Paint 2. This activity is courtesy of Teaching Ideas: teachingideas. co.uk

Art and design resources

Useful resources for art and design include:

- Graphics tablets (e.g. Art Pad) and tablet PCs – which are better options than a mouse when drawing, writing, sketching, colouring and picture editing. *Plus pen and brush styluses.*
- Interactive whiteboards – for whole-class or small group interactive drawing and painting activities. *Plus the whiteboard resource packs.*
- Digital cameras, video cameras, scanners, document cameras and editing software – for the capture and editing of images.
- Digital microscopes to examine textures and patterns of materials.
- Presentation software for the display of finished work.
- Printers – for producing hard copy.
- The Internet – for sourcing artists, craft makers, designers and architects.

Art and design websites

- ArtFund – artfund.org/pages/art-guide-app.
- Artspan – artspan.co.uk.
- Art Web – artweb.com.
- Art.Net – art.net.
- Art Babble – artbabble.org.
- Artcyclopedia – artcyclopedia.com.
- NSEAD – nsead.org/ict/links/links56.aspx.
- The Arts Map – theartsmap.com.

Art and design activity ideas

1. Year 1 children learn what happens when paints of two different colours are mixed. They first try it out using the free online activity Noddy's Paint It and then they confirm their findings using real paint and brushes.

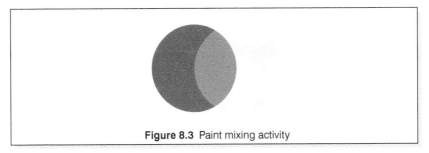

Figure 8.3 Paint mixing activity

2. A Year 1 teacher uses a digital microscope to help her pupils explore the textures of different fabrics that they have brought in from home. The pupils categorise the fabrics by colour, then the teacher prompts them to think of other ways to describe the fabrics. The pupils use the digital microscope in turn to examine their fabric and to describe the appearance of it. The teacher captures pictures of some of the textiles and makes a list of the pupils' descriptive words.

3. Year 4 pupils investigate pattern and symmetry. They use the available shapes in a paint package as simple building blocks. Using copy, paste and grouping they gradually create a number of patterned squares which are reflected in the horizontal and vertical axes of symmetry provided by the package.

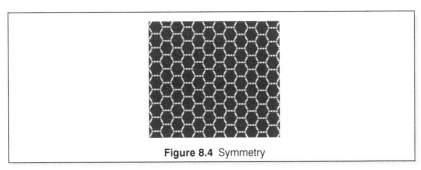

Figure 8.4 Symmetry

4. A Year 5 teacher encourages her pupils to use more shades of colour in their art work. She takes photographs which have many shades of blue and pupils download them to their tablets. They use the eye dropper tool in a painting program to isolate different shades of blue within the picture. In a separate document they flood fill small rectangles and note the red/blue/green values against each. They print-out the second document to use for future reference.

5. Year 3 children use paint software to create their own online art gallery, displaying their own imitations of a famous artist. The paintings are displayed using presentation software (e.g. PowerPoint), photo album software (e.g. Adobe Photoshop) or the Windows Picture and Fax viewer. Finally, they use a word processor to write about the artist.

Boats   Factories

Figure 8.5 Children's art gallery

6. Year 2 pupils create still-life pictures using a range of readily available materials. They each use a digital camera to take photographs of their work and a word processor and prepared word bank to help them write captions and descriptions of what they had created. With the help of an adult, their pictures and writing are imported into a multimedia presentation program template. A slideshow of the work is then played at parents' evening.

7. Year 6 pupils are covering the Second World War. They use their tablets, Smartphones and digital cameras to capture footage of older properties and people in their own location. They then use image enhancement apps to apply effects to their photographs and the 8mm app to turn their videos into old fashioned movies.

8. Year 5 pupils create a theatre set using a backdrop downloaded from the Internet and printed on card. They create a sequence of events by placing Duplo models in the set and moving them bit by bit. They use a digital still camera on a tripod to take photos of the sequence each time they have moved them. All of the photos are then imported into the video-editing software Pivot. Using trial and error they eventually watch their characters come to life.

 Activity

For more activity ideas, link to the Primary ICT site at primaryict.org.uk/icthandbookv2.htm and read the document ICT in Primary Art and Design.

Design and technology

The national curriculum for design and technology aims to ensure that all pupils:

- develop the creative, technical and practical expertise needed to perform everyday tasks confidently and to participate successfully in an increasingly technological world;

- build and apply a repertoire of knowledge, understanding and skills in order to design and make high-quality prototypes and products for a wide range of users;

- critique, evaluate and test their ideas and products and the work of others;

- understand and apply the principles of nutrition and learn how to cook.

At Key Stage 1, through a variety of creative and practical activities, pupils should be taught the knowledge, understanding and skills needed to engage in an iterative process of designing and making. They should work in a range of relevant contexts [for example, the home and school, gardens and playgrounds, the local community, industry and the wider environment].

When designing and making, pupils should be taught to:

Design

■ design purposeful, functional, appealing products for themselves and other users based on design criteria;

■ generate, develop, model and communicate their ideas through talking, drawing, templates, mock-ups and, where appropriate, information and communication technology.

Make

■ select from and use a range of tools and equipment to perform practical tasks [for example, cutting, shaping, joining and finishing];

■ select from and use a wide range of materials and components, including construction materials, textiles and ingredients, according to their characteristics.

Evaluate

■ explore and evaluate a range of existing products;

■ evaluate their ideas and products against design criteria.

Technical knowledge

■ build structures, exploring how they can be made stronger, stiffer and more stable;

■ explore and use mechanisms [for example, levers, sliders, wheels and axles], in their products.

At Key Stage 2, through a variety of creative and practical activities, pupils should be taught the knowledge, understanding and skills needed to engage in an iterative process of designing and making. They should work in a range of relevant contexts [for example, the home, school, leisure, culture, enterprise, industry and the wider environment].

When designing and making, pupils should be taught to:

Design

■ use research and develop design criteria to inform the design of innovative, functional, appealing products that are fit for purpose, aimed at particular individuals or groups;

■ generate, develop, model and communicate their ideas through discussion, annotated sketches, cross-sectional and exploded diagrams, prototypes, pattern pieces and computer-aided design.

Make

■ select from and use a wider range of tools and equipment to perform practical tasks [for example, cutting, shaping, joining and finishing], accurately;

■ select from and use a wider range of materials and components, including construction materials, textiles and ingredients, according to their functional properties and aesthetic qualities.

Evaluate

- investigate and analyse a range of existing products;
- evaluate their ideas and products against their own design criteria and consider the views of others to improve their work;
- understand how key events and individuals in design and technology have helped shape the world.

Technical knowledge

- apply their understanding of how to strengthen, stiffen and reinforce more complex structures;
- understand and use mechanical systems in their products [for example, gears, pulleys, cams, levers and linkages];
- understand and use electrical systems in their products [for example, series circuits incorporating switches, bulbs, buzzers and motors];
- apply their understanding of computing to program, monitor and control their products.

Cooking and nutrition

As part of their work with food, pupils should be taught how to cook and apply the principles of nutrition and healthy eating. Instilling a love of cooking in pupils will also open a door to one of the great expressions of human creativity. Learning how to cook is a crucial life skill that enables pupils to feed themselves and others affordably and well, now and in later life.

ICT in design and technology

ICT allows children to: use appropriate software packages to design products; use hardware such as 2D/3D printers and laser cutters to accurately make products; and use the Internet and CD-ROMs to examine manufacturing processes, explore and evaluate existing products, research key events and individuals, investigate materials and to communicate and discuss their ideas.

ICT can also allow children to simulate and model ideas such as mechanisms and electrical circuits and to apply their understanding of computing to program, monitor and control their products.

Design and technology software

Children can be expected to create designs for simple two- and three-dimensional products such as a photo frame, packaging for a product, house plans and elevations, clothing, models and vehicles. More often than not, a simple paint or drawing package will suffice. Should you wish to use something more elaborate then try one of the following: 2Draw, 2Design and Make, Junior CAD & BoxIT, 2D Design, PE Design, SolidWorks, PhotoVCarve, YouCreate, FlexiCAD or CAD CAM … and don't forget the digital camera and the many banks of clipart such as Clipbank.

They can also use model kits to create electrical circuits, build remote controlled devices and write programs to control models, robots and other systems.

Design and technology resources

Useful resources for design and technology include:

- Software for drawing, painting, design, image editing, CAD, programming, control, embroidery and engraving.
- Industry specific software (such as Focus on the Food Industry, Focus on Mechanisms, Focus on Graphic Products and Focus on Metals).
- Clipart galleries.
- Scanners.

- 2D and 3D printers.
- Laminator.
- Laser Cutters.
- Remote control model kits (such as 4WD).
- Electrics/electronics kits.
- Modelling kits (such as Lego).
- Floor and humanoid robots.
- IWB.
- Digital Camera.

 Activity

Link to the Primary ICT site at primaryict.org.uk/icthandbookv2.htm and try out some of the web-based resources in the D&T Guide. One of the better resources in the guide can be found on the robives site at robives.com/mechs.

Design and technology websites

- Design and technology Association: data.org.uk/for-education/primary.
- Nuffield Primary D&T: nationalstemcentre.org.uk/elibrary/collection/231/nuffield-primary-design-and-technology.
- Ofsted D&T: ofsted.gov.uk/inspection-reports/our-expert-knowledge/design-and-technology.
- Primary Resources (D&T): primaryresources.co.uk/dandt/dandt.htm.
- Robives: robives.com.
- TES Connect: tes.co.uk/teaching-resources.

Design and technology activity ideas

1. Year 3 children design packaging for a set of 6 paint pots. The dimensions are calculated and a drawing package is used to create a template. The template is printed out on card which is cut and glued to form a box.

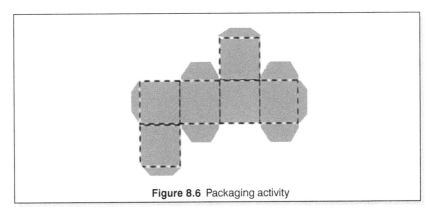

Figure 8.6 Packaging activity

Why is it good to use ICT here? Well, if the first attempt doesn't work, the template can be quickly modified – not so easy if it were done with pencil and paper from the outset!

2. Year 5 pupils are tasked with creating a low-fat menu for the school café. They search the Internet for information on food composition, recommended daily intakes and menu suggestions. A spreadsheet is used to calculate percentage values for carbohydrates, fat and protein and to check that each menu option satisfies the daily nutritional requirements.

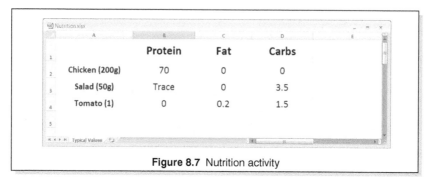

Figure 8.7 Nutrition activity

3. An interactive whiteboard is used with a class of Year 6 children who are required to investigate motors and gear mechanisms that are used to operate fairground rides. They identify the mechanisms involved and work out how they are joined together. The interactive whiteboard allows easy linking to prepared animations and to a number of information websites.

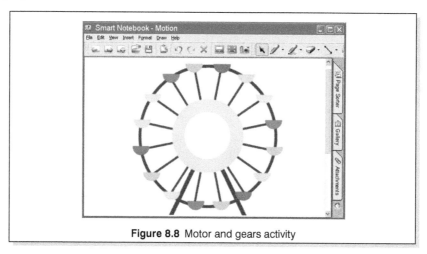

Figure 8.8 Motor and gears activity

 Activity

Link to the Primary ICT site at primaryict.org.uk/icthandbookv2.htm where you'll find the accompanying video for the motor and gears activity (Fairground Rides).

4. Year 3 pupils use 2Design and Make software to create 'nets' of 3D shapes such as houses and vehicles. The designs are coloured using the built-in painting tools. The final designs are printed out onto card, folded and glued.

5. A Year 2 class use a website simulation to explain light and dark (BBC Science Clips website: bbc. co.uk/schools/scienceclips/ages/5_6/light_dark.shtml).

6. Year 5 pupils obtain a recipe and instructional video on the Internet for making bread. They use these to help them make loaves.

Geography

The national curriculum for geography aims to ensure that all pupils:

- develop contextual knowledge of the location of globally significant places – both terrestrial and marine – including their defining physical and human characteristics and how these provide a geographical context for understanding the actions of processes;

- understand the processes that give rise to key physical and human geographical features of the world, how these are interdependent and how they bring about spatial variation and change over time;

- are competent in the geographical skills needed to:

    - collect, analyse and communicate with a range of data gathered through experiences of fieldwork that deepen their understanding of geographical processes;

    - interpret a range of sources of geographical information, including maps, diagrams, globes, aerial photographs and Geographical Information Systems (GIS);

    - communicate geographical information in a variety of ways, including through maps, numerical and quantitative skills and writing at length.

At Key Stage 1 pupils should develop knowledge about the world, the United Kingdom and their locality. They should understand basic subject-specific vocabulary relating to human and physical geography and begin to use geographical skills, including first-hand observation, to enhance their locational awareness. Pupils should be taught to:

Locational knowledge

- name and locate the world's seven continents and five oceans;

- name, locate and identify characteristics of the four countries and capital cities of the United Kingdom and its surrounding seas.

Place knowledge

- understand geographical similarities and differences through studying the human and physical geography of a small area of the United Kingdom, and of a small area in a contrasting non-European country.

Human and physical geography

- identify seasonal and daily weather patterns in the United Kingdom and the location of hot and cold areas of the world in relation to the Equator and the North and South Poles;

- use basic geographical vocabulary to refer to:

    - key physical features, including: beach, cliff, coast, forest, hill, mountain, sea, ocean, river, soil, valley, vegetation, season and weather;

    - key human features, including: city, town, village, factory, farm, house, office, port, harbour and shop.

Geographical skills and fieldwork

- use world maps, atlases and globes to identify the United Kingdom and its countries, as well as the countries, continents and oceans studied at this key stage;

- use simple compass directions (North, South, East and West) and locational and directional language [for example, near and far; left and right], to describe the location of features and routes on a map;

- use aerial photographs and plan perspectives to recognise landmarks and basic human and physical features; devise a simple map; and use and construct basic symbols in a key;

- use simple fieldwork and observational skills to study the geography of their school and its grounds and the key human and physical features of its surrounding environment.

At Key Stage 2 pupils should extend their knowledge and understanding beyond the local area to include the United Kingdom and Europe, North and South America. This will include the location and characteristics of a range of the world's most significant human and physical features. They should develop their use of geographical knowledge, understanding and skills to enhance their locational and place knowledge. Pupils should be taught to:

Locational knowledge

- locate the world's countries, using maps to focus on Europe (including the location of Russia) and North and South America, concentrating on their environmental regions, key physical and human characteristics, countries and major cities;

- name and locate counties and cities of the United Kingdom, geographical regions and their identifying human and physical characteristics, key topographical features (including hills, mountains, coasts and rivers), and land use patterns; and understand how some of these aspects have changed over time;

- identify the position and significance of latitude, longitude, Equator, Northern Hemisphere, Southern Hemisphere, the Tropics of Cancer and Capricorn, Arctic and Antarctic Circle, the Prime/Greenwich Meridian and time zones (including day and night).

Place knowledge

- understand geographical similarities and differences through the study of human and physical geography of a region of the United Kingdom, a region in a European country, and a region within North or South America.

Human and physical geography

- describe and understand key aspects of:

- physical geography, including: climate zones, biomes and vegetation belts, rivers, mountains, volcanoes and earthquakes, and the water cycle;

- human geography, including: types of settlement and land use, economic activity including trade links, and the distribution of natural resources including energy, food, minerals and water.

Geographical skills and fieldwork

- use maps, atlases, globes and digital/computer mapping to locate countries and describe features studied;

- use the eight points of a compass, four and six-figure grid references, symbols and key (including the use of Ordnance Survey maps) to build their knowledge of the United Kingdom and the wider world;

■ use fieldwork to observe, measure, record and present the human and physical features in the local area using a range of methods, including sketch maps, plans and graphs, and digital technologies.

ICT in geography

ICT can be used in a number of ways:

■ Maps and route planners are available in electronic format which allow the scale to be changed to suit the depth of enquiry.

■ Images can be captured and presented in a variety of forms.

■ There are lots of secondary sources of textual and pictorial information on CD-ROM and the Internet.

■ Websites (including Google Maps and Google Earth) provide aerial photographs.

■ Digital cameras can provide permanent records of important features, landmarks, people and places.

■ Completed work can be stored, manipulated and presented in many different ways.

■ Data-logging equipment can be used to investigate 'micro-climates' around the school.

■ An automatic weather station can be used for weather and climate investigations.

■ Since there is also a requirement to communicate geographical knowledge by 'writing at length' then many of the resources for English (writing) will be equally useful here.

Geography software

CD-ROM maps and information sources including: MapCaster; myWorld Geography; Maps of World; 3D World Atlas, Oxford Infant Atlas, BBC Barnaby Bear Atlas of the World E Big Book, BBC Barnaby Bear UK Atlas E Big Book, Worldwise Interactive 3D Atlas, DK Become a British Isles Explorer/DK Become a World Explorer, Eye2eye Britain Panoramic, All about Weather and Seasons, Living Library, Rivers, We are From, Environmental Change, Localities in the UK, Localities around the World, Seeing Geography, Where you Live, Rainforests, Water, BBC Find Out About Our Homes, BBC Find Out About the Seaside.

Geography Apps

There is now an emerging number of Apps for geography including: Google Earth; Maps; GeoMaster Plus; Barefoot World Atlas; World Atlas; Geo Walk; Stack the Countries; OutSide and NOAA Weather Radar.

Global positioning system (GPS)

The GPS is a network of satellites and ground stations that provides a world-wide navigation system. The technology has rapidly developed, becoming cheaper and more accessible. Pupils are increasingly aware of the technology and they respond very well to it when used effectively in the classroom.

GPS has many benefits in education. It can enhance fieldwork or outdoor education, enhance the accuracy and credibility of geographical fieldwork, bring maps and aerial photographs to life and provide opportunities for fun educational activities (e.g. treasure hunts). It is also a useful tool for creating cross-curricular links with maths, science and PE.

There are many available hand-held GPS devices but the specifications vary so do ensure that your intended purchase has the features and connectivity that you require. In fact, you may not need to look any further than your tablet PC or mobile phone because many now include GPS.

Geography resources

Useful resources for geography include:

- ■ Data-logging equipment.
- ■ Automatic weather stations.
- ■ GPS.
- ■ Digital cameras.
- ■ Email and social networking.
- ■ IWB.
- ■ Spreadsheets (for data collection and presentation).

Geography websites

- ■ Barnaby Bear: barnabybear.co.uk.
- ■ BBC Weather: bbc.co.uk/weather.
- ■ Digimap for Schools: digimapforschools.edina.ac.uk.
- ■ Geocaching: geocaching.com.
- ■ Geographical Association: geography.org.uk/eyprimary.
- ■ Google Maps: google.co.uk.
- ■ National Geographic (Education): education.nationalgeographic.com/education.
- ■ National Geographic (Kids): kids.nationalgeographic.com.
- ■ World Atlas: worldatlas.com.

Geography activity ideas

1. Year 2 children explore their local area in search of landmarks. They download a map from the Internet and copy it into a publishing package. Equipped with a print-out of the map and a digital camera they go for a walk and capture images of the library, local shop, school etc. On return to the school the images are superimposed onto the map which is printed out and placed on the classroom wall.

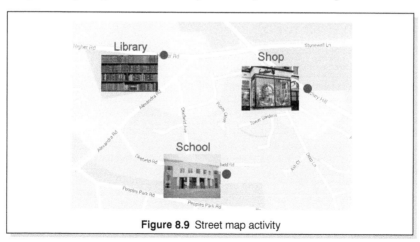

Figure 8.9 Street map activity

2. Year 3 children establish the population of countries around the world using the Internet. The results are presented in a bar chart with a suitable scale and are also added to a database which the children gradually develop as a source of information about countries around the world.

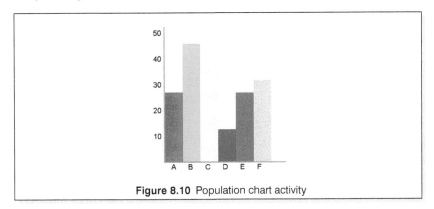

Figure 8.10 Population chart activity

3. Year 6 children carry out a survey to find out about pupils' habits (hobbies, food etc). They use a word processor to devise a questionnaire which is uploaded to the school website. Pupils download and complete the questionnaire, emailing a copy back to the class teacher. Y6 children transfer the information into a spreadsheet, analyse it and present a summary of the results on the school website.

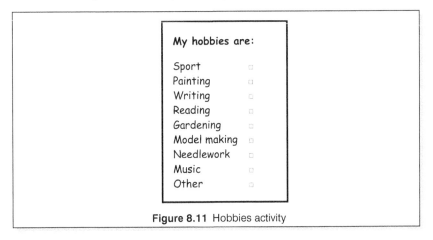

Figure 8.11 Hobbies activity

4. Year 3 pupils check the labels on their clothing, shoes and accessories to find where they are made – the answers surprise them! After they collect the names of the countries, they search an electronic atlas to learn about the locations of the countries and mark them on a map. This gives them a better appreciation of the interdependency of the world's nations.

5. Google Earth is downloaded (from earth.google.co.uk) and displayed on the IWB. Using Q&A, Year 4 pupils learn about the relative locations of countries and then regions within the UK, gradually navigating to the locality around their school. They explore the locality, noting prominent buildings, streets and landmarks. They then use the historical imagery feature to look at how the area around the school has changed in their lifetime.

6. Year 6 pupils use a word processor to write a letter to a fictitious pen friend in another country. The letter describes where they live (including supporting images) and outlines the prominent features.

In a similar, cross-curricular activity they take on the role of their imaginary pen friend and write a similar letter about a foreign location using the foreign language they are learning in school.

 Activity

For a wide selection of presentations on Google Earth, visit the Slideshare site at slideshare.net and search for Google Earth.

 Activity

For more ideas, link to the Primary ICT site at primaryict.org.uk/icthandbookv2.htm and read Using ICT in Geography.

History

The national curriculum for history aims to ensure that all pupils:

- know and understand the history of these islands as a coherent, chronological narrative, from the earliest times to the present day: how people's lives have shaped this nation and how Britain has influenced and been influenced by the wider world;

- know and understand significant aspects of the history of the wider world: the nature of ancient civilisations; the expansion and dissolution of empires; characteristic features of past non-European societies; achievements and follies of mankind;

- gain and deploy a historically grounded understanding of abstract terms such as 'empire', 'civilisation', 'parliament' and 'peasantry';

- understand historical concepts such as continuity and change, cause and consequence, similarity, difference and significance, and use them to make connections, draw contrasts, analyse trends, frame historically valid questions and create their own structured accounts, including written narratives and analyses;

- understand the methods of historical enquiry, including how evidence is used rigorously to make historical claims, and discern how and why contrasting arguments and interpretations of the past have been constructed;

- gain historical perspective by placing their growing knowledge into different contexts, understanding the connections between local, regional, national and international history; between cultural, economic, military, political, religious and social history; and between short- and long-term timescales.

At Key Stage 1 pupils should develop an awareness of the past, using common words and phrases relating to the passing of time. They should know where the people and events they study fit within a chronological framework and identify similarities and differences between ways of life in different periods. They should use a wide vocabulary of everyday historical terms. They should ask and answer questions, choosing and using parts of stories and other sources to show that they know and understand key features of events. They should understand some of the ways in which we find out about the past and identify different ways in which it is represented.

Pupils should be taught about:

- changes within living memory. Where appropriate, these should be used to reveal aspects of change in national life;

- events beyond living memory that are significant nationally or globally [for example, the Great Fire of London, the first aeroplane flight or events commemorated through festivals or anniversaries];

- the lives of significant individuals in the past who have contributed to national and international achievements. Some should be used to compare aspects of life in different periods [for example, Elizabeth I and Queen Victoria, Christopher Columbus and Neil Armstrong, William Caxton and Tim Berners-Lee, Pieter Bruegel the Elder and LS Lowry, Rosa Parks and Emily Davison, Mary Seacole and/or Florence Nightingale and Edith Cavell];

- significant historical events, people and places in their own locality.

At Key Stage 2 pupils should continue to develop a chronologically secure knowledge and understanding of British, local and world history, establishing clear narratives within and across the periods they study. They should note connections, contrasts and trends over time and develop the appropriate use of historical terms. They should regularly address and sometimes devise historically valid questions about change, cause, similarity and difference, and significance. They should construct informed responses that involve thoughtful selection and organisation of relevant historical information. They should understand how our knowledge of the past is constructed from a range of sources.

In planning to ensure the progression described above through teaching the British, local and world history outlined below, teachers should combine overview and depth studies to help pupils understand both the long arc of development and the complexity of specific aspects of the content.

Pupils should be taught about:

- changes in Britain from the Stone Age to the Iron Age which could include:
  - late Neolithic hunter-gatherers and early farmers, for example, Skara Brae;
  - Bronze Age religion, technology and travel, for example, Stonehenge;
  - Iron Age hill forts: tribal kingdoms, farming, art and culture;

- the Roman Empire and its impact on Britain which could include:
  - Julius Caesar's attempted invasion in 55–54 BC;
  - the Roman Empire by AD 42 and the power of its army;
  - successful invasion by Claudius and conquest, including Hadrian's Wall;
  - British resistance, for example, Boudica;
  - 'Romanisation' of Britain: sites such as Caerwent and the impact of technology, culture and beliefs, including early Christianity;

- Britain's settlement by Anglo-Saxons and Scots which could include:
  - Roman withdrawal from Britain in c. AD 410 and the fall of the western Roman Empire;
  - Scots invasions from Ireland to north Britain (now Scotland);
  - Anglo-Saxon invasions, settlements and kingdoms: place names and village life;
  - Anglo-Saxon art and culture;
  - Christian conversion – Canterbury, Iona and Lindisfarne;

- the Viking and Anglo-Saxon struggle for the Kingdom of England to the time of Edward the Confessor which could include:
  - Viking raids and invasion;

- resistance by Alfred the Great and Athelstan, first king of England;
- further Viking invasions and Danegeld;
- Anglo-Saxon laws and justice;
- Edward the Confessor and his death in 1066;

- a local history study which could include:
  - a depth study linked to one of the British areas of study listed above;
  - a study over time tracing how several aspects of national history are reflected in the locality (this can go beyond 1066);
  - a study of an aspect of history or a site dating from a period beyond 1066 that is significant in the locality;

- a study of an aspect or theme in British history that extends pupils' chronological knowledge beyond 1066 which could include:
  - the changing power of monarchs using case studies such as John, Anne and Victoria;
  - changes in an aspect of social history, such as crime and punishment from the Anglo-Saxons to the present or leisure and entertainment in the twentieth century;
  - the legacy of Greek or Roman culture (art, architecture or literature) on later periods in British history, including the present day;
  - a significant turning point in British history, for example, the first railways or the Battle of Britain;

- the achievements of the earliest civilisations – an overview of where and when the first civilisations appeared and a depth study of one of the following: Ancient Sumer; The Indus Valley; Ancient Egypt; The Shang Dynasty of Ancient China;
- Ancient Greece – a study of Greek life and achievements and their influence on the western world;
- a non-European society that provides contrasts with British history – one study chosen from: early Islamic civilisation, including a study of Baghdad c. AD 900; Mayan civilisation c. AD 900; Benin (West Africa) c. AD 900–1300.

ICT in history

ICT provides pupils with opportunities to:

- select and reproduce sources in a range of media;
- contextualise and interpret sources;
- reconstruct and simulate historical events;
- construct narratives;
- identify patterns in large quantities of data;
- develop, organise and communicate historical thinking.

The most useful ICT resources for history are information sources such as websites (particularly those hosted by major libraries, galleries and other public institutions) and DVDs/CD-ROMs.

History software

- **CD-ROMs**: Become A History Explorer, myWorld History, Eyewitness History of the World, Battle Line: a Recorded History of World War 2, Chronicle Encyclopedia of History, History's Great Civilisations, History's Greatest Battles, Hutchinson History Library, The Great War: The Virtual

History Collection, Arcventure The Vikings, Arcventure The Egyptians, A History of the World from the Big Bang to the Present.

- **DVDs:** Horrible Histories, Awesome Egyptians, Terrible Tudors, Groovy Greeks, Vicious Vikings, Rotten Romans, World War II: 1933–1945, BBC History DVDs (Ancient Egypt, Ancient Greece, Aztecs, Britain since 1948, Children in Victorian Britain, Vikings, Famous Events, Life in Tudor Times, Romans in Britain, Children in WW2), Keynotes (The Romans, The Tudors, The Vikings, The Victorians, Life in Ancient Egypt, Life in Ancient Greece, Homes Long Ago, Toys Past & Present), Channel 4 History DVDs (Ancient Egypt & Ancient Greece, Britains at War, Tudor Times, Roman Times, Famous People).

History Apps

Apps for History include: Children's British History Encyclopaedia, A Journey With History's Most Influential People, Britannica Kids – Ancient Rome, Britannica Kids – Aztecs, Streetmuseum Londinium, Virtual History ROMA, British Library Treasures, History: Maps of the World, Timeline World War 2 with Dan Snow, Timeline Eons and Medieval Life.

History resources

Useful resources for history include:

- Word processors (ICT helps to alleviate the constraints of writing and allows pupils to concentrate on the specific topic of discussion. This encourages reflection, analysis and understanding).

- A means of recording fieldwork such as a laptop computer, tablet or mobile phone, a digital camera, a video recorder and a digital voice recorder (mp3/mp4).

- Data-handling software such as spreadsheet or database (using databases to work with large volumes of data can help pupils to look for patterns, frame hypotheses, question accepted theories and place events into wider contexts).

- Computer Mediated Communication – CMC (CMC, including school learning platforms and online discussion groups, enables pupils to better develop and communicate historical arguments, thinking and understanding. These skills can be transferred to essay writing).

History websites

- Active History: activehistory.co.uk.
- BBC History: bbc.co.uk/history.
- British Library: bl.uk.
- British Monarchy: royal.gov.uk.
- British Museum: britishmuseum.org.
- British Pathé: britishpathe.com.
- English Heritage (Education): english-heritage.org.uk/education.
- EyeWitness to History: eyewitnesstohistory.com.
- Historical Association: history.org.uk.
- History of England: historyofengland.net.
- Horrible Histories: horrible-histories.co.uk.
- HSTRY: hstry.co.

- Info Please: infoplease.com.
- Institute of Historical Research: history.ac.uk.
- Keystage History: keystagehistory.co.uk.
- National Archives: nationalarchives.gov.uk.
- Primary Homework Help: primaryhomeworkhelp.co.uk.
- Roman-Britain.org: roman-britain.org.
- Roman Empire: roman-empire.net.
- Spartacus Educational: spartacus-educational.com.
- Student's Friend: studentsfriend.com.
- Tiki-Toki: tiki-toki.com.
- Train History: trainhistory.net/railway-history.
- Webanywhere: webanywhere.co.uk/education/teaching-resources/primary/history.

History activity ideas

1. Year 1 children differentiate between objects used today (new) and objects used in the past (old). Using a content free package they categorise aircraft by dragging and dropping their images into the correct box.

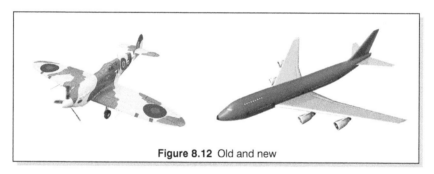

Figure 8.12 Old and new

2. Year 3 pupils research the Internet to find historic archives of their locality. Images and information are transferred onto an old map, printed out and placed on the classroom wall alongside the modern day map that they created in geography activity 1. Children compare the two and use a word processor to write about changes over time.

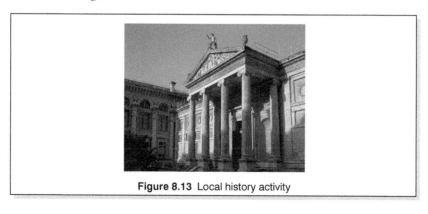

Figure 8.13 Local history activity

3. Year 5 pupils visit the local museum to investigate the influence of the Romans on their town. They capture images of artefacts using digital cameras and other mobile devices and used an mp4 recorder to make verbal notes. They take the opportunity to interview the curator and record this too. Back at school the information collected is collated and added to the history section of the school website. Podcasts are created to provide supporting commentary. A school subscribes to the Keystage History website (keystagehistory.co.uk). Key Stage 1 pupils use it to examine changes within living memory and to look at aspects of life for their parents and grandparents and how they have changed (e.g. new and old toys, washday in the past and grandparent's holidays). Pupils use word processors to devise a questionnaire for their grandparents about where they went on their holidays when they were young children. They scan old photos and feed the information into a simple database. Individual pupil results are displayed on an IWB and discussed.

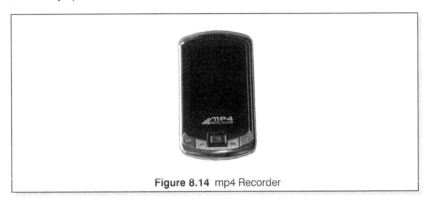

Figure 8.14 mp4 Recorder

4. Year 4 pupils use a simulation of the Battle of Hastings on the BBC History website (bbc.co.uk/history/interactive/games). They play a game to re-enact the Battle of Hastings, which took place on 14 October, 1066. Then they use the Internet to find out more about what caused the confrontation that changed the face of England, as well as the consequences of this historic defeat.

5. Key Stage 2 pupils learn about the Great Fire of London by playing an online game created by the Museum of London in partnership with The National Archives, London Fire Brigade Museum, National Portrait Gallery and London Metropolitan Archives (fireoflondon.org.uk).

Music

The national curriculum for music aims to ensure that all pupils:

- perform, listen to, review and evaluate music across a range of historical periods, genres, styles and traditions, including the works of the great composers and musicians;

- learn to sing and to use their voices, to create and compose music on their own and with others;

- have the opportunity to learn a musical instrument;

- use technology appropriately and have the opportunity to progress to the next level of musical excellence;

- understand and explore how music is created, produced and communicated, including through the inter-related dimensions: pitch, duration, dynamics, tempo, timbre, texture, structure and appropriate musical notations.

At Key Stage 1 pupils should be taught to:

- use their voices expressively and creatively by singing songs and speaking chants and rhymes;
- play tuned and untuned instruments musically;
- listen with concentration and understanding to a range of high-quality live and recorded music;
- experiment with, create, select and combine sounds using the inter-related dimensions of music.

At Key Stage 2 pupils should be taught to sing and play musically with increasing confidence and control. They should develop an understanding of musical composition, organising and manipulating ideas within musical structures and reproducing sounds from aural memory. Pupils should be taught to:

- play and perform in solo and ensemble contexts, using their voices and playing musical instruments with increasing accuracy, fluency, control and expression;
- improvise and compose music for a range of purposes using the inter-related dimensions of music;
- listen with attention to detail and recall sounds with increasing aural memory;
- use and understand staff and other musical notations;
- appreciate and understand a wide range of high-quality live and recorded music drawn from different traditions and from great composers and musicians;
- develop an understanding of the history of music.

ICT in music

ICT helps pupils learn in music by supporting the development of musical skills, knowledge and understanding. ICT also acts as a tool and a distinctive medium for musical expression. For example, pupils can use ICT for recording or listening to music, for simulating the playing of musical instruments, for composing musical scores, for understanding musical processes and for creating and exploring electronic sounds. ICT strongly influences the creative process and enables pupils to compose in a variety of different ways. It allows the composer to assess compositions and revisit them, easily making modifications.

ICT provides the means to access a wide variety of sources of information and provides the opportunity for investigation of the creation of music at various stages, right up to the appreciation of the performance. It provides access to musical experiences from a range of cultures and time periods. This serves to encourage citizenship and the exploration of sameness, difference and diversity.

Music software

2Simple Music Toolkit (a suite of 6 programs: 2Explore, 2Play, 2Compose, 2Beat, 2Sequence and 2Synthesise), GarageBand, Musical Monsters, Mini Musical Monsters, Audacity (free, open source package for audio creation and editing), Super Duper Music Looper, Noisy Things, Target and Touch: Music, Musical School by Charanga (a subscription website that provides a complete scheme of work for years 1 to 6), Compose World Play, Sibelius (Scorch, Auralia, Musition, AudioScore and PhotoScore).

Music Apps

Beatwave, Mibblio, Drums, Tap A Tune, Mugician, Little Fox Music Box, Garage Band, Avid Scorch, Isle of Tune, Staff Wars, Singing Fingers, My First Orchestra, Little Beethoven, Lopy Tunes, Young Person's Guide to the Orchestra, My First Classical Music, SonicPics, Music Theory for Beginners, Pitch Painter, MadPad, Fingerstomp, Noteworks, Rhythm Cat, Bebot, Musyc, Star Composer and Soundbrush.

Virtual instruments

Why not let your pupils try out a range of musical instruments on-screen? Not the real thing perhaps but an excellent introduction to piano, guitar, violin etc. It's a whole load of fun and excitement and all for free!

Tablet PCs and Smartphones are excellent here because of their interactive touch screens. Here are just a few of the many virtual instrument sites:

- Piano: method-behind-the-music.com/piano.
- Piano: onlinepianist.com/virtual_piano.
- Various: bgfl.org/bgfl/custom/resources_ftp/client_ftp/ks2/music/piano.
- Various: virtualmusicalinstruments.com.

Music resources

Useful resources for music include:

- Focused activity software such as pitch and rhythm games.
- Simple pattern sequencing software.
- Software for recording and processing sound.
- Software for exploring style and structure.
- Tape-recorders with counter.
- Keyboards with a selection of voices.
- Digital effects units.
- MIDI keyboards featuring a wide range of preset sounds.
- Beamz Interactive Music System.
- Tablet PCs and Smartphones (touch screen devices).
- IWB.

Music websites

- Apps4PrimarySchools: apps4primaryschools.co.uk/apps/music.
- Audio Network: audionetwork.com.
- Audio Sauna: audiosauna.com.
- BBC Class Clips: bbc.co.uk/learningzone/clips/topics/primary.shtml.
- BBC School Radio: bbc.co.uk/schoolradio.
- Charanga Musical School: charanga.com/site/musical-school.
- Finale: finalemusic.com.
- First School Years: firstschoolyears.com.
- Jam Studio: jamstudio.com.
- Jolly Music: jollylearning.co.uk/overview-about-jolly-music.
- Musescore: musescore.org.
- Music-ITE: music-ite.org.uk.
- Music Monsters: musicmonsters.co.uk.

- Noteflight: noteflight.com.
- O-Music: o-music.tv.
- Out of the Ark Music: outoftheark.co.uk.
- Pop4Schools: pop4schools.com.
- Sing Up: singup.org.
- Songs for Teaching: songsforteaching.com.
- UJam: ujam.com.
- World Music: worldmusic.net.
- YouTube (Hooplakidz): youtube.com/user/hooplakidz.

Music activity ideas

1. Year 5 pupils use the 2Simple Music Toolkit to produce a simple radio jingle using two staves and two different musical instruments. The composition is developed over a period of six weeks using all the staves and different instruments. Pupils are then encouraged to develop and amend ideas and, at the end of each session, pupils evaluate each other's compositions.

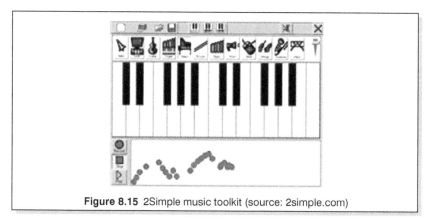

Figure 8.15 2Simple music toolkit (source: 2simple.com)

2. Year 1 children discuss features of sounds they might hear around the school (sounds such as the school bell, rain on a window, an aeroplane flying overhead etc.) noting features (such as loud, quiet, long, short, high pitch, low pitch etc.). Then they locate the source of these sounds and record them using a tape recorder. The sounds are played back later and children have to identify each sound.

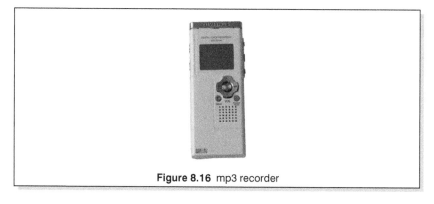

Figure 8.16 mp3 recorder

3.   Having listened to several music samples, Year 4 pupils use simple drag and drop software to produce a structured music composition. A number of instruments are used and each is allocated its own track. The music is critically evaluated (against a set of criteria) and edited accordingly until the children are satisfied with it.

4.   Year 3 pupils make an mp3 recording of themselves singing a number of their favourite songs. They load the songs into Audacity in order to edit them and add a voice commentary.

5.   Year 5 children use an IWB with a musical score background to compose simple music scores for use with their recorders.

6.   A reception class sing along to the Five Little Ducks Nursery Rhyme on YouTube (youtube.com/watch?feature=player_profilepage&v=Tmoebx4gbs4).

7.   A primary school subscribes to Sing Up (singup.org) and uses this subscription website to plan and deliver their music offering across the whole school.

8.   Four Newham primary schools participate in a collaborative music technology project to create a soundtrack for a video game. They use iPads and GarageBand software, utilising a range of effects to produce their own music.
     You can find out more from the Newham Trust website at newham-music.org.uk.

9.   Year 6 pupils write a song and accompanying music score which they then play using virtual instruments on their iPads and keyboards that plug into iPads.

10. A primary school in the midlands create a school band using their iPads. The project involves the whole of year 5 and gets them engaged with digital music using iPads, digital instruments and a small selection of traditional percussion instruments. In just two days the pupils are able to learn and play three complete soundtracks. Technology used includes iPads, an Allen and Heath ZED16FX 36 Channel USB Mixer, five Alesis IO docks and iRig adaptors for connecting the microphones, guitars and MIDI keyboards. Apple TV is used to demonstrate how to play various notes on specific instruments (using the software GarageBand).

See also 'Music technology for SEN' in Chapter 10.

Physical education (PE)

The national curriculum for physical education aims to ensure that all pupils:

- develop competence to excel in a broad range of physical activities;
- are physically active for sustained periods of time;
- engage in competitive sports and activities;
- lead healthy, active lives.

At Key Stage 1 pupils should develop fundamental movement skills, become increasingly competent and confident and access a broad range of opportunities to extend their agility, balance and coordination, individually and with others. They should be able to engage in competitive (both against self and against others) and co-operative physical activities, in a range of increasingly challenging situations. Pupils should be taught to:

- master basic movements including running, jumping, throwing and catching, as well as developing balance, agility and coordination, and begin to apply these in a range of activities;
- participate in team games, developing simple tactics for attacking and defending;
- perform dances using simple movement patterns.

At Key Stage 2 pupils should continue to apply and develop a broader range of skills, learning how to use them in different ways and to link them to make actions and sequences of movement. They should enjoy communicating, collaborating and competing with each other. They should develop an understanding of how to improve in different physical activities and sports and learn how to evaluate and recognise their own success. Pupils should be taught to:

- use running, jumping, throwing and catching in isolation and in combination;
- play competitive games, modified where appropriate [for example, badminton, basketball, cricket, football, hockey, netball, rounders and tennis], and apply basic principles suitable for attacking and defending;
- develop flexibility, strength, technique, control and balance [for example, through athletics and gymnastics];
- perform dances using a range of movement patterns;
- take part in outdoor and adventurous activity challenges both individually and within a team;
- compare their performances with previous ones and demonstrate improvement to achieve their personal best.

Swimming and water safety

All schools must provide swimming instruction either in Key Stage 1 or Key Stage 2. In particular, pupils should be taught to:

- swim competently, confidently and proficiently over a distance of at least 25 metres;
- use a range of strokes effectively [for example, front crawl, backstroke and breaststroke];
- perform safe self-rescue in different water-based situations.

ICT in PE

ICT has traditionally offered a range of tools for teachers and pupils to analyse, evaluate, compare and improve performance across a range of physical activities including dance and swimming. For example, ICT can be used for:

- researching individual sporting techniques using the Internet and DVD;
- making use of a range of audio and visual stimuli;
- analysing performance using software and hardware;
- timing and data collection using software and hardware devices;
- recording and analysing performance;
- tracking participation, involvement and improvement;
- providing constructive and timely feedback;
- creating multimedia productions for reference and for use in other curriculum areas.

Until recently, any work requiring computers has typically been done before and after activities. However, as a result of the increased popularity of mobile devices, software is now widely used in real time as a physical event takes place (on tablet PCs, Smartphones and other mobile devices). As a result, ICT has had a significant and positive effect on pupil motivation in a subject where some children are often reluctant participants.

PE software

There is relatively little software for PE. Here are just a few titles:

- **CD-ROM**: The WarmUp/CoolDown CDs, The Drummin' 'N Dancin' CDs, Dance Dance Dance CDs, The DanceMusic CD Pack, The DanceTechnic CD Pack, 321 Go!, AnyBodyCanDance, Dartfish Motion Analysis, Daydream Education's PE Interactive Content Packs (Nutrition, Physical Education, Principles of Training, Safety in Sport, The Cardiorespiratory System, The Components of Physical Fitness, The Human Skeleton, The Short Term Effects of Exercise, The Long-Term Effects of Exercise, Training Methods and Training Thresholds and Zones).

- **DVD**: Great Activities for Physical Education – Keystage 2, Physical Education Games, Track, Great Activities For Kids – PE. Keystage 2, Dancing Folk: BBC Education, PE Video Analysis Assessment Toolkit, Moving 'N' Grooving, Dancin Time.

PE apps

Coach's Eye, Ubersense Coach: Slow Motion Video Analysis, Team Shake, StopWatch, Giant Scoreboard, Nutrition Tips, Pocket First Aid & CPR, iFitness HD, Pocket Body, Pocket Heart, Teacher's Assistant, Easy Assessment, Timer Tools, Teacher's Roll Call, Class Cards, Bracketmaker, MusicWorkout, Numbers, Educareations, Fotobabble, Snap Guide, Beep Test, Cardiograph, FitnessHD, Touch Stat Lite, Footy Tracker, Coda, Dartfish Easytag, Dartfish Express, Swing Reader, BaM Video Delay, PowerChalk 10 Second Telestrator, Sportscam, Burstmode, Instant Replay Camera, CoachBase, Coachnote, Hudl, Athletes, Pedometer and Coin Toss.

PE resources

Useful resources for physical education include:

- Digital cameras – video and still.
- Mobile devices (incl. Laptops, tablets and Smartphones).
- Large mobile touch screens.
- Interactive whiteboards.
- Sound systems with recording facilities.
- Digital timers, heart rate monitors and timing mats.
- Data-recording and analysis software such as spreadsheets.
- Information CD-ROMs.
- Motion analysis software.
- Film editing.
- Voice projections systems.
- Games consoles (Xbox, Nintendo Wii Fit).
- Dance mat systems.
- Pedometers.
- Internet.
- YouTube.

PE websites

- ASA School Swimming and Water Safety: swimming.org/asa/schoolswimming.
- Association for Physical Education: afpe.org.uk.

- BBC School Radio (Dance): bbc.co.uk/learning/schoolradio/subjects/dance.
- Fitstats: fitstatsweb.com.
- Olympic Videos: olympic.org/videos.
- Kidnetic: kidnetic.com.
- New Lifestyles: new-lifestyles.com.
- PE Central: pecentral.org.
- PE Primary: peprimary.co.uk.
- Physical Education Update: physicaleducationupdate.com.
- Swimming.org: swimming.org.
- Teachnology: teach-nology.com.

PE activity ideas

1. In athletics, Year 4 children work on their running technique. The teacher introduces key principles and the children then explore the Internet for videos of athletes. They examine the athletes' running actions and attempt to emulate these on the playing field. Pupils take videos of themselves and use them to evaluate their own performance.

2. Year 1 children use images projected onto the wall (or onto an interactive whiteboard) to discuss the association between colours and moods and between the weather and our emotions. As part of a dance lesson they act out these emotions using a range of movements.

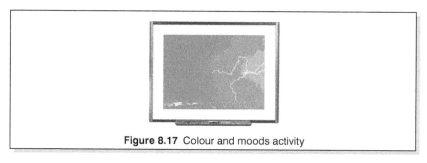

Figure 8.17 Colour and moods activity

3. Year 6 pupils design a 'beeping' stopwatch and a metronome using MS PowerPoint. They are projected onto the wall in the sports hall and can be used in a variety of races, games, gymnastics and dance activities.

Figure 8.18 PowerPoint stopwatch activity

4. Year 6 pupils use GPS to monitor individual performance on the cross country route. Their performance is analysed afterwards to reveal at which points pupils are running faster or slower. The pupils use the data to draw a map of the course indicating which points they found easy or hard. Finally, they discuss their findings and offer ideas about how to improve their performance.

5. Year 2 children use the iPad Mini to create videos of their performance in simple gymnastic and dance sequences (using a range of viewing angles). They play back the videos (including slow motion) and this helps the teacher and the children to evaluate and improve their own performances.

6. Year 3 pupils use CD-ROMs to help develop their understanding of the human body, physiology and health.

7. A number of still images are taken by teachers and pupils over a period of time. Teachers use them to create activity cards, worksheets and presentations. Pupils use software to edit the images and to create a slideshow which highlights their personal and group achievements.

8. During an orienteering activity, Year 5 and 6 pupils use their mobile phones to capture evidence of having visited each point on the course. The images are subsequently used in English to illustrate individual reports on the topic of orienteering.

9. Key Stage 2 pupils make videos of themselves playing tennis. They import the videos into Dartfish motion analysis software and use it to perform a frame by frame analysis of their actions. The teacher uses this to evaluate their performance and provide instant feedback. The software is also used to make annotations and voice-overs so that it can be used subsequently as training media.

10. A primary school uses a Nintendo Wii games console to encourage disaffected pupils in physical education lessons in order to increase fitness levels and to improve pupils' behaviour and teamwork.

    The game consoles Nintendo Wii, Microsoft Xbox, and Sony Playstation all have associated electronic game mats that encourage physical activity through game participation. These mats are typically used in dance games. The Wii also offers a balance board that is used with the Wii Fit game package.

11. A local authority sponsored project uses the CyberCoach Virtual Instructor and Dance Mat Games with a pilot group of 12 schools. The Virtual Instructor software creates a life size dance instructor that leads pupils through routines in much the same way as a human dance instructor would. The system is used in PE, breakfast clubs and after school clubs.

 Activity

Link to the Primary ICT site at primaryict.org.uk/icthandbookv2.htm.
Read the pdf file 'Using Video Cameras in PE' and try out the PowerPoint Stopwatch.

Foreign languages

Learning languages in primary school provides children with early access to foreign people and cultures. It may also improve performance in secondary school.

The national curriculum for languages aims to ensure that all pupils:

■ understand and respond to spoken and written language from a variety of authentic sources;

■ speak with increasing confidence, fluency and spontaneity, finding ways of communicating what they want to say, including through discussion and asking questions, and continually improving the accuracy of their pronunciation and intonation;

- can write at varying length, for different purposes and audiences, using the variety of grammatical structures that they have learnt;

- discover and develop an appreciation of a range of writing in the language studied.

At Key Stage 2, foreign language teaching may be of any modern or ancient foreign language and should focus on enabling pupils to make substantial progress in one language. The teaching should provide an appropriate balance of spoken and written language and should lay the foundations for further foreign language teaching at Key Stage 3. It should enable pupils to understand and communicate ideas, facts and feelings in speech and writing, focused on familiar and routine matters, using their knowledge of phonology, grammatical structures and vocabulary.

The focus of study in modern languages will be on practical communication. If an ancient language is chosen the focus will be to provide a linguistic foundation for reading comprehension and an appreciation of classical civilisation. Pupils studying ancient languages may take part in simple oral exchanges, while discussion of what they read will be conducted in English. A linguistic foundation in ancient languages may support the study of modern languages at Key Stage 3.

Pupils should be taught to:

- listen attentively to spoken language and show understanding by joining in and responding;

- explore the patterns and sounds of language through songs and rhymes and link the spelling, sound and meaning of words;

- engage in conversations; ask and answer questions; express opinions and respond to those of others; seek clarification and help★;

- speak in sentences, using familiar vocabulary, phrases and basic language structures;

- develop accurate pronunciation and intonation so that others understand when they are reading aloud or using familiar words and phrases★;

- present ideas and information orally to a range of audiences★;

- read carefully and show understanding of words, phrases and simple writing;

- appreciate stories, songs, poems and rhymes in the language;

- broaden their vocabulary and develop their ability to understand new words that are introduced into familiar written material, including through using a dictionary;

- write phrases from memory, and adapt these to create new sentences, to express ideas clearly;

- describe people, places, things and actions orally★ and in writing;

- understand basic grammar appropriate to the language being studied, including (where relevant): feminine, masculine and neuter forms and the conjugation of high-frequency verbs; key features and patterns of the language; how to apply these, for instance, to build sentences; and how these differ from or are similar to English.

The starred (★) content above is not applicable to ancient languages.

ICT in foreign languages

There are a number of ways in which ICT might be used in foreign languages. Interactive whiteboards enable improved delivery and pacing, whole-class teaching, interaction and discussion. Digital resources from the Internet and CD-ROMs give access to a vast number of learning opportunities, allowing pupils to work at their own pace and replay audio/video repeatedly according to individual needs. International communication projects via video conferencing, email and discussion forums facilitate cultural awareness and impact positively on grammar, vocabulary and tenses. Multimedia presentation software enables a range of foreign language skills to be practised. Digital video and audio recordings of pupils (whilst speaking) provide feedback opportunities on performance and the opportunity for critique and evaluation by teachers, peers and pupils themselves. Films in DVD format with subtitles and audio tracks in different languages are useful for language translation.

Foreign language software

- **CD-ROM:** 2Simple French, 2Simple Spanish, Rosetta Stone (range of languages), StarFrench, Teaching-You French, Ecoutez Bien, Kids French, Start To Learn French, Jump Ahead 2000 French, George the Goldfish, Chatter Chatter Primary Spanish, Spanish Lessons for Kids, Start To Learn Spanish, Chatter Chatter Primary German, German Lessons for Kids, Kids Language Lessons, Talk Now (French, Italian, Spanish, German, Mandarin), Clicker MFL, Fluenz (French, Spanish, Italian, German, Mandarin and Portuguese), Human Japanese, Byki, Anki.

- **DVD:** Learn A Language, First Fun With French, Talk French, French for Kids, First Fun With Spanish, Talk Spanish, Spanish For Kids: Simple Words, Italian For Beginners, Italian for Kids Beginning Level 1, Early Start Mandarin Chinese With Bao Bei The Panda, Ni Hao Kai Lan: Super Special Days, Culture Cubs – Mandarin Chinese for Kids (Time to Swim, Time to Meet the Animals, Time to Eat).

Foreign language apps

Babbel, Human Japanese, ConjuVerb, Busuu, Keewords.

Foreign language resources

Useful resources for foreign languages include:

- Interactive whiteboards.
- Presentation software.
- Audio/Video CDs and DVDs.
- CD-ROMs with phonetics and language activities.
- Video conferencing, email, discussion boards and blogs.
- Language labs.
- Web-based resources.

Foreign language websites

- BBC Languages: bbc.co.uk/languages.
- Busuu: busuu.com/enc.
- Duolingo: duolingo.com.
- Early Start Languages: earlystart.co.uk.
- Education City: educationcity.com/uk/primary-schools/foreign-languages.
- Fonetiks: fonetiks.org.
- Grow Story Grow: growstorygrow.com.
- Language Software Reviews: languagesoftware.net.
- LingQ: lingq.com.
- Livemocha: livemocha.com
- Living Language: livinglanguage.com.

- Memrise: memrise.com.
- Open Culture (Languages): openculture.com/freelanguagelessons.
- Pimsleur: pimsleur.com.
- Primary Languages: primarylanguages.org.uk.
- Rosetta Stone: rosettastone.co.uk.
- SmartClass+ Language Lab: robotel.com/en/smartclass_language.php.
- TeacherTube: teachertube.com.
- The Language Investigator: language-investigator.co.uk.
- Transparent Language: transparent.com/education.

Foreign language activity ideas

1. A Year 3 class use a web-based resource as part of their French lesson. The children watch the animated sequence which is projected onto an IWB. The sequence is repeated and the children repeat the phrases. The teacher supports the spoken word with speech bubbles created in the Smart Notepad. Later, children play individual parts and act out the sequence themselves.

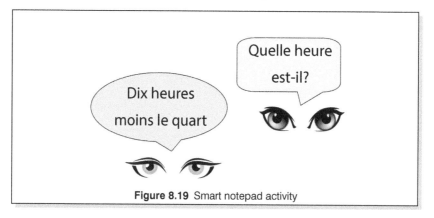

Figure 8.19 Smart notepad activity

2. Year 4 children take a PowerPoint talking story book of Goldilocks (which they previously created in English) and adapt it into a French language version (Boucle d'Or et les Trois Ours). As an extension, the class are split into three groups with each group working on a different language (Spanish, French and German).

Figure 8.20 The Three Bears (Boucle d'Or et les Trois Ours)

3. A Year 5 teacher introduces German vocabulary and common phrases using the software title Chatter Chatter. Emphasis is placed on learning vocabulary in a fun and motivating way by listening to the spoken language and practising newly acquired words using some of the many games and focused lesson activities.

4. A primary school subscribes to the website Grow Story Grow (growstorygrow.com). The site teaches languages through stories and games that uniquely 'grow' in length and structure, allowing for progression, inclusion and transition. There are over a hundred stories designed to help pupils to learn French, Spanish, German, Mandarin and English (TEFL, ESL). The stories, which have cross-curricular themes (such as history, RE, science and citizenship) include interactive games and sentence-building using high-frequency words.

 Activity

Link to the Primary ICT site at primaryict.org.uk/icthandbookv2.htm and watch the video Grow Story Grow. If you wish you can register at growstorygrow.com/freestories to try out some free stories.

5. Year 3 pupils practise French numbers, days of the week etc. using a pre-prepared PowerPoint presentation with recorded voice over.

 Activity

Link to the Primary ICT site at primaryict.org.uk/icthandbookv2.htm and try out the French Days of the Week PowerPoint.

The PowerPoint resource is something you could easily make yourself. Perhaps you could modify it so that it speaks the English days too.

You could easily record the sounds yourself using the Windows Sound Recorder.

6. A primary language specialist incorporates videos from TeacherTube into a range of her foreign language lesson plans.

Religious education (RE)

Religious education for children and young people:

■ provokes challenging questions about the meaning and purpose of life, beliefs, the self, issues of right and wrong, and what it means to be human. It develops pupils' knowledge and understanding of Christianity, other principal religions, and religious traditions that examine these questions, fostering personal reflection and spiritual development;

■ encourages pupils to explore their own beliefs (whether they are religious or non-religious), in the light of what they learn, as they examine issues of religious belief and faith and how these impact on personal, institutional and social ethics; and to express their responses. This also builds resilience to anti-democratic or extremist narratives;

■ enables pupils to build their sense of identity and belonging, which helps them flourish within their communities and as citizens in a diverse society;

- teaches pupils to develop respect for others, including people with different faiths and beliefs, and helps to challenge prejudice;

- prompts pupils to consider their responsibilities to themselves and to others, and to explore how they might contribute to their communities and to wider society. It encourages empathy, generosity and compassion.

RE has an important role to play as part of a broad, balanced and coherent curriculum to which all pupils are entitled.

ICT in Religious education

Religious education can make use of a number of digital sources of information and activities on CD-ROM, Apps and on the Internet. It can also utilise a wide range of generic ICT resources for gathering, analysing and presenting data.

Religious education software

- **CD-ROM**: Religious Education in the Early Years, Badger Religious Education for Key Stage 1, Badger Assembly Stories with Christian Themes Ages 5–7, Kar2ouche Understanding Religion; Encyclopaedia Britannica: World Religions, Religious Studies: Religions of the World, Investigating World Religions, Modern World Religions, Interactive Bible Study Guide, Ready Resources Religious Education [1 and 2], Daydream Education: Religious Education (various titles).

- **DVD**: Paws & Tales, My Religion, The Miracle Maker, Religious Education (The Primary Teachers Guide), Primary Religious Education – A New Approach: Conceptual Enquiry in Primary RE, Religious Education KS2.

Religious education apps

Children's Bible, Festivals and Holy Days, Salah for Kids, iRosary, Encyclopaedia of Religions, iPieta, Bible.is: Audio Bible, Prayer HD, World Religions Pocketbook, Oxford Dictionary of World Mythology, Religion Trainer, Bible Promises, Sturgeon's Faith Devotional, 100 Great Muslims, 12 World Religions, Analects of Mythology, Bible, Bible Memory, Bible Stories, Bible Stories – Word Search, Daily Koran, Daily Prayer, Holy Bible, Jesus Evangalism Tool, John the Baptist, Logos Bible, Logos Bible Reader, New Mass, NIV Bible, Noah's Ark, Men of the Bible, Moral Compass, Oxford Dictionary of the Bible, Pilgrim App, Priests for Life, Religion Trivia, Religion Tube, St Francis of Assisi, Stories of the Quran.

Religious education resources

Useful resources for RE include:

- Software on CD-ROM and DVD.
- Educational Apps.
- Websites including: Holy days and festivals; Religion online; Christianity [Hinduism, Judaism, Islam, Sikhism] for Children; and Teddy's day out.
- Generic word-processing, spreadsheet, database, presentation and publication software.

Religious education websites

- BBC Bitesize: bbc.co.uk/schools/gcsebitesize/rs.
- BBC Class Clips: bbc.co.uk/learningzone/clips.
- BBC Religion: bbc.co.uk/religion.
- Cracking RE: crackingre.co.uk.

- Crickweb: crickweb.co.uk/ks2re.html.

- Discovery RE: discoveryschemeofwork.com.

- The National Association of Teachers of Religious Education: natre.org.uk.

- RE Online: reonline.org.uk.

- Religious Education Handbook: re-handbook.org.uk.

- TeachersMedia: teachersmedia.co.uk.

Religious education activity ideas

1. Year 2 children learn that religious organisations do work to protect our world. They use the Internet to access religious websites and explore threats to the environment and to the survival of people and animals in some parts of the world. Finally, they use MS Publisher to design a poster to draw attention to issues in the UK.

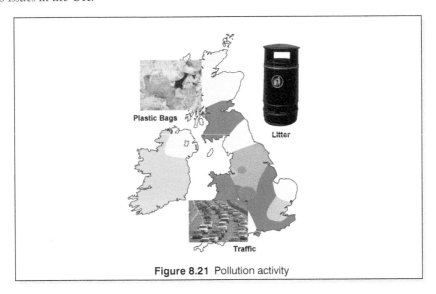

Figure 8.21 Pollution activity

2. Guided by a prepared activity sheet, Year 4 pupils use the CD-ROM World Religions to develop an understanding of unfamiliar religions. In particular, they are required to identify a number of shared beliefs, values and practices within and between the religions.

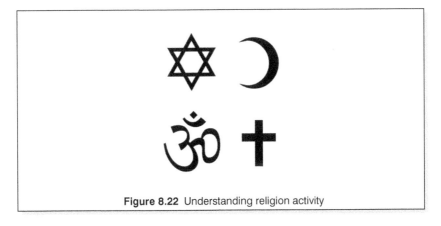

Figure 8.22 Understanding religion activity

3. Year 3 children carry out a school survey to ascertain individual's values and opinions on a number of moral issues. A simple spreadsheet is prepared and copied to pupils' tablet PCs. Pupils use the tablets in the playground and dining hall, recording responses from children across school. The results are analysed and presented using a stacked bar chart.

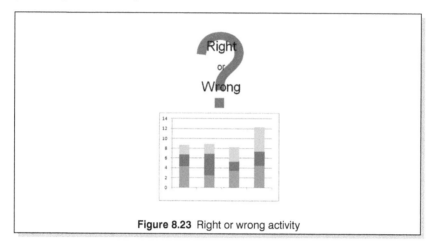

Figure 8.23 Right or wrong activity

Personal, social, health and economic education (PSHE)

Personal, social, health and economic (PSHE) education is an important and necessary part of all pupils' education. All schools should teach PSHE though it is a non-statutory subject. PSHE can encompass many areas of study. Teachers are best placed to understand the needs of their pupils and do not need central government prescription.

However, while schools may tailor their local PSHE programme to reflect the needs of their pupils, they are expected to use their PSHE education programme to equip pupils with a sound understanding of risk and with the knowledge and skills necessary to make safe and informed decisions.

Schools should seek to use PSHE education to build, where appropriate, on the statutory content already outlined in the national curriculum, the basic school curriculum and in statutory guidance on: drug education, financial education, sex and relationship education (SRE) and the importance of physical activity and diet for a healthy lifestyle.

Sex and relationship education

Sex and relationship education (SRE) is an important part of PSHE education and is statutory in maintained secondary schools.

ICT in PSHE

Finding resources for these subjects can prove tricky. However, there are a number of appropriate CD-ROM/web-based offerings and Teachers TV (via TES Connect) provides some particularly useful coverage of a range of PSHE issues.

PSHE software

- **CD-ROM**: Ace Monkey Drug Education Pack, Kar2ouche PSHE [Bullying, Drug Awareness, Respecting Diversity, Relationships: School and the Wider World], Health & Wellbeing, Growing & Developing and The Developing Child, Sex and relationship education (7–9 & 9–11), Inspirational

Ideas (PSHE and Citizenship [7–9 & 9–11], Moving On Up: All You Need to Ease the Transition from Primary to Secondary School).

■ **DVD**:You, your body and sex, Stolen Lives: Children of Addicts, New Zoo Revue: School Drugs & Money, Real Life Teens: Drug Abuse Beyond Marijuana & Alcohol – Crossing The Thin Line, Teen Guidance – Drug & Alcohol Awareness, Your Body Your Health & Drugs, The truth about drugs, Drugs – Keeping Your Head, Saying no to alcohol and drugs, You can choose – saying no to smoking, Teeth: Some Facts to Chew On.

PSHE resources

Useful resources for PHSE/citizenship include:

■ Software on CD-ROM.

■ DVD video.

■ Web-based materials.

■ Teachers TV (TES Connect).

PSHE websites

■ Association for Teaching Citizenship: teachingcitizenship.org.uk.

■ Bamzonia: bamzonia.com (Personal Financial Education).

■ BBC Learning Zone: bbc.co.uk/learningzone/clips/topics/primary.shtml#pshe.

■ Childline: childline.org.uk.

■ Eco Schools: eco-schools.org.uk.

■ Go Givers: gogivers.org.

■ Grid Club: gridclub.com.

■ KidsHealth: kidshealth.org.

■ National Association for Pastoral Care in Education: napce.org.uk.

■ Nationwide Education: nationwideeducation.co.uk (Finance, Sustainability, Safety, Employability).

■ Netmums: netmums.com.

■ Red Cross: redcross.org.uk/What-we-do/Teaching-resources/Teaching-packages/Microsite/Life-Live-it-first-aid-education-for-children (First Aid).

■ Schoolzone: schoolzone.co.uk.

■ Small World: smlworld.co.uk.

■ Uniview: uniview.co.uk/acatalog/health-resources.html.

■ World E-Citizens: worldecitizens.net.

PSHE activity ideas

1. Over a period of time, a primary school uses video cameras (in a variety of forms) to create a collection of audio and video clips of children expressing their views on a wide range of moral and social issues. The clips form part of subsequent PSHE lessons and are used to stimulate discussion on a whole range of topics. Cameras are ideal in this respect for reflection and consolidation.

Figure 8.24 Video camera activity

2. A Year 4 class use an interactive whiteboard to create a mind map of ideas on reactive and preventive measures with regard to smoking. The file is saved and revisited from time to time so that children can review the topic.

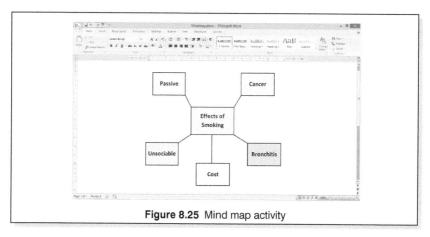

Figure 8.25 Mind map activity

3. Year 5 pupils use the Ace Monkey Drug Education Pack to explore the topic of drugs. They interview each other and record their responses to important questions using the free podcasting package Audacity. The resulting mp3 files are shared on the school learning platform.

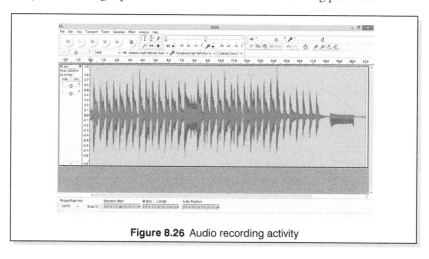

Figure 8.26 Audio recording activity

9

Models of digital learning

Introduction

For the purposes of this book, digital learning is defined as 'technology-based learning' whether the method of presentation is in a face-to-face environment, at a distance, online or a blended approach.

There is no single 'best practice' when using ICT to enhance teaching and learning and, not surprisingly, a variety of 'models' have emerged. This chapter examines these models which may be used in isolation or in combination. They include:

- Interactive whiteboards
- The Internet and World Wide Web
- Mobile learning (including tablet PCs and Educational apps)
- Learning platforms
- Computer-mediated communication
- Podcasting and vidcasting
- Video conferencing
- Computer games
- Subscription websites
- Play-based learning
- Visualisers and document cameras
- Computer configurations.

It must be stressed however that, whichever model is adopted, it is the learning that is important; the technology simply helps provide the means by which it is achieved.

Interactive whiteboards (IWB)

Interactive whiteboards enable improved delivery and pacing, whole-class teaching, interaction and discussion, and relate to increased motivation for both teachers and pupils. Boys in particular are captivated by the IWB. It captures their interest, holds their attention and offers them a degree of control.

What is an interactive whiteboard?

An interactive whiteboard is a touch-sensitive screen that works in conjunction with a PC and a data projector.

This combination of technologies not only turns the IWB into a huge computer screen, it also provides a range of features which allow teachers and children to perform functions and carry out activities which would otherwise be impossible or inferior when reliant upon conventional whiteboards and computer displays alone. In the right hands, the IWB is a very valuable resource.

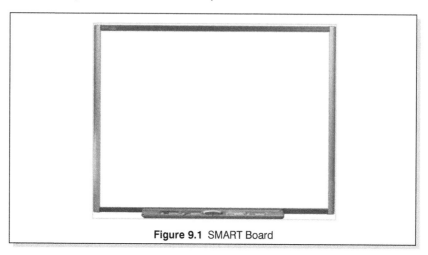

Figure 9.1 SMART Board

History of the interactive whiteboard

The IWB has been around for many years (in one form or another) but only began to make a major impression in primary schools from the early part of the twenty-first century and particularly from 2003 when the Department for Children, Schools and Families (DCSF) Primary Schools Whiteboard Expansion project (PSWE) was launched. It provided substantial funding to 21 local authorities to support the acquisition and use of interactive whiteboards. Research on IWBs has found that:

- the more experience the teacher has of using the interactive whiteboard, the greater the likelihood of positive attainment gains for pupils;
- in primary maths, science and English, both boys and girls that have been taught extensively with the interactive whiteboard have made several months' additional progress over the course of the two key stages.

What are the benefits of the interactive whiteboards?

Using your finger as a pointer you can do anything that a mouse can do (including left and right click). You can also write on the board, on top of open applications and within applications which support writing. This makes IWBs ideal for whole-class teaching because everyone is able to see the large screen from their own seats. IWBs have specific educational value and offer a whole variety of benefits (though some of these result solely from projection onto a large screen):

- They provide all the familiar features of a traditional whiteboard without the mess, without the need to clean them and with an infinite amount of working space.
- Lessons can be enhanced by augmenting the teacher's personal presentation with a range of formatting and multimedia features.
- Anything on the screen can be saved or printed as required.
- Teachers and children can interact directly with the board creating lessons and activities that benefit from a graphical user interface including the movement of objects (drag and drop), input of text, navigation and hyperlinks.
- They allow learners to absorb information more easily.

- They promote better learner participation by freeing them from note taking.
- They allow learners to work collaboratively around a shared task/work area.
- When used for whole-class interactive testing of understanding, they can provide learner feedback rapidly.
- They link to other applications (e.g. MS PowerPoint and Interactive Voting Systems), providing them with additional features.
- They are well supported by a huge assortment of interactive educational software packages (both free and commercial).
- They come with additional, advanced features, for example, you can record and playback a whole lesson.
- As with many other ICT resources they are extremely motivating both for teachers and pupils.

They do of course have their downside:

- Simply installing the technology doesn't guarantee its use. There needs to be a positive investment by staff in terms of training and practice.
- Some teachers can become prepossessed to the extent that:
    - They use the IWB at any available opportunity, whether it is appropriate to do so or not!
    - They 'hog' the board and don't provide sufficient opportunity for children to interact.
- Interactive whiteboards are more expensive than conventional whiteboards or projector/screen combinations.
- Their surface can become damaged, necessitating expensive replacement.
- Front projection boards can be obscured by the user.
- Inadvertent eye contact with the projector is potentially harmful. Children should be supervised at all times when a projector is being used.
- Fixed-height boards are often too high to reach the top or too low for their bottom to be readily visible.

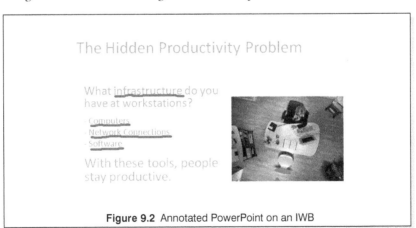

Figure 9.2 Annotated PowerPoint on an IWB

Making good use of interactive whiteboards

To maximise the impact of IWBs, teachers should invest time and energy in training and practice. Before considering specific software resources, the inherent features of the IWB should be mastered.

Whatever you are projecting you can make annotations on top. Great for thought sharing, building up key points and highlighting text and images. The pens and highlighters have a wide range of colours and, of course, your notes can be saved, printed or wiped clean at a stroke. The 'floating tools' is a useful feature too.

Make use of the features linked to MS PowerPoint. These include: a special toolbar with navigation and menu options, the option to advance (and rewind) the presentation with your finger (using single or double touch), pens or floating tools to make annotations (which may be permanently incorporated if desired), inserting notes and drawings on the fly and incorporating hyperlinks.

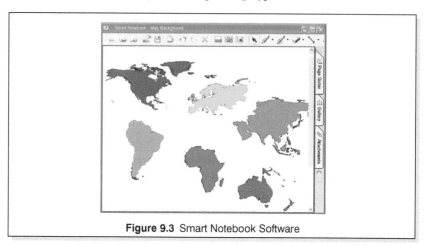

Figure 9.3 Smart Notebook Software

All boards come with useful software (e.g. Smart Notebook or ACTIVstudio). These are multi-page notebooks which include a variety of tools, such as drawing objects, photos, rulers, flipchart functions, protractors, playback features, diagrams, animations, backgrounds, text conversion, screen capture and more.

Activity ideas

1. Key Stage 1 children work in small groups on a number of interactive literacy activities provided free from the Crickweb website. Here they drag and drop the names of vegetables onto the picture. The name box turns green if correctly placed.

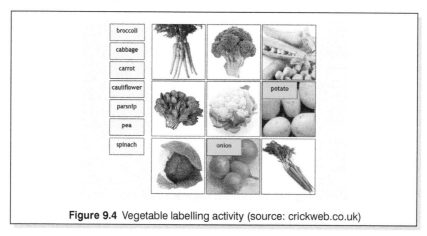

Figure 9.4 Vegetable labelling activity (source: crickweb.co.uk)

2. A Year 1 teacher designs her own simple maths activity using the Smart Notebook. Children count green and red apples (whilst dragging and dropping them from baskets into the answer box). The children are

invited to write the corresponding numbers below each group of apples. More able children do the same with words to form a number sentence.

The words and numbers are then grouped and dragged onto a separate slide so that the exercise can be repeated over and over for all number bonds to 10. Other than the apples, all objects are fixed to the screen to prevent them being accidentally moved.

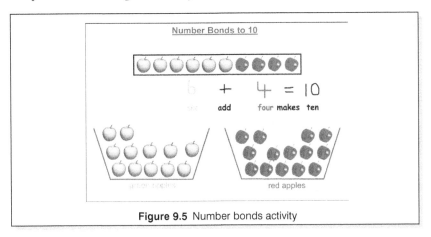

Figure 9.5 Number bonds activity

3. Using one of Smart Notebook's handwriting backgrounds, a Key Stage 1 group practise their writing skills (given pictures and typed words as clues). Their writing is then converted automatically into typed text in order to provide confirmation that they are achieving their goal.

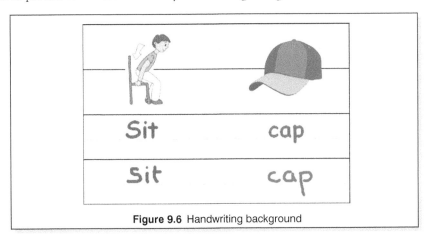

Figure 9.6 Handwriting background

4. A Year 6 teacher uses several features of the IWB to demonstrate forces and movement. Using a content free software package she imports a number of useful images and builds up a word bank. With these objects, and some built-in drawing tools, she builds up key points as the demo progresses. Using hyperlinks to pre-selected science websites, children are invited to carry out further reading and research and to confirm the knowledge and understanding they have acquired.

5. Year 5 children participate in a mind-mapping activity on the effects of bullying. They use MS Word to organise their ideas and input them using a radio-linked remote keyboard. Their handwriting is then converted to text, formatted, colour coded and printed as an aide-memoire for a subsequent off screen activity.

6. A primary school uses Whiteboard Wizard's Time Teller, one of many commercial packages designed specifically for IWBs. It is used in whole-class teaching for time-telling on analogue and digital clock faces. Tasks are made incrementally more difficult to suit ability and progress through years 1 to 6.

7. A Reception/Year 1 teacher uses TextEase to set up a lesson on small numbers and number order using money as the theme. The available clipart provides the drag and drop money images and the features of grouping and rotating are used to help establish the principles involved.

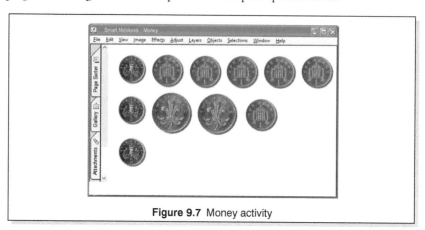

Figure 9.7 Money activity

8. A Year 5 teacher uses the IWB to make annotations on top of a spreadsheet in order to help explain the use of tables, formatting and simple formulas. When used with the whole-class (or to overcome problems for small groups) this saves the time which would otherwise have been expended dealing one-to-one with each pupil in turn.

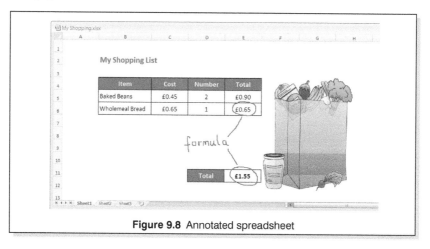

Figure 9.8 Annotated spreadsheet

Types of interactive whiteboards

There are several types of IWB to choose from. Options include front projection, rear projection, interactive displays, boards incorporating projectors, boards that use existing dry erase boards and adjustable height boards (very useful when you need to position the board close to the floor for young children at circle time). Some have associated Interactive Response systems. The main brands are:

Table 9.1 Types of Interactive Whiteboard

Smartboard from smarttech.com	Touch activated. It comes with the Smart Notebook, Smart Classroom Suite and a wide array of other associated software and hardware resources. Probably the most popular.
Promethean ACTIVboard from prometheanworld.com	Available as ActivPen, intuitive touch, or a combination of both types of interactivity. Comes with ActivInspire and ActivOffice software.
MimioTeach from mimio.com	An interactive whiteboard system that uses existing dry erase boards. Includes MimioStudio classroom software, wireless capability, and a range of other MimioClassroom products.
StarBoard from eu.hitachi-solutions.com	Offers complete whiteboards and those that use existing dry erase boards. Comes with StarBoard, StarCloud and Advanced Collaboration software.
RM Classboard from rmeducation.com	Comes with Easiteach Studio software and offers a powerful teaching product for both primary and secondary schools.
Clasus Interactive Smart Board from clasus.com.tr/en	Comes with A-migo software specifically developed for training and education.

The Internet and World Wide Web

Introduction

The Internet has become an increasingly important feature of the learning environment for pupils and teachers. Despite concerns over e-safeguarding, it is now an essential and often vital study aid both inside and outside the classroom, an important means of communication and a way to access and share resources.

    ★ *E-safeguarding is covered in Chapter 11.*

Most schools now have fast Internet access via the SuperJANET network and many pupils now use the Internet as their primary source of information.

This section will briefly examine uses of the Internet in schools and social networking.

Uses of the Internet in schools

 Activity

You might begin by listing:

- all the ways in which your school currently uses the Internet;
- any further possible uses of the Internet you can think of.

You can compare your list with Table 9.2.

Table 9.2 School-related use of the Internet (pupils and teachers)

General research by searching ('Googling').	Electronic submission of work.
Information for a school project.	Email project with other schools.
Accessing museums and art galleries.	Collaborating in group work.
Downloading a study aid, image, sound or video.	Social networking (blogs, discussions etc.).
Creating a web page for a school or pupil.	Accessing teacher resources.
Pupils/parents emailing teachers.	Linking to web-based activities (e.g. CBeebies).
External access to school learning platform.	Sharing school resources with others.
Keeping abreast of policy and practice.	Linking the school MIS to the local authority.
Using LEA portals and Grids for Learning.	Instant messaging – pupil to teacher (e.g. Skype).
Video conferencing.	News and current events.

Searching and learning

The Internet is most frequently used as a tool for 'searching and learning' and, whilst children are particularly adept, there are some useful rules to be followed if searches are to be effective. For example, attaching a '+' immediately before a word asks the search engine to match that word precisely as you typed it. Using quotes " " tells the search engine to carry out a phrase search to find all the words in the exact order you typed them. These simple rules (and more) are covered in Google's Search Help pages.

 Activity

Visit Google's Basic Search Help pages:

■ Basic: google.co.uk/support/websearch/bin/answer.py?answer=134479

■ Advanced: google.co.uk/support/websearch/bin/answer.py?answer=136861

Familiarise yourself with the search techniques.

Now select the tips which you think are important for your own year group and compile a 'child-friendly' guide for your class.

Social bookmarking

Having found useful information on the web it's wise to keep track of where you found it. You could bookmark sites in your web browser but it can quickly become messy and bookmarks are tied to the computer you're using at the time. A better alternative is to use social bookmarking.

To do this you simply subscribe to a social bookmarking site. One of the most popular is Delicious (delicious.com). Your bookmarks are then stored in that site and will be available on any connected device that you may use and from wherever you may use it.

 Activity

For an overview of social bookmarking, watch the video on the YouTube website at

youtube.com/watch?v=HeBmvDpVbWc&noredirect=1.

Web 2.0

The term Web 2.0 describes a number of developments on the World Wide Web that mark a shift in the way it is used. Most notably it signifies a move from accessing static content (information) to dynamic, interactive participation by way of communicating, collaborating and sharing. Examples of services include: social networking sites, weblogs (blogs), wikis, social bookmarking, RSS and media sharing sites.

Whilst accessing these services is predominantly a leisure pursuit, many teachers have identified benefits for young learners including: enabling access anytime and anywhere, encouraging participation and online collaboration, extending children's use of media, providing opportunities for assessment and extending learning beyond the school. The ensuing 'sense of ownership' promotes increased attention to detail and an improvement in the quality of work.

It is true to say however that many teachers have yet to use Web 2.0 services in their teaching and learning because they are not yet familiar with the technology or they have concerns about using the Internet in class.

Let's take a look at one of the Web 2.0 tools, the weblog (or blog). A blog is basically a personal journal that is available on the web. The activity of updating a blog is "blogging" and someone who keeps a blog is a "blogger." Blogs are typically updated on a frequent basis using software that allows people with little or no technical background to update and maintain the blog. Postings on a blog are almost always arranged in chronological order with the most recent additions featured most prominently.

Wikis are much like blogs but are set up in order that groups, rather than individuals, can add entries. In this way they act as shared spaces and discussion forums.

 Activity/

There are a number of free blogging sites such as Primary Blogger: primaryblogger.co.uk, eThink: ethink. org.uk and Edublogs: edublogs.org.
   Take a look at the blog at St Leonards CE Primary, Bridgnorth: stleonardsprimarybridgnorth.ethink.org.uk/ to see how they use them.

Social networking

Social networking sites provide new and varied ways to communicate via the Internet and mobile phone. Users can easily create their own online page and personal profile which they display to a network of contacts ('friends'). Users of these sites can communicate with friends and others and share resources. Communication may be one-to-one (like email) or one-to-many (postings, comments etc. that everyone can see).

Social networking services (SNS) have been around for over a decade. They began with services that allowed users to build personal profiles (for a variety of reasons) and have now grown to include media sharing. The term networking relates to contact with people who share similar interests and pursuits and not to making deliberate contact with strangers. Some of the more popular examples are:

- **Facebook** – the leader in social networking websites that provide users with personal profiles, a network of friends, blogs, photos, music and videos.
- **MySpace –** the predecessor to Facebook. Now focuses mainly on music.
- **YouTube** and **TrueTube** – video sharing websites where users can upload, view and share video clips.
- **Bebo** – once a popular social networking website that was relaunched on mobile only in 2014.
- **Twitter** – a social networking and micro-blogging service using mobile phones to send text-based posts of up to 140 characters in length.
- **Flickr** – a photo and video hosting and sharing website.

Most schools block access to these sites although research by Childnet suggests that there is good reason to explore their potential.

 Activity

Childnet's mission is to help make the Internet a great and safe place for children. If you'd like to read The Benefits and Opportunities of Social Networking (extract from Childnet report) there's a copy on the Primary ICT site at primaryict.org.uk/icthandbookv2.htm.

The report looks at how social networking services can support learning in schools and colleges. The report also includes an evaluation tool, produced in conjunction with major service providers, designed to walk teachers through key features of sites that they are considering for use in support of their teaching and learning practice.

The report finds that young people are well acquainted with social networking services and regard them as just another part of their social and school-related activities. Many children from 5 years and upwards are believed to have a profile on a social networking site and there is an indication that education-related topics are the most commonly discussed. However, teachers are often wary about social networking because of the negative press. They may not recognise the educational potential of social networking and are more likely to need support than their pupils.

What are the risks?

The two most obvious risks are making friends with strangers who turn out to be predators and the opportunity for cyber-bullying or trolling (not to mention the downside of increased time spent online and over-exposure to advertising). This presents teachers (and parents) with a dilemma; banning social networking completely may appear to be the only safe option but it also denies any opportunity to exploit possible educational potential.

What are the benefits?

Despite the concerns, children are really enthusiastic about social networking and independent research shows that it has significant benefits and helps raise standards.

Communicating via personal profiles, emails and blogs builds friendships around the world and, in doing so, promotes reading and writing skills and allows children to present information in a variety of formats.

Forums get pupils involved in discussing ideas on a variety of topics of personal and educational interest. They can collaborate on projects, building and confirming knowledge. They can form partnerships and buddying schemes with other schools in the UK and abroad, broadening their understanding of local, national and global issues. Children can also join (or set up) shared interest groups.

Social networking helps to encourage creativity and develops authoring and publishing skills through the creation of personal websites on hobbies, personal interests and school work.

Doing all of this improves children's knowledge and skills in ICT – and there is often support for teachers too!

 Activity

You may wish to read a report on Benefits of Social Networking (copy on the Primary ICT site at primaryict. org.uk/icthandbookv2.htm).
Research was conducted in 2006 but is nevertheless just as relevant today.

Safe social networking

It may be that your school will err on the safe side and stay clear of general social networking services. However, in truth, networking can be kept within the confines of the school network/learning platform for extra safety. A good compromise, which has been adopted by many, is to use a system which is designed specifically for schools. This will help to overcome most of the problems.

The main advantages are that only the school itself can register users and every user can be monitored. Good systems will incorporate both automatic and manual monitoring in order to identify inappropriate material and possible instances of bullying. The best systems will also provide real time intervention and someone to contact.

However, the very features which make such systems attractive to teachers (e.g. control) often make them less attractive to children because they will not be the systems of choice (such as Facebook).

There are several systems available, some are web-based and others are run from the school server. Examples include:

SuperClubs Plus

A Safe Social Learning Network where 6–12 year olds can meet friends across the UK and around the world, be creative, have fun and learn ICT, Literacy and Global Citizenship together. All members are validated through their own schools. Professional mediators monitor all communication and content and constantly watch out for your children and keep them safe. The communities are available from breakfast to bedtime – on school and home computers and mobile devices, so it's non-stop learning for children at school and at home. Children from different backgrounds and cultures keep in touch with friends, share interests and help each other. The home-school projects help parents get involved with their children's school work. The communities are ideal for elective home education (superclubsplus.com).

Learner journey

A safe space to post, share and discuss pupils' work, while learning about e-safety and appropriate conduct online. You can instigate and guide discussions or set reflective writing tasks so that pupils can learn skills for use across the curriculum.

Other safe sites

Other safe social networking sites include Togetherville and What's What (by Facebook), ScuttlePad (https://www.facebook.com/scuttlepad), Club Penguin (clubpenguin.com), iTwixie (itwixie.com), Yourshere (yoursphere.com), Franktown Rocks (franktownrocks.com), Jabbersmack (jabbersmack.com), Sweety High (sweetyhigh.com), Kidzworld (kidzworld.com) and giantHello (gianthello.com).

You can also access Educators Technology for up-to-date advice: educatorstechnology.com/2012/12/social-networking-sites-teachers.html.

 Activity

Visit the Primary ICT site at primaryict.org.uk/icthandbookv2.htm and explore a range of social networking applications and guides in the document Social Networking Guides.

Summary

- The Internet has many potential uses in education.
- It has now become the most widely used source of information.
- New tools including Web 2.0 and social networking offer increased opportunities for a range of educational activities.

Mobile learning

Introduction

Mobile learning has evolved much in the last decade as a result of the extremely fast pace of change in technology. At the turn of the decade (2010) the latest devices included personal digital assistants (PDAs), NetBooks, Play Station Portables (PSPs) and mobile phones. Tablet PCs were on the decline.

Five years later and the PDA is pretty much obsolete, Netbooks have been pushed aside by an array of laptop and notebook computers, the reign of the PSP, faced by vast competition from other mobile devices, is coming to an end and the mobile phone has morphed into the Smartphone. Tablet PCs have made an upturn, largely because of decreasing cost, and are now prevalent in homes and classrooms across the globe.

In this section you will examine the potential of mobile devices in the classroom.

E-Readers

Research shows that pupils are engaging more than ever with electronic devices. For both study and for fun, students read eBooks at a higher rate than ever before, and the numbers continue to climb.

This digital shift is sometimes met by schools with uncertainty and an unwillingness to adapt. However, many schools are embracing the challenge of incorporating eBooks into the learning environment to complement traditional methods. This is surely a step forward in getting more children to read.

There is a plethora of e-reading devices available including the Kindle, Nook and Kobo, not to mention the e-reading capability of some tablets and PCs.

There is also a free Kindle reading app available from the Apple App Store (for iPad and iPhone), Google Play (for Android) and Windows Store (for PCs).

 Activity

Read the success story of Kindle e-Readers in Shepherd Primary (copy on the Primary ICT site at primaryict.org.uk/icthandbookv2.htm).

Tablet PCs

A tablet PC is a slate-shaped mobile computer equipped with touch screen technology that allows the user to operate the computer with their finger, a stylus or a digital pen. Some are 'hybrids' and also include a keyboard (which can be detached as required). Some tablets can be housed in a docking station which provides a CD drive and additional ports.

Only five or so years ago, and despite showing early promise, tablet PCs were not taking off in a significant way because of the prohibitive cost (better models sold for around £2000). However, just like the PC and other devices, costs have now reduced dramatically and the tablet has re-emerged with a vengeance!

Advantages

Tablets have many advantages over PCs and laptops:

- Same functionality as a normal computer.
- Portability (can work from everywhere and small enough to put into schoolbags).
- Connection to the Internet from anywhere.
- Light weight (lighter than most laptops).
- Smaller in size.
- Flexible screen (can be oriented in landscape or portrait).
- Can be connected to a keyboard if required.
- Longer battery life.
- Quicker to boot up (and shut down).
- Intuitive to use.
- Touch screen allows for better interaction with websites and other subject matter.
- Allow for handwriting and handwriting recognition.
- Can be laid flat on the working surface and easily shared within a group.
- Various sizes (most common are 10" and 7").
- An effective learning and teaching enhancement tool.
- An interactive teaching aid for tutorials and external student consultation.
- 1000s of available apps.

Figure 9.9 Tablet PC

Disadvantages

They also have a number of disadvantages:

- Hardware is prone to damage (particularly the screen).
- Computers with traditional keyboards are much more comfortable.
- The screen size is sometimes small in comparison with a laptop.
- Some people prefer a mouse.

- They do not come with optical drives for use with CDs/DVDs.
- Difficulties working on the small screen as compared to larger screen size of a laptop.
- Less storage than a laptop (some have no means of adding additional storage).
- Fewer ports.
- Restrictions on file types.

It is therefore true to say that, whilst a tablet has many advantages, it is not necessarily a replacement for a laptop.

Tablet PCs in the primary classroom

Tablet PCs can be used to address all three main learning styles (visual, auditory and kinaesthetic) using applications such as educational games, music and drawing.

As a result, we are seeing an increasing number of educational tablets appear in primary schools, giving children easy access to new applications and providing them with engaging, inspirational material that encourages them to learn. The traditional methods of hands-on classroom activity are being complemented by advancements in technology.

When evaluating whether to make the investment in tablets, here are a few points to consider:

Pros:

- Tablets are user-friendly for both children and teachers with a touch-sensitive interface.
- Children can learn to count, do simple subtraction and addition problems, listen to stories, learn the alphabet whilst most importantly, making learning fun.
- Tablets are very interactive pieces of technology that enable children to access an increasingly engaging learning experience by using a combination of learning styles.
- A provider of audio visual tools in the classroom (camera, video and voice recorder) which can be used creatively across a high number of apps.
- Access to eBooks which allow the child to highlight and look up the meaning of words without having to rely on constant support from the teacher.
- The creative apps on tablets for drawing, video editing and composing music encourage the children to contribute creatively instead of getting into the habit of solely consuming information.
- Tablets are mobile, this encourages pupils to be more active in and around the classroom, providing memorable learning experiences that engage all three styles of learning.
- They can be used effectively to replace an ICT suite and thus free up space.
- They increase motivation and hence likely to have a positive impact on learning outcomes.
- They support independent and collaborative study.
- They are more versatile than laptops.

Cons:

- Schools require the financial support to be able to provide their pupils with tablets, which can prove to be a significant investment.
- They may simply run out of power and therefore disrupt a lesson.
- They suffer poor multi-tasking – some tablet ranges are unable to open multiple windows and files cannot be kept open side by side.

In the next few years, it is likely that most school budgets will cater for tablet devices in order to ensure that their pupils are equipped with the latest educational tools. Supporting teachers with training is essential in order to realise the potential of this technology in the classroom. Being able to use tablet devices to enhance visual, auditory and kinaesthetic teaching could prove to have great potential for the development of education.

Which tablet?

Perhaps the most well-known tablet is the iPad (and iPad Mini) though there are many other options available such as Google Nexus, Microsoft Surface Windows and Samsung Galaxy Tab. It very much depends of course on your budget and your preference regarding operating system and specification. Here are some of the things you need to consider:

- Look for the features of each tablet. See whether it has the features you will need like a music player, video chat capabilities (check its resolution), a good camera (check the pixels of the camera) in front and back, GPS and a built-in e-Reader.
- Check what operating system it has and what version is available.
- Look at the processor and make sure it offers the speed you need.
- See the memory capacity and make sure that it is enough to store your photos, videos and music collections.
- Check the display of each tablet. See whether it has a responsive touchscreen and a beautiful resolution for viewing photos and videos in HD.
- Portability is the distinctive feature tablets bring to the computing world. See if the device is easy enough to navigate, whether it has a built-in stand to hold it for easy viewing or whether it has other accessories like a digital pen, stylus etc.

If you are considering tablets for younger children then you might consider the Challenger Colour Tablet or InnoTab 3S (from VTech), the LeapPad2 or LeapPad Ultra (from LeapFrog), the nabi2 (from Fuhu) or the Galaxy Tab 3 Kids (from Samsung).

Figure 9.10 Challenger colour tablet (source: vtechuk.com)

 Activity

If you're not convinced that tablets have a place in the classroom then visit the Primary ICT site at primaryict.org.uk/icthandbookv2.htm and read the article Should we use iPads in Schools and watch the video iPads in Primary.

Case Study: Swansea tablet computer project boosts pupils' reading

A new way of using tablet computers in schools could change how children are taught in Wales. It follows a project at Casllwchwr Primary which was then tested at Sea View Primary (both in Swansea).

Year 6 children saw average reading ages leap from 9 to 13. Teachers say they have never seen such a dramatic turnaround in pupils. They were much more interested in learning, there was a lot more questioning and they were more interested in coming to school.

Sea View rolled out the experiences of Casllwchwr and other technologically advanced schools, both primary and secondary, in Wales. They started using the "LIFE" programme developed for tablet computers. Pupils quickly became confident and their self-esteem was raised. Their parents then became interested and wanted to come in and see what was happening.

The LIFE programme, which stands for Lifelong Intergenerational Furthering Education, has been a partnership between Swansea Council and Casllwchwr Primary.

Simon Pridham, the executive head at Casllwchwr, said it was clear to him that the technology was becoming crucial in the classroom. "I think it's totally unacceptable for a teacher today to say 'I don't do ITC (information technology)'" he said. "They might as well say 'I don't do literacy' – because it's so integral to our learning. If you engage, enthuse and inspire a child, you can take him anywhere. But engaging, enthusing and inspiring the teaching profession is another thing. But that's why the children have to be at the centre of this. We can't preach to them."

BBC (2013)

 Activity

If you would like to know more about the LIFE Programme you can access their website at life1881.co.uk.

Mobile phones

Mobile phones are more than communications devices, they are mini computers which are no longer simply classroom distractions, they are now powerful classroom tools.

Pupils can use their mobile phones to document science experiments, record oral exams and research information. Teachers can use mobile phones to poll students, communicate with parents and update class blogs.

For most pupils, mobile phones are indispensable and are always turned on. So why not make use of their redeeming features, treat them as powerful learning devices and use the opportunity to everyone's educational advantage? Even with the existence of a digital divide, most pupils in the UK already own their own phone and many have the latest Smartphones.

Educational use of mobile phones will need to sit alongside school policy for the use of mobiles devices in order that the privilege is not abused.

Pupils will undoubtedly welcome using their phones, just as they have done with other technology. However, making effective use of mobile phones in learning will require considerable rethinking by teachers.

Opportunities for learning with phones will depend upon their included features. Most phones have text input, voice recording and cameras (still and video) and the latest Smartphones provide a whole lot more.

In addition, phones provide a convenient way for schools to communicate with pupils using web-based SMS services (text messaging). Such services can provide for coordinated activities and also provide a means of sending reminders, test results etc. One example is janet.txt (pageonejanettxt.com).

Mobile phones and smaller tablet PCs have taken over where Personal Digital Assistants (PDAs) left off.

Learning-related ideas for mobile phones

- Using educational apps (see next section).
- Timing experiments with stopwatch.
- Photographing apparatus and results of experiments for reports.
- Photographing development of design models for e-portfolios.
- Photographing texts/whiteboards for future review.
- Bluetoothing project material between group members.
- Receiving SMS and email reminders from teachers.
- Synchronising calendar/timetable and setting reminders.
- Connecting remotely to school learning platform.
- Recording a teacher reading a poem for revision.
- Accessing revision sites on the Internet.
- Creating short narrative movies.
- Downloading and listening to foreign language podcasts.
- Logging into the school email system.
- Using GPS to identify locations.
- Transferring files between school and home.

Activity ideas using mobile phones

1. Year 5 and 6 children took mobile phones and small tablet PCs on a field trip to the Black Country Museum. The features of the phone were used to capture images and short videos and to store textual descriptions of some of the museums artefacts. Back at the school, all the information was uploaded to PCs and used to compile a web page which served as a portfolio of work to share with all the children and their parents.

   As a result, the trip was all the more interesting and motivating. The quality of the images was extremely high and it served to demonstrate how such small mobile devices can be used without the need for larger laptops or notebooks.

Figure 9.11 Black Country Museum (source: bclm.co.uk)

2. A school in Australia, looking for ways to connect with their disengaged pupils, decided to employ mobile phones in literacy. The pupils, who found writing difficult, were invited to use their phones to develop their writing and reading skills: capturing images, writing about them, and emailing the work to friends, families and teachers. The school's principal said he had been overwhelmed by the pupils' enthusiasm and resulting progress.

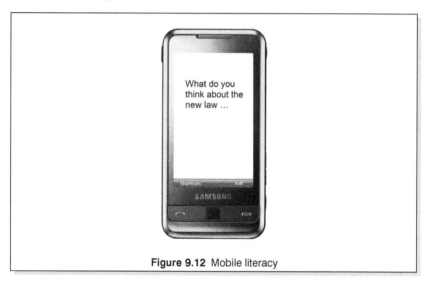

Figure 9.12 Mobile literacy

3. A Year 6 class teacher decided to incorporate mobile phones and Twitter into her classroom. She introduced a history topic and asked her pupils to research it on the Internet (both in class and then later, outside school). The result was that, rather than a few pupils entering into a face-to-face discussion, every pupil contributed something to Twitter using a mobile phone. Having contributed, pupils responded eagerly and a discussion that might have lasted for one lesson continued over several days and more.

Interestingly, the activity attracted followers from other schools and, recognising this new found potential, the class teacher created further networking activities that would include other schools in the locality.

Educational apps

A mobile app is a computer program designed to run on a Smartphone, tablet PC, laptop and other mobile devices.

Apps are usually available through application distribution platforms and are typically operated by the owner of the mobile operating system, such as the Apple App Store, Google Play, Windows Phone Store and BlackBerry App World. Some apps are free, while others must be purchased. Usually, they are downloaded from the platform to a target device, such as an iPad, iPhone, BlackBerry, Android phone or Windows Phone, but sometimes they can be downloaded to laptops or desktop computers.

There is a growing list of educational apps. Some of the most popular are listed in the Table 9.3

Table 9.3 Educational apps

Title	Description	Cost/Platform★
Letterschool	Learn how to trace letters and numbers.	£1.99 iPhone and iPad.
Reading Raven	Teaches phonics.	£2.99 iTunes – Version 2 now out. There is demand for an Android version too.
Meteor Math	An explosive maths challenge with an arcade game feel.	Free on iTunes and Meteor Math: Planet Defence free on Android.
Endless alphabet	Pick word, find the letters and pop them in the right place.	Free iPhone and iPad.
Percy Parker	Times tables.	69p for each table or cheaper if you buy in a bundle. iPhone.
Barefoot Atlas	Explore an interactive 3D globe.	£2.99 Best on the iPad because of the larger screen.
Bee-Bot	Software version of the popular floor robot.	Free iTunes.
Duo Lingo	Helps you learn Spanish, French, German, Portuguese, Italian and English.	Free on iTunes and Android.
Math Bingo	Tests children on their mental addition, subtraction, multiplication and division.	99p on iTunes and there is an app with the same name and design free on Android.
Magic Piano	Play a variety of tunes on its three keyboards.	Free iTunes and Android.
Super Why	Recognise and read letters and words.	£1.99 – android and iPhone.
Little Writer	Trace letters and learn all the sounds and letter formation of the alphabet.	Free iTunes.
Star Walk	Find out what stars you can see from your garden.	£1.99 iTunes. If you want to try a free app that teaches you all about the night sky, try SkyView Free – Explore the Universe.
Eggs on Legs	Solve maths problems to crack open quirky eggs on legs.	69p iTunes.
Music Sparkles	Learn about and 'play' different musical instruments.	Free iTunes.
Pop Math	Learn maths and get to grips with addition, subtraction, multiplication and division.	69p iTunes and Android. Pop Math Lite is free.
Monster Time	Telling the time – analogue and digital.	£1.49 iTunes If you want to try a free app, try Interactive Telling Time Lite, which is good as well.
Lola's Alphabet Train	Solve letter matching and reading puzzles.	£1.49 iPad and Android – Lite version is free.

★ As of June 2014

Activity

For more apps and ideas about using them you can read Apps for Primary School (copy on the Primary ICT website) and visit Apps4Primary at apps4primaryschools.co.uk, Primary Apps at primaryapps.wordpress.com, Teaching Appz at teachingappz.co.uk and Appcrawlr at appcrawlr.com/ios-apps/best-apps-video-analysis.

App and iPad sources

- iPad apps for school – ipadapps4school.com.
- Blippit: blippit.co.uk.
- 20 amazing apps for educators – teachhub.com/20-amazing-ipad-apps-educators.
- 107 apps for learning – innovatemyschool.com/industry-expert-articles/item/166-107-favourite-ipad-apps-for-learning.html.
- iPads for Educators – ipadeducators.com/#!curriculum-apps/c2t8.
- Teach with your iPad – teachwithyouripad.wikispaces.com.
- Apps for primary schools – apps4primaryschools.co.uk.
- iPads in Primary by Mr Andrews – mrandrewsonline.blogspot.co.uk/2012/03/apps-for-primary-education-apps-for.html.
- Apps in Education – appsineducation.blogspot.co.uk.
- Ed Tech iPad resources pages – educatorstechnology.com/p/blog-page_9.html.
- Mr P's ICT blog – mrparkinsonict.blogspot.co.uk.
- 200 Apps for Special Education – educatorstechnology.com/2012/10/top-200-special-education-apps.html.

Creating apps

Some primary schools create their own apps as collaborative, cross-curricular projects that link ICT with other subjects. Pupils can find out what an app does and how it works, research potential uses of Apps for children in their school and design apps using software such as Apps4PrimarySchools: apps4primaryschools.co.uk (free) and Blippit: blippit.co.uk.

 Activity

You are now invited to devise learning activities which incorporate mobile devices.
Perhaps you can design an activity that helps resolve the issues posed in the scenario below ?

Scenario:
Paul is a Year 4 pupil and is classed as a 'reluctant writer'. He has great difficulty producing legible, coherent writing. His writing is difficult to assess due to lack of written work. His motor control is adequate and his spelling is reasonable. He is of average speaking and listening age yet he lacks interest in committing pencil to paper.

Paul is occasionally absent from school and this exacerbates his problem because he has fallen behind his peers in several subjects.

How might mobile technology help this pupil?

Summary

- Handheld mobile technology can play a significant part in children's learning.

- Pupils adapt easily to such devices, some of which they already use outside school.

- Teachers often feel uncomfortable getting to grips with these devices. However, they should be encouraged to take the plunge – their own pupils will be pleased to show them how to operate the devices!

- Some devices are still quite expensive though prices are dropping all the time.

Learning platforms

The evolution of online learning

Online learning is not a new phenomenon. It dates back to the advent of the Internet in the early to mid-1990s and before that on network-based learning environments and CD-ROMs. However, the advent of online education in primary schools began only in the last 5–10 years.

The majority of schools have networked resources and broadband connectivity to the Internet. Not only can pupils and teachers access learning and share information and resources within the school, the possibility exists to do this from outside the school too – via a learning platform.

This section will briefly introduce the notion of learning platforms and their potential benefits.

★ It was once a part of the government's e-strategy that, by 2010, every pupil should have access to their own personalised learning space inside a learning platform. However, following a change in policy in 2010, schools are no longer required to do this.

What is a learning platform

In its simplest form a learning platform or virtual learning environment (VLE) is a means of accessing learning across a network and the Internet. It might be no more than the school website though there are more sophisticated packages available which take the form of integrated learning environments.

Learning platforms combine a number of features including the presentation of learning materials, assessment, discussion forums and links to other resources. Learning environments can also be linked to school management information systems for the purpose of enrolment, records of achievement etc. These are known as Managed Learning Environments (MLEs).

School learning platforms

Some schools (including primary) use MOODLE because it is a free, open source package.

 Activity

If you would like to try out MOODLE you can do so by visiting their demo site at demo.moodle.net.

Many primary schools have elected to install one of the child-friendly versions now available on the market. These include:

- DB Primary
- FrogLearn

- RM Learning Platform
- eSchools
- itslearning
- Learnanywhere

You will find links to the providers of learning platforms in Appendix 3.

 Activity

Visit the Primary ICT site at primaryict.org.uk/icthandbookv2.htm and watch the first half of the Learning Platforms Video (courtesy of Teachers TV). This may help to generate some ideas with regard to the choices of platform available and the uses that they can be put to.

It is evident that it's not easy to choose a platform for your school. What is clear is that you will probably need to find help from a private company or your education authority.

Benefits of learning platforms

A learning platform not only promotes learning, it serves a number of other purposes too. It helps promote extended learning and, in doing so, connects with parents and the outside community. Within the school it provides a range of features which are helpful to administration and management. The main benefits are summarised in Table 9.4.

Table 9.4 Benefits of a learning platform

Teachers will: Deliver online tutorials, access email and hold online discussions with learners and colleagues. Participate in a collaborative approach to the development of lesson plans, schemes of work and learning plans. Access learning resources and content designed to support learners in groups or individually.

Learners will: Access learning materials and tutor support before, during or after school. Study from home or other locations. Submit homework and assessment activities in electronic format. Work in a secure and safe virtual environment. Take part in discussions with other children (perhaps live!).

Management/administration will: Have online access to up-to-date learner data, thus improving efficiency and effectiveness. Communicate quickly and effectively with parents via email, electronic bulletins and discussion groups. Deliver personalised learning plans and materials. Contribute to the adaptation and development of web-based and electronic learning resources.

Parents will: Access online portfolios and information. Support children accessing online resources and homework. Access school bulletins online and join discussion groups. Feedback information to school and contribute to the school community. Play a greater role in supporting their children's learning.

Ideas for using a learning platform

Learning platforms are extremely versatile and can be used for any number of learning activities from bitesize chunks (e.g. homework exercises and revision) to full blown learning units (e.g. a history project or a self-paced module on PSHE). Here are a few ideas:

Staff Room

Staff share ideas and resources using an area of the learning platform which they have named the 'Staff Room'. The Staff Room has several functions: it acts as a repository (for lesson plans, presentations, videos etc.); as a discussion area; and as a collaborative space which can be used for team working (e.g. joint contributions to a policy document).

The Tudors

A Key Stage 2 teacher sets up a learning space as part of a history project. The space is available to pupils, teachers and parents so that children can carry out some of the work from home and parents can take an active interest in what their children are doing. The space contains guidance on how to go about the project, choices of tasks they might perform, links to resources (both on the school server and on the Internet), and how they will be assessed (in this case they are to compile a short presentation).

Noticeboard

Children from Year 1 to Year 6, by way of an exercise in social interaction, are given ownership of an area of their learning platform. Each week the children contribute useful information to their electronic 'notice board' including reviews of books they have read, films they have seen, recipes for healthy eating etc. They are responsible for deciding the content and for updating it on a periodic basis. The area also contains a safe chat room which allows them to discuss issues they have raised.

My Parents

A primary school identifies their learning platform as an ideal way to communicate with parents. The announcements page of the 'My Parents' area provides parents with their first point of contact and acts as an up to the moment message system. Discussion forums allow parents to have their say on a variety of issues. Their comments are constructive and they feel involved in the development of the school and can truly influence proceedings.

Content creation

Increasingly, learning platform providers are offering their own content packages (either pre-loaded or as add-ons). Many teachers will, however, create their own content in familiar formats such as MS Word documents, PDFs, PowerPoint presentations, images, audio and video (including podcasts and vidcasts) and so on.

To help create units of learning and assessment there are a number of available content creation tools (some free, some at a cost).

You will find an extensive list of authoring tools at the Centre for Learning and Performance Technologies (c4lpt.co.uk/directory-of-learning-performance-tools).

 Activity

Link to the Primary ICT site at primaryict.org.uk/icthandbookv2.htm and look at the simple Wimba Create (Learning Unit) and the original document Wimba Create (MS Word Original) on which it is based.

Lesson creation is simple with packages like this. Type the content and assessment into MS Word and Wimba Create will do the rest. The word document is instantly converted into a series of linked web pages together with a SCORM-compliant zipped version which can be uploaded into many learning platforms.

Summary

- It is not a statutory requirement for schools to implement a learning platform but it would be beneficial to do so.

- It is not easy to choose a platform and schools are advised to seek help from private companies or their education authority. If your school has good technical support you may decide to 'go it alone'.

- There is clear evidence that learning platforms provide many potential benefits to pupils. They also allow parents to engage with their children's education and, when they do, achievement levels rise. When parents have timely and accessible information about their children at school it has a significant effect in stimulating the children's engagement with learning.

Computer-mediated communication (CMC)

Introduction

Computer-mediated communication, mainly in the form of discussion forums, has become an integral part of many e-learning courses. It is seen as an effective means of providing students and teachers with a means for discussion (often the only means) and, more appropriately, a way to collaborate in order to construct and confirm learning. Communication is mainly asynchronous with students and teachers posting messages (threads) to online forums. The discussion can be between teacher and students (one-to-many), between students themselves (many-to-many) and between the teacher and a single student (one-to-one). Messages posted are visible to the entire group and can be searched, sorted and archived.

What started out in further and higher education has now begun to spread into primary schools. After all, children make much use of social interaction and are equally able to construct learning. Since most all learning platforms incorporate discussion boards then the opportunity exists to employ CMC as one means of promoting learning.

The teacher's role

Whilst children are the main participants in discussions, teachers have a specific role to play. Here are their main responsibilities:

- Presenting content/questions.
- Focusing the discussion on specific issues.
- Identifying areas of agreement/disagreement.
- Seeking to reach consensus/understanding.
- Encouraging, acknowledging or reinforcing children's contributions.
- Setting the climate for learning.
- Drawing in reluctant participants.
- Prompting discussion.
- Assessing the efficacy of the process.
- Summarising the discussion.
- Confirming understanding through assessment and explanatory feedback.
- Injecting knowledge from diverse sources (e.g. books, Internet and personal experiences).
- Responding to technical concerns.

A CMC activity for Year 1

Children share their ideas and thoughts about characters from traditional stories that they have read in a book. They can continue the chat from home because the platform and its features are accessible remotely – they are however secure and the children are therefore protected.

Podcasting and vidcasting

In Chapter 6, podcasting was hailed as a great ICT resource for supporting speaking and listening. In truth, podcasting, and indeed vidcasting, lends itself well across the curriculum. Podcasts can be used independently as part of the mobile learning revolution or incorporated into the school learning platform. The use of RSS feeds further extends their capability allowing automatic downloading of 'episodes' of learning as and when they become available (or at pre-determined times). For example, a pupil with a Smartphone or tablet PC which incorporates an RSS reader could automatically receive 'chunks' of learning which are periodically downloaded from their school learning platform or website.

There are many potential benefits both for teachers and for pupils.

For teachers:

- A new and dynamic element to teaching and learning.
- Convenience of listening anywhere, anytime.
- Teacher absence – when away at a conference etc., a podcast could replace a conventional lesson.
- Economic on resources – most resources are freely available.
- May suit particular learning styles – most children are 'plugged in' to mp3/mp4 players everywhere they go.
- Supports or extends the work of any pupil with special needs – useful for those with a reading difficulty or for English as a second or third language.
- Useful for children who miss lessons (e.g. disengaged or ill).
- Great community/school link potential and an effective way to communicate with parents (e.g. regular broadcasts instead of/as well as newsletters).
- New approach to homework (e.g. audio notes to reinforce learning).
- Enables schools to celebrate their school's achievement and events.

For pupils

- The benefits of podcasting extend much further than simply listening to educationally charged content. The process of creating podcasts themselves gives children a whole new outlook and opportunity to exploit their creative talents, share what schools are doing with other schools as well as the wider community, and showcase their work with a potential audience of thousands.
- Pupils concentrate on their speaking and listening skills which will have consequential effects on their writing skills (writing scripts, setting up interviews etc.).
- Publishing their own podcast is hugely motivating for pupils and also gives them a sense of ownership.
- In learning how to create a podcast, pupils are extending their ICT skills and capabilities to embrace new technologies.
- Podcasting can be tailored to a number of curriculum areas and is also great for developing teamwork skills.

Activity

There are three podcasts on the Primary ICT website at primaryict.org.uk/icthandbookv2.htm (Ch6). They are part of a literacy activity. If you have not already listened to these you may like to do so now. These may give you some ideas for the next activity in this chapter.

Creating a podcast

Creating podcasts is quite simple. You can use your mobile phone or mp3 recorder to make a recording and then upload it to your PC as an .mp3 or a .wav file.

These are convenient, ready-made solutions for recording when out in the field, however, for better quality recording, and editing capability, you will need podcasting software and a good quality microphone. There are numerous Open Source and commercial software packages. Here are just a few:

- Podium
- Propaganda
- Odeo Studio (free)
- Evoca
- Audacity (free)
- ePodcast Creator
- WebPod Studio
- Voice2Page
- Gabcast
- Hipcast
- Phone Blogz

A podcast usually comprises one or more mp3 files, each file representing an 'episode' of the podcast.

For the following activity you will need Audacity software installed on your PC. If you don't own it you can download it free from audacity.sourceforge.net.

Finally, if you want to go a step further then you could produce the video version of the podcast – the vidcast (or vodcast). The principles are much the same but the video will be captured using a camcorder, webcam, mobile phone, tablet etc. and the format will likely be .mp4, .avi or .wmv.

Windows Movie Maker, SAM Animation and Photostory 3 are free software applications that pupils can use to create their own videos.

Playing podcasts and vidcasts will rely on you having an appropriate player installed on your PC. The most common are Windows Media Player, QuickTime (by Apple) and Flash (by Adobe). If you don't already have these they are free to download from the Internet.

 Activity

Access the Primary ICT site at primaryict.org.uk/icthandbookv2.htm and carry out the Podcasting Activity.

You can download Audacity for free from audacity.sourceforge.net and you'll find help and tutorials at audacity.sourceforge.net/help/documentation.

Do you think you might use podcasting in your own teaching and learning?

There are plenty of plus points with podcasting but there are some disadvantages too:

- As with all ICT activities, their creation is time consuming and schools may need to invest in training for their staff.
- Without reasonable resources quality may be jeopardised.
- Broadcasts are one-way only; there is no immediate opportunity for interaction.
- File size can be large and downloading consumes bandwidth.

In addition, some staff are not comfortable recording their own voices and there may be issues around intellectual property rights.

If you are beginning to feel that this discipline is the preserve of the real enthusiast then do keep in mind the many benefits that are to be had and, all said and done, it won't harm to have a go. Even if you don't create your own learning podcasts, you should strongly consider allowing children to develop them as a class or school project.

RSS Feeds

As listeners to popular radio stations will already know, podcasts can also be made available as RSS feeds from a website. Doing this from your school website will allow pupils, and others, to subscribe to your podcasts by linking their RSS reader (e.g. iTunes) to your website. Many school websites already provide RSS feeds.

 Activity

For more ideas on Podcasting, visit the Teaching Ideas website at teachingideas.co.uk/ict/podcasting. htm.

Video conferencing

Benefits of video conferencing

Video conferencing has become quite commonplace in many primary schools and enriches learning by:

- giving children easier access to distant people and places;
- elimination of travel costs and subsequent time saving;
- allowing several schools to share the same teacher;
- developing speaking and listening skills;
- developing questioning skills;
- encouraging collaboration between schools (both locally and worldwide);
- bringing expertise into the classroom.

Video conferencing can be used to support traditional teaching and learning in many ways. For example:

- in PSHE, children can compare their diet with that of learners in another country;
- in foreign languages, children can chat with native speakers;
- in science, pupils can talk to experts about a topic they are studying, or share a scientific event with users elsewhere.

Activity

Visit the Primary ICT site at primaryict.org.uk/icthandbookv2.htm and watch the video Video Conferencing.
Do you know of any places (e.g. museums) that provide video conferencing services for pupils?

Setting up a video conferencing system

You may decide to set up your own conferencing system independently but, before embarking on such a project, you should check with your Local Education Authority to find out what expertise they have to offer and whether they have a regional conferencing service available to you.

Equipment needed

There are a several options from cheap 'low end' systems to expensive 'high end' systems.

Table 9.5 Comparison of video conferencing systems

Type	Equipment	Comments
Basic	Flash Meeting software or Skype and a webcam	Cheap, cheerful and reliable – a good place to start. A good quality webcam can be purchased from £50 upwards.
Intermediate	Polycom PVX software and webcam	Runs on fast PCs. Picture quality depends on webcam. Software and camera bundles cost around £200 upwards.
Higher	Video Phone	Like a telephone with a built-in screen. Allows you to call other video phones or other intermediate and higher systems, but is only really suitable for one-to-one conferences. Cost around £500.
	All-in-one camera and monitor	A flat-panel monitor with a built-in camera at the top that works independently of a PC. Better for one-to-one or small group. From around £1700.
Top	Desk top video conferencing unit (DVC) e.g. Polycom, Cisco Jabber or Aethra	Top of the range all-in-one solutions with frills such as ability to zoom and pan camera from remote end. Cost from around £2000 upwards. Now available with High Definition video (HD) – at a higher price!

To some extent, quality depends on price. However, many schools, having invested in an expensive system, have found that it doesn't get the level of use that its cost would justify. As a start up you may find an intermediate system to be perfectly adequate.

Intermediate solutions such as Polycom PVX run from a PC or laptop computer with a broadband connection. DVC solutions do not require a PC or laptop, they connect directly to a TV or data projector and have a network point to access the school's broadband.

Video conferencing was originally conducted over leased telephone lines and, whilst this is still an option (known as ISDN video conferencing), it is relatively expensive. You are most likely to use your broadband connection and conference across the Internet (known as IP video conferencing).

Conferencing sessions can be set up between any two parties that have video conferencing systems. You will most likely participate with other schools and video content providers such as the many museums and galleries that offer video conference programmes to schools.

It is possible to connect directly to another party but this will often give you problems resulting in picture and sound break up. You are better advised to make use of the National Education Network (NEN) which has been set up to connect schools in England and Wales. The NEN uses the JANET network (or superJANET) to allow video conferences to take place between sites around the world. (JANET – Joint Academic Network – is a private British government-funded computer network dedicated to education and research.)

Video conferencing connectivity is managed by the JANET Video Conferencing Service (JVCS) which is based in Edinburgh. You first need to register with them (at ja.net/products-services/janet-collaborate/janet-videoconferencing-service) and then you may book a connection in advance of each of your intended conferencing sessions. JVCS provide support during the school day. There is no charge for this service.

Activity ideas

1. As part of its Foreign Language programme, a local authority employs a language specialist to teach French to several primary schools from a small conferencing room in a central location. The class teachers observe the lessons with a view to taking on the role themselves the following year. Classes are often delivered to individual schools but occasionally, more than one school joins in the same lesson. Equipment can be expensive though simple systems such as webcams and Skype can be effective too.

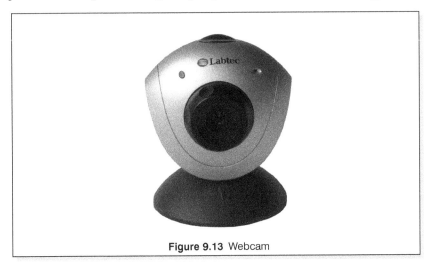

Figure 9.13 Webcam

2. Year 5 and 6 pupils learn about the solar system and space travel via a pre-booked video conferencing session with the National Maritime Museum. They also take the opportunity to question an expert from the Royal Observatory with astronomy-related questions (which they have prepared in advance).

Computer games

There is much concern that computer games are bad for children. They expend an inordinate amount of time; they can become addictive; many include unnecessary violence; they can be sexist and promote stereotypical views; they can have physically harmful side effects; and they can deny children the benefits of a fully active lifestyle.

Since 2010 however, the purposeful use of computer games as educational tools has become much more prevalent in UK schools.

Computer games are accessible in a number of forms including: CD-ROM based games (which are played on a computer); television-based consoles such as the Sony PlayStation® and Microsoft's Xbox®; handheld devices such as the Nintendo DS™ series; Sony PSP; tablet PCs; Smartphones; and online games via the Internet or other networks.

Traditionally, most games have been designed for entertainment. More recently it has been recognised that aspects of some games are inherently educational: responding to challenge; achieving goals; applying logic; reasoning; problem solving; and, in some cases, literacy skills. Above all they are extremely motivating. Indeed, there are now a number of games that are designed with education in mind. Notable examples include Minecraft (for reluctant writers), Angry Birds (for maths, science, music, language, arts and crafts, physical education and social interaction) and The Sims (for social science).

Research suggests that playing games is an important part of our social and mental development. Pupils prefer 3D adventure and strategy games and rate game elements such as logic, memory, visualisation and problem solving as the most important. Such elements are integral to adventure games and are also required during the learning process. Games that include such elements can provide stimulation to engage learners in knowledge discovery, while at the same time developing new skills.

Some of the software houses that now produce games have a specific educational focus and base their designs on accepted educational philosophy and valid educational objectives. In doing so they:

- involve teachers in the design and evaluation process;
- include a wide range of aptitudes and abilities;
- provide support and guidance for learners and teachers;
- ensure that the route through the software is clear;
- design software to be interactive and purposeful.

In using the software, teachers should:

- thoroughly evaluate its educational value;
- use it for a specific purpose (i.e. to achieve a set of desired learning outcomes);
- monitor pupil performance;
- provide learners with opportunities for reflection and evaluation;
- provide learners with feedback on performance;
- offer the chance to correct and to learn from errors in order to improve performance and achieve goals.

Success stories

Minecraft

Minecraft is a game where players create their own virtual world. There are no rules so players are able to be very creative. The game was invented several years ago but the designer is now tailoring Minecraft for use in education.

The game uses very basic graphics and yet it is highly addictive. Whilst this may be perceived as problematic, supporters claim that it simply harnesses what pupils are already doing at home. It capitalises on the skills that pupils will need in the future.

In Year 6 of a primary school in the Midlands, Minecraft was trialled and targeted at pupils (particularly boys) who found it difficult to engage with books. They played the game and then wrote stories inspired by the outcomes. The result was that otherwise reluctant readers and writers produced some high quality pieces of work.

More than 200 UK schools are now using Minecraft (June 2014) and, internationally, 200 schools per month are adopting it as a learning tool.

Angry Birds

In a speech to an audience of teachers at Brighton College in 2013, education secretary Michael Gove made a scathing attack on teachers' enthusiasm for providing pupils with 'relevant' material.

> You see your son is totally absorbed, hunched over the family laptop. You steal a look over his shoulder – and what would please you more – to see him playing Angry Birds, or coding?
>
> Politics.co.uk (2013)

This rather naive comment assumes that game playing has no place in education, that playing a popular game and learning to code are mutually exclusive, and that the designers of such games have not considered their use as educational tools.

Indeed, the designers have worked with National Geographic, NASA and the European Organization for Nuclear Research (CERN) on science-related books and educational materials and Angry Birds is based on the Finnish national curriculum (covering maths, science, music, language, arts and crafts, physical education and social interaction).

 Activity

Visit the Primary ICT site at primaryict.org.uk/icthandbookv2.htm where you'll find some ideas for activities using the Angry Birds game.

Nintendo

As part of an experiment on 600 pupils in 32 Scottish schools, test groups of pupils used the commercially available 'Nintendo's Brain Training' for 20 minutes every day over nine weeks. A control group continued their lessons as normal.

Testing, before and after the experiment, revealed that all groups had improved their scores but those using the game had improved by a further 50 per cent and had taken less time to complete tests. Teachers also intimated that a combination of good teaching and the impact of the computer games had brought about marked improvements in behaviour, class morale, time-keeping and even handwriting.

Critics might argue that a maths game, whether done on a computer or done by paper and pencil, is going to improve pupil capabilities. However, the success of the trial is attributed to a number of factors: children responded to the targets set and the desire to improve with each successive attempt; the games were simple to use; and the children were motivated to play (Cairns, 2008).

Myst III Exile

The fantasy puzzle game 'Myst III Exile' was introduced to a primary school class who used it as part of structured lessons for over a year. It has helped to improve their literacy, particularly boys who are reluctant writers.

Teachers have described it as 'Motivational and inspirational ... Pupils are so engaged with the game that they were writing without any pressure'.

The game, which was also used for music, art, science and problem solving, has had a number of benefits including: promoting collaborative working; inspiring creativity through drawing, writing and discussion; encouraging children's art; promoting prolonged writing; improvement of vocabulary; and the acquisition of better speaking and listening skills (McLeish, 2008).

For additional ideas on gaming, try the Marc Prensky website at marcprensky.com.

Subscription websites

Some schools invest in subscription websites either in addition to conventional software or as a complete solution in itself. There are a number of available sites that charge a small subscription per pupil per year. Some are devoted to specific topic areas whilst others cover the whole of the National Curriculum. Some are available online whereas others are downloaded to the school server and updated on a regular basis. Each has its own strengths and weaknesses. Perhaps the two most popular are Espresso and Education City.

Subscription sites include:

- **At School**: atschool.co.uk.
- **Brain POP**: brainpop.co.uk.
- **Busy Things**: busythings.co.uk.
- **Charanga Musical School**: charanga.com/site/musical-school.
- **Education City**: educationcity.com.
- **Espresso**: espresso.co.uk.
- **My Maths**: mymaths.co.uk.
- **Sing Up**: singup.org.
- **Spark Island**: sparkisland.com.

Figure 9.14 Espresso (source: www.espresso.co.uk)

Play-based learning

Introduction

When playing, children experiment with new ideas, develop their physical abilities and practise social and language skills. They use their imagination and learn to think and express themselves creatively, enhancing their self-confidence and increasing their sense of self and identity. Much has been written about what children may learn through play (Vygotsky, 1978; Clements and Fiorentino, 2004; Montessori, 2007) and there are those who adopt the Reggio Emilia approach, a philosophy where children delight in taking responsibility for their own learning (Brunton and Thornton, 2005).

Few would argue against the premise that play-based activity is an important way to promote active learning – where children use their brains in lots of ways. Play is the means by which young children make sense of their world. In this respect, children may be self-directed (unstructured play) or may follow pre-determined rules (structured play). There are sound reasons for doing both, just as there are for playing on their own, alongside others in independent parallel play or with other children in cooperative play.

Teachers can facilitate play by programming opportunities into the curriculum or by allowing it to develop and flow naturally during more formalised activities. The teacher's role will be one of supporting children's development, observing their actions and responding where necessary. They should raise children's awareness of technology in the world around them and create safe settings which model a range of real world scenarios and include a choice of appropriate resources such as safe household items and materials.

There are many suitable ICT resources that lend themselves well to role play situations and, with adult support, children can:

- develop an interest in ICT equipment and apparatus;
- identify and explore everyday uses of information technology in a meaningful context;
- talk about uses for ICT in their own lives and represent experiences through role play;
- understand how to operate simple equipment and perform simple functions independently;
- turn to appropriate equipment in their play in order to communicate information;
- be aware of the dangers associated with some equipment, such as electrical switches, and of the need to work within simple safety guidelines;
- use correct technical vocabulary.

Resources

Possible resources, from a cast of hundreds, include:

- Battery operated toys
- Food mixer/blender
- Electronic till
- Telephone/mobile phone
- Washing machine
- Walkie-talkies
- Computer/keyboard
- Drill/screwdriver
- Heart monitor
- Tape recorder/headphones
- X-ray light box
- Clock radio
- Credit card/ticket machine
- Franking machine
- Radio
- Metal detector

- Television/remote control
- Patient buzzer
- Microwave
- Telephone/answer phone
- Digital microscope
- Calculator
- Digital weighing scales
- On/off controls
- Digital camera
- Video/DVD player
- Scanning equipment
- Buzzers/lights
- Cash dispenser
- Light toys
- Traffic lights
- Sensory devices

Activity ideas

These activities are aimed primarily at the Foundation Stage/Reception Classes.

1. Children set up a role play shop by assembling a selection of readily available items (for purchase) and a model electronic till with electronic keypad and display, swipe card facility and toy money. The items are labelled with price tags which have been prepared in a previous lesson using the simple software toolkit – Tizzy's First Tools.

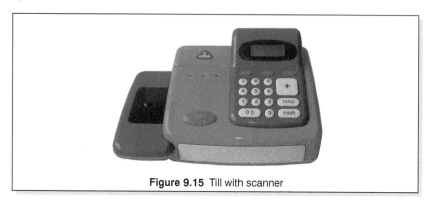

Figure 9.15 Till with scanner

2. A set of model traffic lights (fully working) is set up in the safety of the school playground and used to help children conduct a role play activity on traffic awareness and how to cross the road safely. A prior walk around the local area has already raised the children's awareness of traffic lights and pelican crossings and they are familiar with their sequence of operation.

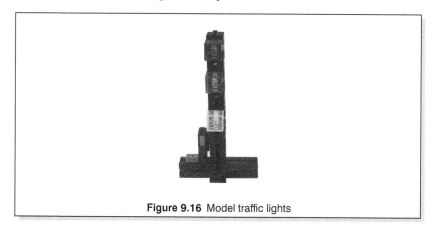

Figure 9.16 Model traffic lights

3. Airport security is simulated when children adopt a range of roles and utilise familiar equipment such as walkie-talkies, metal detectors, light systems scanners, security systems, mobile phones, TV monitors, and buzzers.

    Other role play situations include: 'the bank', 'the office', 'the supermarket', 'the café', 'the music studio', 'the hospital', 'the post office', 'the travel agent', 'outer space', 'the police station' and so on …

Activity

There are many sources of good information on the web. Try the following:

- Nursery World: nurseryworld.co.uk
- ICT in the Early Years: ictearlyyears.e2bn.org

You will also find the following useful reading on the Primary ICT site:

- Using ICT in the Early Years
- ICT in Role Play
- Opportunities for ICT in the EYFS

Visualisers and document cameras

The visualiser is a major item of ICT equipment and, whilst it is not a new technology, it has become popular in some schools in recent years. It's more of a teaching aid than a learning resource and it's not exactly a 'model' of e-learning. However, it is very much a favourite with a number of teachers and is used on such a frequent basis that it is perhaps deserving of a place in this chapter.

What is a visualiser?

If you haven't come across one before, a visualiser is essentially a movable digital colour camera mounted above a display platform. It is similar in appearance to an overhead projector but it is a much more powerful device in terms of its technical and pedagogical capabilities. Solid objects on the platform can be displayed on a computer and/or projected onto an IWB or large screen. The resulting images have superior clarity. The camera can zoom in to magnify the object and display it in microscopic proportion.

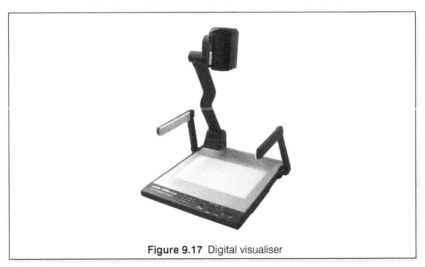

Figure 9.17 Digital visualiser

Visualisers come with a whole range of additional features such as: the ability to freeze a screen shot whilst still displaying the object; allowing the object to be moved and captured in a sequence of different positions; splitting the screen into two or more areas thus allowing the user to display a complete object whilst simultaneously viewing a portion of it in fine detail; capturing still and moving images; and displaying 'negatives' of an object.

How can a visualiser be used?

Some examples of use include:

- Numeracy: place coins under the visualiser to practise counting money; easily add and remove coins to change the amount.

- Literacy: display the page of a book and zoom in on particular paragraphs or words.

- Science: use the zoom to display an insect in great detail to observe its features.

- History: display artefacts to the class quickly and easily.

- Geography: display maps, zoom in on particular features and symbols.

- Music: display sheet music and zoom in on features such as clef, key signature, rests etc.

- Art: use the visualiser to highlight different brush stroke techniques in great detail.

- Assembly: if you have a projector in your assembly hall you can use a visualiser to present certificates, good work etc. to the whole school.

Computer configurations

In an ideal school, the preferred teaching approach of staff would dictate the deployment of their ICT resources. However, in some cases it is the other way around! Typical organisational models include:

- Fixed computer suites: large numbers of computers assembled in one dedicated teaching space.

- Computer clusters: small groups (clusters) of computers within classrooms or in areas close by.

- Classroom computers: a small number of computers within the classroom itself.

- Mobile computing: sets of laptop computers or tablet PCs that can be configured as a 'suite' (and stowed away/moved from room to room as required).

You will of course be faced with practical constraints which will ultimately dictate the outcome. The availability of appropriate accommodation, cost of building or refurbishment, cost of ICT resources (capital and maintenance) and availability of technical support will all play a part. Your main aim however should be to achieve appropriate and equitable access to ICT resources. This is not necessarily about the quantity of resources but more importantly it is about their organisation.

 Activity

Given the choice, which model of computer configuration would you prefer?

It is certainly a matter of preference but hopefully you would base your decision on some sound fundamental criteria including: the learning experiences you want for your pupils; their preferred learning styles; the range of teaching methods you wish to employ; the balance between individual, paired, small groups and whole-class teaching; the balance between discrete ICT subject teaching and the use of ICT to support learning across the curriculum; and health and safety issues. All these should be reflected in the school's ICT policy and its vision for the future.

Fixed computer suites

If you want to allow large groups or whole-classes to work simultaneously in ICT 'lessons' then fixed computer suites offer a solution. They are self-contained environments which, together with a data projector and interactive whiteboard, lend themselves nicely to the teaching of ICT as a discrete subject and to the acquisition of important basic skills.

Some however would argue that these skills should not be taught in isolation and should be placed within the context of chosen curriculum areas. If pupils are removed from their customary working environment they may perceive computer work as something separate and out of the ordinary.

Whilst computer suites do offer some organisational advantages they require dedicated space (a premium in most schools) and hamper pupil mobility when, as is often the case, their activities require them to move around, inside and outside the school.

Mobile computer suites

A good solution is a portable trolley full of laptop computers or tablet PCs. There are several types on the market and various sizes. They provide secure and rechargeable storage and can easily be moved from one classroom to another. The devices can then connect to the school's existing network via wireless links and, overall, provide a significant saving over a cable network solution.

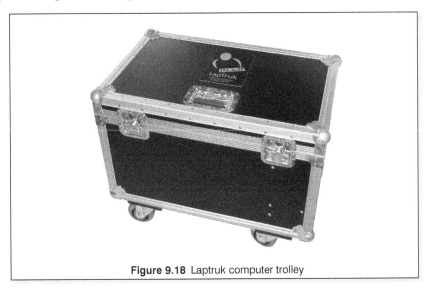

Figure 9.18 Laptruk computer trolley

They allow existing classrooms to be turned into temporary computer suites with minimal disruption and are much less obtrusive than desktop PCs. This makes it easier to integrate ICT into the curriculum, easy to expand the system (additional PCs and trolleys can be added as required) and there are no obtrusive cables. In addition, the laptops and tablets can be used in other locations. For example, they can be used in the school surrounds and pupils and teachers could take them home.

There are of course some disadvantages too. Laptops can be less robust, they can be slower in operation due to the bandwidth limitations of their wireless connection and they need to be recharged on a regular basis.

Overall, the advantages generally outweigh the disadvantages and issues such as bandwidth are improving steadily as technology continues to develop. Indeed, most pupils now own their own laptop or tablet and might view traditional PCs as archaic.

Many schools now implement a Bring Your Own Devices (BYOD) scheme to give pupils and staff access to personal devices such as laptops, tablets and Smartphones in classrooms. This helps alleviate schools budget constraints and further supports the case for the mobile computing option.

Computer clusters

Another option is to incorporate space-saving small clusters of computers for occasional access. Most desks within clusters are hybrid and can be used as an IT work station and also as a paper-based work station. The desks usually fold down to a convenient size and can be stowed away conveniently in a corner. They are also transportable between rooms.

Whatever your choice, research shows that ICT resources have maximum impact when organised around whole-class or small group work which allows for differentiated learning.

ICT infrastructure

Having covered various models of digital learning, and the deployment of assets, this chapter would not be complete without at least a mention of the infrastructure that supports it. That is to say, a computer network and other associated equipment, applications, services and data.

Most schools will already have a network in place but those schools that are considering the purchase, upgrade or expansion of ICT infrastructure are recommended to do so through their local authority. LEAs may have a collective policy for networking and broadband connectivity.

Before completely relinquishing control to others it would serve you well to compile your own 'outline specification' for the school's infrastructure based upon your organisational and pedagogical needs. This will avoid having to accept something you don't actually want or need. The specification will include the types of resource, their deployment and your preference for cabled networking, wireless or a hybrid (and perhaps the use of cloud computing). The most important point here is that the resulting change should bring about significant improvement to teaching and learning and afford everyone reasonable access to, and sharing of, resources.

It should also enhance communication and improve connectivity with the outside world. This is not simply about linking to the Internet, it is also about accessing the school learning platform and thus increasing the possibilities for extended learning. In addition, if you have access to the National Education Network (NEN), you will benefit both from the widening access it provides and the high bandwidth dedicated connections provided by the SuperJANET backbone.

Health and safety

ICT resources pose specific health and safety issues. These issues are outlined briefly in Chapter 10 and you may also seek advice from more appropriate sources such as the Health and Safety Executive (HSE) and the Schools Building and Design Unit (SBDU).

10

ICT and special educational needs

Introduction

One in every five children are considered to have special educational needs (SEN) because they either have greater difficulty in learning than the majority of children of the same age or they have a disability which prevents or hinders them from making use of educational facilities.

Since the latter years of the last century, moves have been made to include all SEN pupils, other than those with severe problems, into mainstream schools. This has placed additional demands on teachers and teaching assistants who are now responsible for pupils with a diverse range of personal needs. Staff need access to a greater range of tools and the use of ICT in advancing and enabling access to learning is therefore pivotal in meeting the needs of these learners (at all educational levels).

It should be recognised that children with SEN rarely fit into one specific category. Similarly, many ICT resources can be used for a multitude of needs – and for all children who just require that bit of additional support!

Communication and interaction

Children with communication and interaction problems may have difficulty understanding others and/or making others understand them. Problems include delayed speech or language development, inability to articulate or to form certain speech sounds, speech impediments (such as stammer) and those who do not speak at all.

There are also those with language difficulties who cannot understand words or cannot use them in the right context. They will generally have limited vocabulary or find it hard to recall words and express ideas.

Technology can aid these children in order that they can participate in lessons and gain access to the same curriculum as their peers. For some learners with speech and language difficulties, ICT is a lifeline, enabling them to communicate with the world around them. For others, it can support their classroom work and therapy.

 Activity

You might like to take a look at the simple approach taken by one primary school teacher from The Cape Primary School, Sandwell.

On the Primary ICT site at primaryict.org.uk/icthandbookv2.htm you'll find a video (ICT and SEN), associated lesson plans and a report.

The activity clearly demonstrates three things:

1. ICT has an effective role to play for children with special needs.
2. The approach need not be complex – it pays to keep it simple.
3. Even a novice teacher can acquire the necessary skills.

Augmentative and alternative communication (AAC).

Those with speech problems may benefit from AAC resources. These range from high-tech voice output communication aids (VOCAs) and software equivalents, to simple paper-based symbols which illustrate words or phrases.

Symbols

There are a number of sets of symbols. The most common are the Widgit Literacy Symbols (previously known as Rebus) and the Pictorial Communication System (PCS). Others include Makaton, PECS and Bliss. Teachers can of course make their own symbol set if so desired.

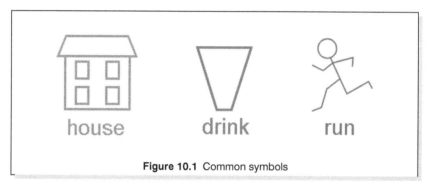

Figure 10.1 Common symbols

There are also graphic symbol systems associated with specific high-tech communication aids, for example, Minsymbols (multi-meaning icons) and Dynasyms.

Practitioners and pupils will need ready access to printed symbols. There are several publications available to purchase though many teachers create their own books, wall posters, laminated flash cards and streamers (which they hang from their belts).

Children can make use of software programs such as Widgit's Writing with Symbols 2000, Widgit Essentials, SymWriter and Communicate in Print 2. These symbol-based word processor programs not only associate words with a choice of symbols, they also include speech, writing grids, word banks and scanning capability.

If you don't own a copy of these programs you can download trial versions from the Widgit website at widgit.com.

 Activity

Visit the Widgit website at widgit.com and browse the resources. You can try some out for free. You might also look at the online resources which provide links to websites that use symbols or provide free resources.

Voice output communication aids (VOCAs)

These hardware devices come in a number of formats displaying up to 128 symbols at a time. Symbols are provided on sets of overlays (with some devices, additional overlays can be self-designed using specific software).

Teachers can record words and messages which are replayed whenever a symbol is touched (either with the finger or using external switches). These devices are designed to be durable but come at a hefty cost.

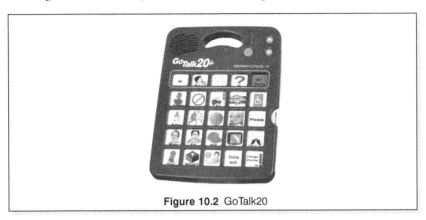

Figure 10.2 GoTalk20

Software communication aids

Software versions of communications devices can be created easily and cheaply using familiar applications such as MS PowerPoint.

Children with communication problems often suffer from other learning difficulties or physical disabilities. The type of communication solution selected will therefore depend on their ability to interact with devices and their understanding of the spoken word.

 Activity

Visit the Primary ICT website at primaryict.org.uk/icthandbookv2.htm and try out the PowerPoint Communication Aid. What are the advantages and disadvantages of developing simple resources of this type?

The PowerPoint communicator emulates the expensive high-tech devices. It is simple to make, scalable and low cost. Resources of this type lack mobility although they could be loaded onto notebook computers, tablets and Smartphones (which are much cheaper than VOCAs and have the added versatility to host other software solutions too). In addition, software equivalents may require their own set of symbols if copyright is an issue.

Language difficulties

Children who have difficulty in formulating language will benefit from the visual stimulus that can be provided by software. Care must be taken when selecting software because it is not always suitable and many content rich software programs for young children are rich in visual stimuli but offer too many distractions. However, using well designed software can have huge benefits.

Applications such as concept mapping can help them to plan and organise their ideas before moving on to communicate them vocally and in writing.

Up-to-date packages like Rationale include tools to guide, develop and enhance thinking, questioning and reasoning skills. These help pupils to build projects using visual objects which can eventually be converted to textual (essay) format.

Children with writing problems will benefit from word banks, talking word processors, talking books, overlay keyboards, predictive words and spelling and grammar checkers.

Word processors with banks of words and phrases together with story grids can be used to support structured language activities. A popular title in this respect is Clicker 6, a switch compliant writing-support tool for every subject area (including EAL). It builds sentences (by selecting words, phrases and pictures) and speaks them back using a selection of voices.

Most word processors include predictive text and spelling/grammar checkers. These can be extremely helpful for children with speech and language difficulties though practitioners should be cautious not to overuse them. Examples include Co:Writer, Penfriend and WordAid.

Another extremely versatile and well respected package to help pupils with reading and writing is textHelp Read and Write Gold. It works alongside mainstream Windows applications and offers a wide range of features including text-to-speech, word prediction, phonetic spell checker and a speaking dictionary.

The Visual Learning For Life website provides over 2000 worksheets on CD-ROM that cover ten visual perception areas. They are designed to strengthen weak areas of visual perception and sharpen mental skills.

Autistic spectrum disorders

Autistic spectrum disorder (ASD) is a lifelong condition that affects how a person communicates with, and relates to other people. It also affects how they make sense of the world around them.

ASD is the term that is used to describe a group of disorders, including autism and Asperger's syndrome. The word 'spectrum' is used because the characteristics of the condition vary from one person to another. Those with autism may also have a learning disability. Those who have Asperger's syndrome tend to have average or above average intelligence but still have difficulty making sense of the world (NHS, 2007).

Autistic children are often unable or unwilling to engage in activities which rely on social or verbal interaction. The computer will therefore offer an attractive alternative. However, whilst ICT can offer a range of useful tools, the National Autistic Society (2006) stress that ICT does not by itself provide a magic solution for people with autism; it must be embedded in a wider care and/or educational system to be effective.

Autism software

The computer should be used purely as an occasional support tool and not allowed to become a dominant part of learning activities. Care should also be taken not to overuse the computer as a means of curbing bad behaviour as this may ultimately appear to condone it!

The main advantages of computers are that:

- they don't require interaction with other people;
- they offer autonomy and a 'safe' environment;
- they are non-judgemental;
- they provide a focal point to hold concentration;
- they are consistent and predictable;
- they enable errors to be easily corrected;
- they can provide instant feedback;
- interacting with a computer can create an awareness of self;
- simple games promote communication with others.

Here are some ideas:

The company 'Raising Horizons' has researched and produced training materials specifically to help people with ASD. Your School Day is aimed at children aged 5–10 years and, with teacher assistance, takes them through the school day including getting ready for school, recognising 'danger zones' when travelling to school, recognising faces and working with others.

Figure 10.3 Your School Day (source: raisinghorizons.com)

Social and life skills training software for younger children includes software packages like Smart Alex which can be used to learn how to recognise facial expressions and emotions from an animated character. At a higher level, keyboard users can hold a simple conversation with Alex and talk about their likes and dislikes. Try also Streetwise.

Figure 10.4 Smart Alex (source: inclusive.co.uk)

Researched by professionals, Gaining Face helps people with Asperger's syndrome, high-functioning autism and similar issues to learn to recognise facial expressions and associated moods and emotions. A free demonstration can be downloaded from ccoder.com/GainingFace.

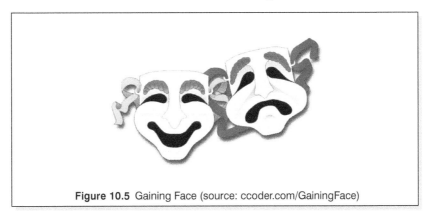

Figure 10.5 Gaining Face (source: ccoder.com/GainingFace)

Other titles include Mouse Trial, Mind Reading, Being Me, Connections, ISPEEK at home, ISPEEK at school, Blooming Kids (series), Story Builder, Just Like (series) and Out and About.

You may also find the following sources useful:

- Accelerations Educational Software: dttrainer.com.
- Autism Speaks: autismspeaks.org.
- Autism today: autismtoday.com.
- Brain Pro: brainsparklearning.com/brainpro-autism.
- Mouse Trial: mousetrial.com/autism_software_database.php.
- Social Skill Builder: socialskillbuilder.com.
- TeachTown: web.teachtown.com.
- The National Autistic Society: autism.org.uk.
- University of Iowa: openautismsoftware.org.
- Zac Browser: zacbrowser.com.

Video conferencing

Pupils who experience difficulty interacting with others have been shown to respond much better when communicating using indirect methods such as video conferencing. They seem to feel less intimidated and are able to open up more freely. As a result, they can work together on projects and build up strong relationships with pupils in other schools.

Computer-mediated communication

Computer-mediated communication (CMC) was covered in Chapter 9 and includes the use of discussion forums, social media and email. Children on the autistic spectrum should excel using CMC because they can work in an environment which does not require face to face interaction and is therefore more comfortable for them. In addition, some of the weaknesses of CMC are implicitly turned to advantage. For example, children with autism rarely have the ability to read body language and are therefore not penalised by its absence.

Video cameras

A Key Stage 1 child with Asperger's syndrome was given a simple video camera as a tool for self-expression. She was asked to explore the classroom and talk about the things she liked and disliked about school. The activity motivated her and the outcomes were astonishing. The audio was very clear and she expressed herself in a way that she would never have done when talking to the teacher or to other children.

Cognition and learning

Children requiring help in this category come under the general headings of specific learning difficulty (SpLD), moderate learning difficulty (MLD), severe learning difficulty (SLD) and profound and multiple learning difficulty (PMLD).

SpLD pupils may have a particular difficulty in one learning area (e.g. reading or writing) but not in others. They may also suffer from short-term memory loss and with coordination. Pupils with SpLD cover the whole ability range and the severity of their impairment varies widely. Specific learning difficulties include dyslexia, dyscalculia and dyspraxia.

MLD pupils will have difficulties with most or all areas of the curriculum and with basic literacy and numeracy skills. They may also have associated speech and language delay, low self-esteem, low levels of concentration and under-developed social skills. Their needs cannot be met by normal differentiation.

SLD pupils will have significant intellectual or cognitive impairments which have a major effect on their ability to participate in school without support. They will need support in all areas of the curriculum and they may also require teaching of self-help, independence and social skills. Some pupils may use signs and symbols but most will be able to hold simple conversations and gain some literacy skills.

PMLD pupils have severe and complex learning needs. In addition they have other significant difficulties, such as physical disabilities or a sensory impairment. They require a high level of adult support, both for their learning needs and also for personal care. They are likely to need sensory stimulation and a curriculum broken down into very small steps. Some pupils communicate by gesture, eye pointing or symbols, others by very simple language.

This section will address the needs of SpLD/MLD children. The more specialist needs of SLD/PMLD children are not addressed specifically in this book except where they overlap with other needs such as sensory, physical and medical requirements.

Dyslexia

Dyslexia is a term to describe a learning difficulty associated with words (reading, writing and spelling). It affects some 4 per cent of the population severely and a further 6 per cent have mild to moderate difficulties across the whole ability range. Symptoms are wide ranging and children with dyslexia may have poor reading comprehension, handwriting, spelling, punctuation and pronunciation. They may also reverse or jumble letters and sounds in words and mistake similarly shaped words. As a result, their work may be untidy and full of errors and crossing out and they may become reluctant writers. They can suffer from memory loss, have difficulty organising thoughts and manage time poorly. ICT can help with these issues and can also be directed toward the strengths of dyslexics which include innovation, lateral thinking and creativity.

Memory loss

One very simple idea is to provide an area on the computer to store ideas, notes and reminders to help with memory loss. MS Windows includes 'Sticky Notes' and there are several, similar free packages for download from the Internet. Try sticky-notes.net.

Figure 10.6 Sticky notes

Organising

Mind mapping helps children to organise, plan and present ideas in pictorial form using words which they find are familiar. This provides a structure for writing. Some software titles provide tools to transform mind maps into sequential text which helps to begin the writing process. Titles include Inspiration, IdeasMap, Kidspiration, Visual Mind and 2Connect.

Writing

Touch typing and keyboard skills are invaluable for dyslexic children. They reduce the need for handwriting (which is commonly a disliked or a challenging area for many) and help children to learn spelling, word recognition, comprehension and vocabulary. Effective products include 2Type, Englishtype Junior, First Keys 3, Speedy Keys and Nessy Keys.

Figure 10.7 2Type (source: 2simple.com)

 Activity

Link to the Sense Lang site at sense-lang.org/teachers/signup.php. You will need to sign up and then you will have access to many online tutorials and touch typing activities.

Dyslexic children who struggle to scribble down notes will benefit from electronic note taking devices. There are plenty to choose from. Sound recording can be done using dictaphones, mobile phones, mp3 recorders, Smartphones, tablet PCs and other hand-held devices. Notebooks and tablets with spellcheckers and other useful features can be used to type notes directly.

Pupils with dyslexia are often frustrated because they know what they want to write but they have great difficulty in committing it to paper. Word processors and 'add-ons' provide a range of features to alleviate the problem. Programs such as SOLO 6 add word prediction, word banks, a dictionary and other tools to any word processor or email program.

For severe dyslexia, voice recognition may provide a much needed alternative input (these are covered fully in the section 'Sensory, physical and medical' below). However, these should not be used frequently for mild dyslexics or it may impede development.

Reading

Reading can be improved in a number of ways. When presenting written material, try to keep to continuous and consistent lines of text. Avoid centre and right justification, try to reduce unnecessary clutter on the screen and don't wrap text around images. Block capitals and underlining are often tricky for children with dyslexia too.

Reading rulers will help to focus readers on specific lines of text either as paper versions or free screen utility programs such as VU-Bar or Virtual Reading Ruler.

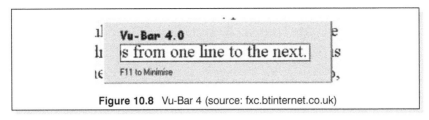

Figure 10.8 Vu-Bar 4 (source: fxc.btinternet.co.uk)

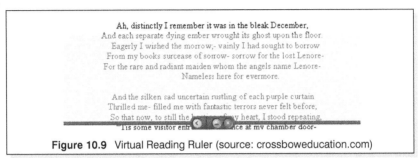

Figure 10.9 Virtual Reading Ruler (source: crossboweducation.com)

Changing background colours and fonts can be beneficial and each individual will have their own preference. Computer operating systems will have limited features. For example, Windows Control Panel provides Accessibility/Ease of access options such as 'ClearType' and 'High-Contrast' which offer a range of colours and fonts and a sharper picture for easy reading. However, it is cumbersome to change settings and limited in operation.

Individual software applications may have reading options as do some websites. There are also a number of software programs which provide more efficient solutions.

Screen Tinter Lite, one of a number of useful products by Thomson Software Solutions, is a free download which allows for easy adjustment of the colour properties of a Windows display. It helps with reading difficulties and reduces glare from the screen. Changing a screen's colour scheme can also motivate learners with cognitive difficulties.

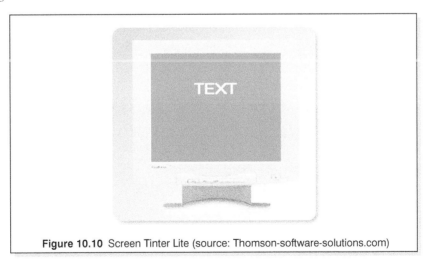

Figure 10.10 Screen Tinter Lite (source: Thomson-software-solutions.com)

A large and ever-increasing number of e-books are available to download from digital bookstores such as ebooks.com and Amazon. There is also a large collection of free out-of-copyright e-books available at Project Gutenberg.

Pronunciation

Reading pens (scanning pens) help children to read words that they can't spell, pronounce or comprehend. The pen is scanned across printed text and the word is displayed on an LCD screen and spoken (or spelled out) using clear English voices. Oxford Dictionary pens can recognise up to 240,000 definitions from the Oxford Concise Dictionary.

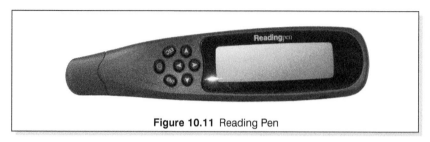

Figure 10.11 Reading Pen

Screen readers and text-to-speech converters can perform the same function with on-screen text. Text can also be scanned in from printed documents if required (these are covered fully in the section 'Sensory, physical and medical').

Another way to help with pronunciation and spelling is to provide materials such as podcasts together with accompanying printed copy and a reading ruler. Children play the files using an mp3(4) player, iPod or mobile device. They can work at their own pace, in their own time and repeat the process as many times as they require.

Other software and teaching programs

A number of computer teaching programs have been designed to provide multi-sensory support. Examples include:

- The Nessy Learning Programme: a complete teaching scheme including worksheets, puzzles and activities for developing reading and spelling skills.
- AcceleRead AcceleWrite: a complete programme using speech output to develop reading.
- Spinout Stories: talking stories to get poor readers reading the same information as their peers.
- Eye Track: visual discrimination, pattern recognition, memory and spatial relationships.
- Phoneme Track: relates sounds to letter combinations and phonemes.
- Wordshark: reinforces spelling rules through fun games.
- Starspell: look-cover-write-check approach to spelling (words are spoken).
- Oxford Reading Tree Talking Stories: reading scheme for infants.
- Lexion: helps children to unravel the reading and spelling process.
- Learning Access Suite: a complete learning suite for reading, writing and accessibility.

Dyscalculia

Dyscalculia is a condition that affects the ability to acquire mathematical skills. It is not as widely understood as dyslexia, perhaps because there is less shame attached to being poor at sums than there is to not being able to read.

Dyscalculic learners may have trouble learning and recalling number facts, counting up or down, relating multiples of ten, dealing with money, rote learning the times tables, telling the time and understanding direction. There is no direct link between dyscalculia and dyslexia though some dyslexic children have difficulty with maths because of the language surrounding it.

In terms of ICT resources you might begin by listing the general ways in which teachers can help dyscalculic learners. For example, you could provide fact sheets, encourage children to set out work neatly, offer pictorial representations of numbers and provide physical (or virtual) objects which can be manipulated. With these in mind, consider whether ICT can be used to create these types of resource. It may be that you simply use basic office packages to produce printed materials or perhaps you can be more ambitious.

Fact sheets

It is helpful to provide basic fact sheets (number grids, times tables, formula lists) to help children to visualise number pattern and position. ICT is useful here because fact sheets created using word processors and spreadsheets can be stored and printed out easily and will not be lost as frequently. There are also many websites that provide free sheets together with other useful resources. Try the BBC Skillswise site for fact sheets, work sheets, quizzes and games.

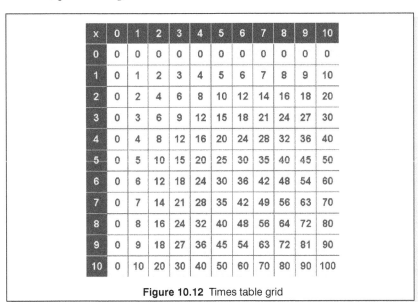

x	0	1	2	3	4	5	6	7	8	9	10
0	0	0	0	0	0	0	0	0	0	0	0
1	0	1	2	3	4	5	6	7	8	9	10
2	0	2	4	6	8	10	12	14	16	18	20
3	0	3	6	9	12	15	18	21	24	27	30
4	0	4	8	12	16	20	24	28	32	36	40
5	0	5	10	15	20	25	30	35	40	45	50
6	0	6	12	18	24	30	36	42	48	54	60
7	0	7	14	21	28	35	42	49	56	63	70
8	0	8	16	24	32	40	48	56	64	72	80
9	0	9	18	27	36	45	54	63	72	81	90
10	0	10	20	30	40	50	60	70	80	90	100

Figure 10.12 Times table grid

 Activity

Try out the Fact Sheets, Work Sheets, Quizzes and Games on the BBC skills site at bbc.co.uk/skillswise/maths

Number lines

Number lines can be created in a variety of formats to help with number position and counting up and down. Sets of numbers and mathematical symbols are available commercially though you can improvise and create your own printed and laminated versions (children could make them as part of a structured activity). The use of ICT here is highly appropriate because you are in a position to create individual solutions which fit the personal requirements of children with particular needs. If you are ambitious and creative then you might also consider designing simple on-screen versions using software which allows drag and drop. The Smart Notebook and TextEase Studio CT are two contenders.

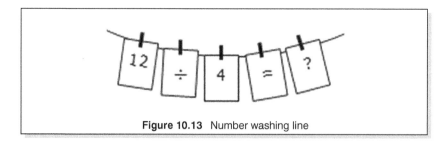

Figure 10.13 Number washing line

Websites

If experimenting isn't your style or you simply don't have the time on your hands then search the Internet or visit some of the sites listed in Appendix 3. English and maths resources are abundant and many of them, whilst not necessarily designed with SEN in mind, are quite suitable for dyslexic and dyscalculic children. Two good examples from the popular Primary Resources website are Number Line and Number Order. Both have a range of activities which are both effective and very motivating.

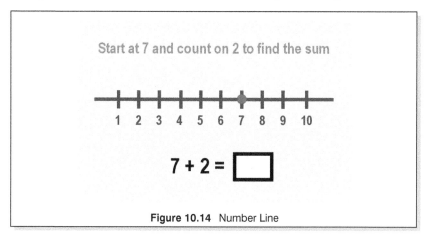

Figure 10.14 Number Line

Figure 10.15 Number order

Activity

Link to the Primary ICT site at primaryict.org.uk/icthandbookv2.htm and try out the Numbers to 10 activity. This is an example of a game you can create yourself using a spreadsheet (in this case the spreadsheet is MS Excel though you could use a child-friendly version such as TextEase Studio CT).

Such games are simple to design and easy to adapt. Once you have created one game or activity you quickly realise that the possibilities are endless.

Calculators

Using a calculator can be very helpful. The keys provide a guide to number order and it can be easier to perform simple calculations than using pencil and paper. However, there are more issues than solutions with calculators. Whilst most people can estimate what to expect for an answer, dyscalculic learners cannot. One remedy is to perform the calculation more than once and see whether the answer comes out the same each time. Also, computer keypads are laid out as the inverse of calculator keypads (7,8,9 at the top rather than 1,2,3). This leads to confusion as do the numerous superfluous keys. Talking calculators are available but these are extremely expensive.

Commercial software

There are many maths software titles which are suitable for dyscalculic learners. There are also programs for identifying children who might have dyscalculic tendencies. One example is Dyscalculia Screener, designed by Professor Brian Butterworth, a leading UK authority on dyscalculia.

Some software applications rely on reading skills and will therefore require teacher support. Others, like Numbershark 4, include audio instructions. Popular titles include The Number Race, Bubble Reef, Knowlsey Woods, Star Fractions, Time and Money and Dynamo Maths. Try also some of the school websites such as Priory Woods (priorywoods.middlesbrough.sch.uk).

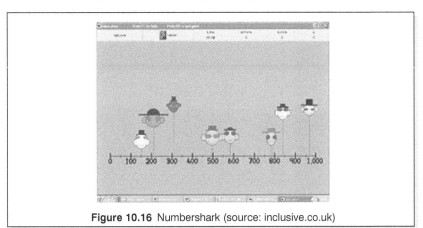

Figure 10.16 Numbershark (source: inclusive.co.uk)

Dyspraxia

The term dyspraxia is used to describe impairment or immaturity in the organisation of movement. Children with dyspraxia have difficulty developing fine motor skills and often appear clumsy. As a result, they may have problems with handwriting, drawing and articulation. This will often lead to a lack of confidence and poor social skills.

With some dyspraxic children there is a definite overlap with dyslexia and dyscalculia and the ICT solutions that can be applied to these will often help dyspraxic children too. In addition, ICT can help with:

- fine motor skills;
- mouse, keyboard and graphic tablet activities;
- presentation: word processors, DTP applications, presentation software etc.;
- privacy: computers allow for self-paced work without fear of embarrassment or intimidation;
- social interaction: the motivational impact of ICT draws children naturally into group participation.

As a result there may also be an accompanying increase in motivation and self-esteem.

Behavioural, emotional and social difficulties

The SEN Code of Practice (2014) describes children with behavioural, emotional and social difficulties (BESD) as children who demonstrate behaviour such as being withdrawn or isolated, disruptive and disturbing, being hyperactive and lacking concentration, having immature social skills or presenting challenging behaviour arising from other complex special needs.

BESD includes children with emotional disorders and hyperkinetic disorders including attention deficit disorder or attention deficit hyperactivity disorder (ADD/ADHD). It also includes children with anxiety, school phobia, depression and those who self-harm.

Pupils with BESD cover the full range of ability and a continuum of severity. They are considered to have SEN if their behaviour presents a barrier to learning and persists despite the implementation of an effective school behaviour policy and personal/social curriculum. They may be withdrawn or isolated, disruptive and disturbing, hyperactive and lack concentration, have immature social skills or present challenging behaviour.

With this category of pupil, ICT in general can have a positive impact on motivation, self-esteem and achievement, just as it can with any pupil. The level of impact will depend upon the capability of teachers in making effective use of ICT to provide exciting lessons and to offer opportunities for autonomous learning. As a result, pupils become more engaged in their work, their standards rise, they become motivated to continue learning in their own time and behaviour improves.

Interactive whiteboards

When considering how to use ICT to help BESD pupils a good starting point is the interactive whiteboard. Teachers indicate that the IWB is especially motivating for pupils who respond badly to, or choose not to take part in, whole class activities.

The success of the IWB is in part due to its striking visual impact and also to its numerous interactive features. BESD pupils, particularly visual or kinesthetic learners, relish the opportunity to carry out exercises involving writing and moving objects on the board. This in itself improves concentration and participation and the incentive to take part has a tendency to improve behaviour. For very bad behaviour it can act as both carrot and stick!

> Several teachers report spectacular initial results with children with attention deficit disorder and those on the autistic spectrum; the highly visual nature of the tasks [on the Interactive Whiteboard] seems to attract their attention and keeps them attentive in ways that tasks presented at a desk cannot.
>
> (Sparrowhawk and Heald, 2007)

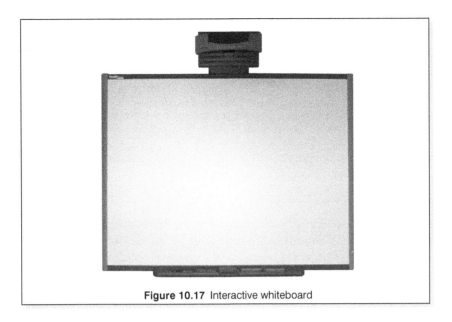

Figure 10.17 Interactive whiteboard

Software

Garagouni-Areou and Solomonidou (2004) carried out a controlled study which involved primary school pupils with and without ADHD. Both groups worked on computers on a series of specially designed software activities. The results indicated that the software's specific features stimulated the ADHD students' attention far more than it did the other group. Such software will have sound, graphics and animations that hold a pupil's attention in a way that the teacher cannot. In addition, computers allow greater independence, privacy and are non-judgemental – 'the computer doesn't shout at me!'.

Several suitable software titles have already been mentioned in this chapter. Here are just a few more:

- Talking Animated Alphabet: presents letters of the alphabet, with graphics and sound feedback, to help children learn letter sounds and shapes.

- Tizzy's Toybox/Tizzy's First Tools: stimulating and enchanting resources that introduce early learners to essential basic literacy and numeracy skills.

- Wellington Square: talking books including supporting activities.

- Clockwise 2: practise telling and perceiving time.

- Making sense with number: provides practice in early number work.

- Maths Circus Act: practise and enhance a wide range of maths and problem solving skills.

- Think About: helps develop literal, inferential and evaluative comprehension and aids concentration and memory skills.

- Letter Olympics: covers recognition, discrimination and differentiation of lower case letters b and d, with auditory and visual instructions emphasising accurate sound production of the b and d phonemes.

- Penfriend: helps children with words they can't read or spell.

- NumberTrain: over 20 carefully structured practical and mental maths activities. You might of course consider designing activities yourself.

Activity

Link to the Primary ICT site at primaryict.org.uk/icthandbookv2.htm and try out the Emotions Game. It was created by a PGCE student and has yet to be finished. You might like to do this yourself.

The activity was designed using MS PowerPoint to augment a social use of language programme (SULP). If you evaluate it you will find plenty to criticise. For example, you may feel that there is far too much distraction and that the synthetic voice could be improved. There are plenty good points too. Evaluation of software and hardware will be covered fully in Chapter 12.

Interactive voting systems

Interactive voting systems are an ideal way to motivate pupils with learning difficulties and engage them in lessons. They are suitable for a range of activities including quizzes, multiple choice mental arithmetic (or spelling), surveys on their own preferences for music and discussions stimulated by posing a question and then voting on the possible answers. Since responses during most activities are quite simple (Yes/No; A, B or C etc.), the majority of pupils will not have difficulty in operating the hand-held devices.

Pupils who normally lack confidence and are reluctant to respond in conventional lessons are able to provide anonymous answers. This allows teachers to facilitate learning and assess outcomes in a way that they would otherwise find tricky. In order that this approach remains effective over time it should not be overused and should be one element of a blended system which incorporates a range of ICT and non-ICT activities.

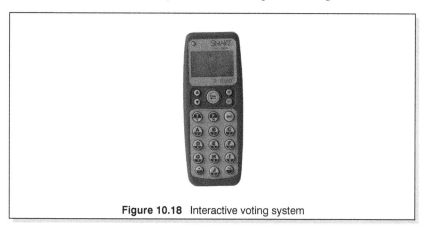

Figure 10.18 Interactive voting system

Mobile devices

Tablet PCs, Smartphones and other mobile/hand-held devices provide opportunities for autonomous learning. They can also motivate and include pupils who fail to attend.

Learners nowadays are mobile, and with good pedagogy and good support, hand-held devices can help them fulfil their full potential.

Examples of mobile activities include:

- A mobile phone activity: pupils are sent instructions for a literacy activity using SMS (text messaging). The activity requires them to read a passage of text and summarise its meaning. Each summary is returned, via a specified mobile number, to a website which collates and presents the results. These are used to stimulate a subsequent group discussion once the pupils return to school.

■ Nintendo DS: together with its associated packages, Brain Training and Big Brain Academy, this hand-held game console helps to improve numeracy skills.

■ Weather Willy: pupils with learning difficulties use this simple wireless device to help to choose what clothing to wear prior to setting out on a nature trail. Some children use a map and compass to navigate and others make use of a Smartphone with a built-in global positioning system (GPS).

For further ideas, visit the Mobile Learning Network (MoLeNET) site at molenet.org.uk.

The choice of teaching method, whether it be whole group (using the IWB, video conferencing and interactive voting systems) or individual (using PCs and mobile devices) will depend on each child's preferred learning style. This is something which needs to be established at the outset. In some cases, the degree of privacy required by a child might warrant the use of screening around the computer (this could be achieved by setting up your suite as a number of carousels).

Multi-sensory rooms

Multi-sensory rooms offer a safe, relaxing and fascinating environment which potentially stimulates children to explore, develop awareness and learn. They can also reduce behavioural difficulty, stimulate conversation and act as a reward.

The concept of sensory rooms is accepted by practitioners as an effective therapy for special needs children if they are designed well and used correctly because learners are affected by their environment.

Having spent a limited amount of time in a sensory room, the effects can carry over into other learning spaces and other activities.

Correct supervision is essential and staff should always be adequately trained to ensure that they are conversant with technical, pedagogical and health and safety issues.

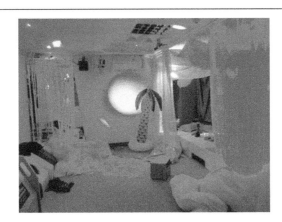

Figure 10.19 Multi-sensory room (source: experia-innovations.co.uk)

Sensory rooms have been used for people with behavioural issues, learning difficulties, physical disabilities, autism, ADHD and other problems. The potential benefits include: developing a sense of cause and effect; controlling events; improving hand/eye coordination; developing language; promoting communication and sharing; encouraging human touch; reactivating hearing, sight, smell, touch and taste and relaxation.

Sensory rooms may be designed to cater for a range of needs or for one specific need. They may take the form of light rooms, dark rooms or soft play areas and general multi-sensory rooms. In some schools the sensory environment takes up only part of a room or other designated area and, for those with restricted facilities or funding, a sensory 'trolley' or 'tub' may be the preferred option.

Figure 10.20 Sensory trolley (source: mikeayresdesign.co.uk)

The focus in sensory sessions may be on calming, relaxing and generally having fun or it may be to achieve a number of specified objectives. Equipment will include:

- Lighting effects such as projectors, spotlights, UV lights, bubble lamps, mirror balls, fibre optics, glow lines, glow sticks, torches and visual software. They are often used in conjunction with wheels and other devices which disburse light patterns throughout the room.

- Sound effects such as music, nature sounds, animal sounds and soothing rhythmic music.

- Cause and effect equipment such as switches and sensors (including remote controlled).

- Sensory surfaces which comprise interactive floor and wall projection systems.

Sensory equipment can be expensive though you can start quite cheaply with some soft lighting, simple torches, switches and your own existing sound system.

Sensory, physical and medical impairment

Visual impairment

Visual impairment includes a range of difficulties from partial sight through to blindness. For educational purposes, a pupil is considered to be visually impaired if they require adaptations to their environment or specific differentiation of learning materials in order to access the curriculum.

As with other special needs, the first step should be to establish the exact nature of the impairment and the problems faced by each individual pupil. Some pupils are registered as blind whilst others will have partial sight which manifests itself in a number of ways including: poor central vision; poor peripheral vision; blurred vision; a mixture of blank areas and defined areas and colour blindness. It may therefore be necessary to obtain medical advice from health professionals and qualified teachers for the visually impaired before exploring possible solutions.

This section presents a number of resources which may prove useful in enhancing the learning of children with visual impairment. The best place to start would be the computer display settings. However, since this applies to all users, it has been incorporated into the final section of this chapter 'Environmental health and safety'.

Windows accessibility options

Windows operating systems incorporate a number of accessibility options. It would be prudent to explore these first since they are available free of charge. The options have grown with the release of each new version of Windows.

You can usually access them via the Control Panel (Windows XP), Ease of Access Center (Windows Vista and Windows 7) or Search (Windows 8).

Magnifier

Magnifier (XP and Vista) enlarges selected text and other on-screen items for easier viewing. When launched, the enlarged view appears in a designated pane. The magnified portion can also invert colours (i.e. black on white becomes white on black).

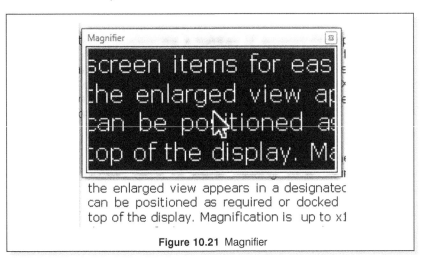

Figure 10.21 Magnifier

Narrator

Narrator reads on-screen text, dialogue boxes, menus and buttons. It will also read text as it is typed. A choice of synthetic voices are available and, whilst they might seem unrealistic at first, frequent users will quickly get used to them.

Speech recognition

Speech recognition allows the user to dictate text and control the computer using voice. The user can train his/her voice and, the more training carried out, the more accurate the conversion process. The same feature is available in MS Word.

Display options

Some computer display options can be modified. These include: font style, colour, and size of items on the desktop; icon size; screen resolution; high-contrast schemes (for colour combinations that are easier to see); cursor width and blink rate (to make the cursor easier to locate) plus other personalised settings.

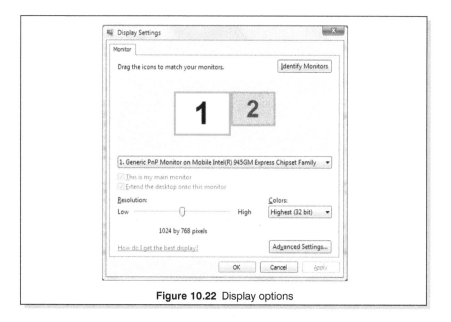

Figure 10.22 Display options

Sound schemes and themes

Sound schemes/themes can be assigned to many program events. Every sound scheme consists of a set of events and sounds associated with them. These will benefit pupils who rely on sounds to get information from their computers including those who are blind or have other visual impairments.

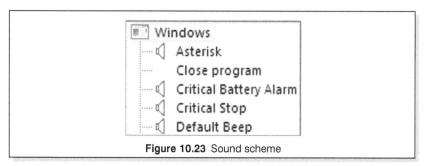

Figure 10.23 Sound scheme

Internet Explorer

Internet Explorer includes a number of useful features: zoom – to magnify text, images, and controls; change colours of text, background, links and hover; change text size from small to medium to large and Internet options to change font and accessibility settings.

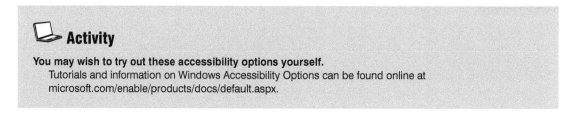

Activity

You may wish to try out these accessibility options yourself.
Tutorials and information on Windows Accessibility Options can be found online at microsoft.com/enable/products/docs/default.aspx.

Educational materials

When presenting materials for your pupils you can:

- provide access to existing electronic materials (e.g. websites and e-books);
- create your own electronic texts (e.g. word processed, PDF and html);
- convert existing printed materials into electronic format (by scanning with optical character recognition);
- produce printed materials which are more accessible than the norm;
- produce audio materials (and/or allow pupils to record lessons and dictate their own notes);
- produce Braille books.

Electronic materials are a good option because they are readily accessible using good screen reading software. The Windows narrator will suffice for some pupils but those who are heavily dependent on such software will benefit from a better offering. There are several on the market including, LookOUT, Window-Eyes, ProTalk, JAWS, Wordread, SuperNova and THUNDER (free); but perhaps the best is HAL.

For more information try the Screenreader website at screenreader.net.

If you create your own texts and web pages then you should incorporate alternative text in order that your chosen screen reader can decipher images too (all good authoring packages, including MS Word, will provide this feature).

Converting printed materials to electronic format is quite simple and requires a flatbed scanner with optical character recognition (OCR) software. Most scanners will include OCR software but it may not entirely meet your needs. If you are to avoid tedious editing, a quality package will be needed; titles include OmniPage, FineReader and IRIS. For 99%+ accuracy choose Kurzweil 1000.

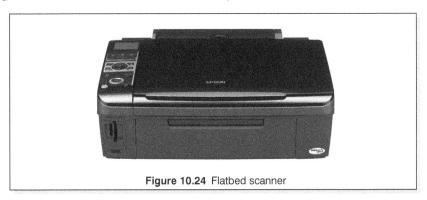

Figure 10.24 Flatbed scanner

Blind pupils may rely heavily on quality OCR software which will allow them to scan books (and other documents) and have them read back directly using a screen reader (or a standalone reading machine which integrates a scanner, OCR software and speech software).

Partially sighted pupils will still need access to printed materials. It's all too easy to administer standard materials which have been prepared for other children in the class. However, it is very important for the partially sighted to receive materials in clear print. Each individual's needs will differ but, in general, print should be of adequate size (12 – 14 point minimum), contrasting with the background colour (e.g. black on green), simple typeface (e.g. Arial), and consistent word and line spacing. The Royal National Institute of Blind People (rnib.org.uk) offer more detailed advice on the topic.

You should also be conscious of any colour deficiency (colour blindness); red and green are the most common colours affected. Blue on yellow and white on black are best for significant features.

Braille

Developments in ICT have led to the emergence of many useful resources for the visually impaired. These have augmented, though not entirely replaced Braille. However, for many people, Braille is their natural way of working and it is an essential medium for the deaf-blind.

Braille note takers assist the blind in several aspects of their work including note taking, sending emails and acting as personal organisers. They come in a variety of forms and their essential features are a refreshable Braille display and a Braille keyboard with voice output. Some have a computer style keyboard. Using screen reading software the BrailleNote can also be used as a Braille terminal.

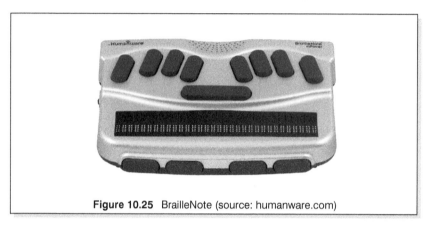

Figure 10.25 BrailleNote (source: humanware.com)

Braille translation software (such as the Duxbury Braille Translator) will convert text from any type of document into Braille. Reading the converted Braille will require either an electronic Braille display or a Braille printer (embosser).

Voice recognition

Voice recognition is useful for pupils with physical access difficulties, reading, writing or spelling difficulties and for those with visual impairment. There are two types of recognition system – discrete and continuous.

Discrete systems require words to be spoken one at a time with a distinct pause in between. These are useful for pupils with speech impairments that are due to other problems such as cerebral palsy or dysarthria. The most widely known system is DragonDictate.

Continuous systems are now the most widely used because they allow pupils to speak in a more natural way. The most popular continuous speech systems are Dragon NaturallySpeaking and IBM ViaVoice. Microsoft has incorporated speech recognition into its Windows operating system (from Windows XP on) although it is not as accurate as the dedicated products.

Whichever system is used it must be trained by each individual user. This usually takes a small number of 10–15 minute sessions; the more training carried out, the more accurate the system becomes.

MS Word offers simple speech recognition that allows you to dictate and Windows 7/8 provides speech recognition that allows you to control your computer by voice.

 Activity

You may wish to try out the speech recognition in MS Word and Windows.

Hand-held computers

Hand-held computers are also available for blind people. They come with an integrated tactile keyboard, audio recording, voice playback, Wi-Fi, infrared, Bluetooth and Internet access. Some will also have built-in GPS which can afford users increased independence.

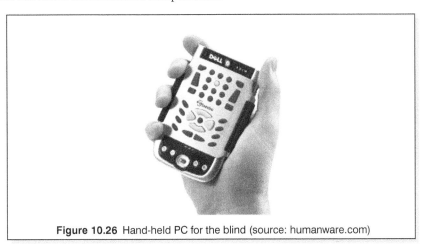

Figure 10.26 Hand-held PC for the blind (source: humanware.com)

Global positioning systems (GPS)

A GPS has many applications and can be invaluable to a blind or partially sighted person who may find it difficult to read signs and maps. Users can tell exactly where they are at the touch of a button, navigate their way around with precision and follow familiar, pre-stored routes. Directions are given using voice announcements and these devices offer a much valued degree of independence, freedom and dignity which may otherwise be denied.

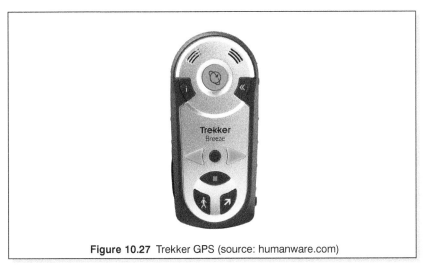

Figure 10.27 Trekker GPS (source: humanware.com)

Hearing Impairment

Pupils with a hearing impairment range from those with a mild hearing loss to those who are profoundly deaf. They may have a complex range of needs and those with significant impairment will receive support from a specialist teacher of the deaf. Some children will rely on lip reading, some will use hearing aids and some will have British Sign Language (BSL) as their primary means of communication. There are also emerging derivatives of sign language which are used in conjunction with lip reading and known as 'Visual Phonics'.

In education, children are regarded as having a hearing impairment if they need communication aids or alternative approaches to teaching in order to access the curriculum. Most will require help with communication and associated language and literacy support.

Windows accessibility options

Recent versions of Windows operating systems include a number of accessibility options that are suitable for those with hearing impairment. They are usually available via the Control Panel.

- ShowSounds is an accessibility feature which instructs programs that usually convey information only by sound to also provide all information visually, such as by displaying text captions or informative icons.

- SoundSentry is an accessibility feature designed for people who have difficulty hearing system sounds generated by the computer. SoundSentry allows them to change the settings to generate visual warnings, such as a blinking title bar or a screen flash, whenever the computer they are using generates a sound. They will be able to choose visual warnings (for example, a flashing border) for sounds made by windowed programs and for sounds made by full-screen text programs.

 Activity

You may wish to try out the accessibility options in MS Word and Windows.

Software

Since hearing impairment results in communication difficulties, much of the software already covered for reading, writing and language difficulties is useful here too. Content free packages, especially word processors, allow text, images (and clipart), animations and symbols to convey information. This mixture of media gives additional meaning and visual clues to written material.

Hearing impaired children may not be able to work at the same pace as other pupils because they may require more time to assimilate information. Electronic delivery of information allows pupils to work at their own pace and to revisit parts of lessons they do not fully comprehend.

Good examples of content free packages are Writing with Symbols 2000, Symwriter, Communicate in Print, Clicker 6, Co: Writer and TextEase. Content rich packages include Wordshark, Fun with Texts and THRASS.

Sign language

Images or video clips of signing (BSL or letter signing) can be added to software activities, multimedia presentations, TV programmes and other media which incorporate sound as a means of conveying information.

Deaf books are a good example. There are lots available to purchase from commercial vendors and plenty of free offerings too if you care to search the Internet. Most will have been created on CD-ROM or using simple multimedia packages such as PowerPoint. Examples include: Let's Sign (series), Centre Stage and Level 2 BSL Stories. Some software activities have built-in signing. A good example is To Market.

Activity

Link to the Primary ICT site at primaryict.org.uk/icthandbookv2.htm and look at the Five Little Ducks activity. It is one example of a multimedia deaf book produced using MS PowerPoint and incorporating BSL images (sign boxes).

This is yet another instance of a type of resource that you can easily develop yourself and tailor to the exact needs of your own hearing impaired learners. You can add sign boxes to your printed materials too in order to aid the learning of sign language.

There are also multimedia dictionaries, software and online courses for learning sign language. These include The Standard Dictionary of The British Sign Language (multimedia dictionary), Sign to Me (software) and Introducing British Sign Language (online course by British-sign.co.uk).

Text and video communication

Email, discussion forums, social media and SMS (text messaging) facilitate easy text communication using computers and mobile phones. Video conferencing and video-capable hand-held devices allow children to communicate using sign language. Learning platforms and associated systems can ensure that children receive all information, even if they miss out on other visual clues.

Interactive whiteboards

Once again, this versatile device can prove extremely useful. It facilitates clear presentation of information and, by its very nature, it allows teachers to face the class whilst delivering a lesson and this will help lip-readers.

Hearing aids

The term 'hearing aid' now applies to conventional hearing aids and also to technologies such as loop systems and sound field systems which can greatly improve the range and quality of sound received by pupils in the classroom. With induction loop systems the teacher will communicate with hearing impaired pupils using the amplified signal from a radio microphone to connect with pupils' hearing aids via a pre-installed loop (wire installed around the classroom being served). An alternative is an infrared induction hearing system.

With the sound field system, the teacher communicates using a microphone which links, using Bluetooth, to a number of pre-positioned loudspeakers around the classroom. The idea is that all children will receive the same volume of sound regardless of their position. For small numbers of hearing impaired children the teacher can use a radio microphone to transmit to individual receivers which hang around pupils necks.

Not only do these systems provide sound amplification, they also remove the need to continually lip read and, if teachers occasionally turn their backs on the class, pupils can still hear what they have to say.

Physical disabilities

The traditional mouse and keyboard provides suitable access to a computer for most pupils but not for those with physical disabilities or impaired fine or gross motor skills. ICT can however provide these children with assistive technology which can enhance their learning.

Windows accessibility options

Windows provides a number of accessibility options which may be suitable for some pupils with physical disabilities.

Children with motor impairments including Motor Neurone Disease (MND) and cerebral palsy may need help with devices such as the mouse and keyboard which require motor control.

Mouse options include:

- Double-click speed allows control over the speed of a mouse click. It may be beneficial to slow the process down (particularly when it comes to double-clicking).
- ClickLock allows users to highlight and drag objects without having to continually hold down the mouse button.
- Pointer schemes alter the size and colour of the pointer for better visibility.
- Pointer speed controls the speed of the mouse pointer as it moves across the screen. Slowing it down allows for easier location of objects.
- Pointer trails gives better visibility when set to 'long'.
- SnapTo helps users to locate buttons by forcing the pointer to move to the default button in a dialogue box.
- Button reversal allows the functions of the right and left mouse buttons to be reversed if users are more competent with their left hand.

Keyboard options include:

- Character repeat rate sets how quickly a character repeats when a key is struck.
- StickyKeys removes character repeat and allows one key to be pressed at a time.
- Dvorak keyboard layout offers alternative keyboard layouts for people who type with one hand or finger.
- FilterKeys ignores brief or repeated keystrokes and slows down the repeat rate.
- MouseKeys allows the mouse pointer to be moved using the four arrows on the keyboard.
- On-screen keyboard displays a virtual keyboard on the computer screen. It has scanning capability which allows users to type data by using switches or a pointing device.

 Activity

Experiment with the mouse and keyboard options. You will usually find these in the Control Panel Accessibility Options (Windows XP), the Ease of Access area (Windows Vista and Windows 7) or Search (Windows 8).

Keyboard access

Poor motor skills may result in pressing the wrong key or fingers slipping from one key to another. A standard keyboard fitted with a key guard can help prevent unintended key presses and can provide support for the hands between key presses.

Figure 10.28 Keyboard with key guard

Another way to cater for unsteady hands is to choose a keyboard with bigger keys. The model in Figure 10.30 has 1" square keys with striking lettering and helpful colour coding. It has a simple ABC layout (though some would argue that children should use QWERTY layouts to avoid confusion). The best judge is you.

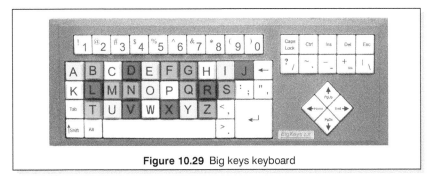

Figure 10.29 Big keys keyboard

Keyboard gloves are an inexpensive way to turn an existing keyboard into a more accessible option. Gloves will normally come in sets with picture symbols and colour coding. Additional blank gloves and stickers allow you to add colour coding, convert a standard keyboard to lower case or to 'ABC'. They also offer protection to the keyboard from spills and drips.

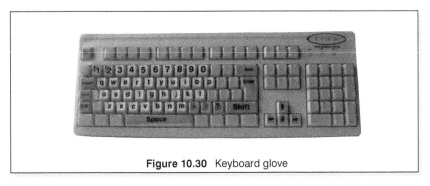

Figure 10.30 Keyboard glove

If your children are learning lower case letters and words then you can also obtain lower case keyboards. Again, colour coding and other options are available.

Ergonomic keyboards compel users to continually adjust their hand and arm position. They were originally designed to prevent repetitive strain injury (RSI) but were subsequently found to be helpful to SEN children with limited hand control or who suffer pain when typing.

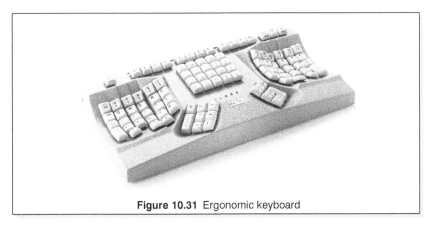

Figure 10.31 Ergonomic keyboard

Pointing devices

A conventional mouse is often difficult for children to use because of their small hands. A number of alternatives exist including rollerballs (including those with a large ball such as Big Trak) and joysticks. There are also mice for very small hands and ergonomic mice too.

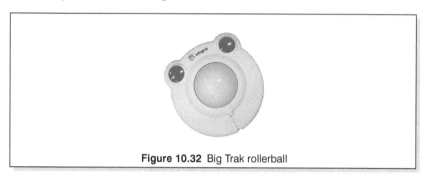

Figure 10.32 Big Trak rollerball

Special software exists to make clicking a mouse easier (e.g. one click to select and move without having to hold the button down and then a second click to release; or make a single click equivalent to a double-click).

Switch access

Pupils with severe disabilities may not be able to use a keyboard or mouse at all. They can however interact with a computer via a combination of one or more switches. Switches are provided in a number of different forms suitable for all parts of the body. They can be mounted on furniture or on a wheelchair (with adaptations if required). Switches are normally connected via a USB switch interface which allows for connection of multiple switches.

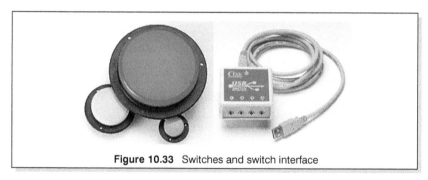

Figure 10.33 Switches and switch interface

Switches may also prove useful for children with learning difficulties because they simplify the menu selection process. Buttons such as the spacebar and mouse buttons can also be used as switches.

Scanning access

Switches interact with any software that has 'scanning' access. Scanning refers to the process of highlighting consecutive menu options or items on the screen (not to be confused with scanning of documents).

When the desired item is highlighted, the switch is pressed in order to select it. The principle extends to the selection of letters, words, punctuation and images such that pupils are able to carry out word processing and other activities. One of the best examples of SEN software with scanning capability is Clicker 6.

Most scanning software applications provide a number of scanning options. Autoscan puts the computer in control and automatically cycles through items on the screen (with an adjustable pause between items).

Some children become anxious when using this method and better alternatives might be Userscan and Stepscan which put the user in control, allowing them to start, stop and pause the process.

Scanning can be 'simple scan' where individual items are highlighted in succession or 'group scanning' where complete rows or columns are highlighted followed by individual items within the row or column once it has been selected. Group scanning speeds up the selection process.

A pupil's ability to successfully operate one or more switches will depend upon the degree of their disability, the speed and method of the scanning process and the pupil's positioning with respect to the switch and the screen (seating, comfort, switch mounting etc.). Children's capability should always be assessed prior to engaging in scanning activities in order to make them as effective as possible and to avoid frustration. All scanning software is capable of accepting single switch access. Some however will permit two or more. If a child is capable of using two or more switches then this can speed up the scanning process.

Software with scanning access

Wide provision has been made with regard to scanning software and, as with other applications, it comes in both content rich and content free forms (including online offerings). Much of the commercial software (e.g. Clicker 6 and Communicate in Print) and some of the Windows accessibility options (e.g. the on-screen keyboard) already mentioned in this chapter incorporate scanning. For more comprehensive listings, visit the SEN suppliers listed in Appendix 4. There are plenty of free resources too. For example, you might try the SEN Teacher website at senteacher.org.

Activity

Link to the Assist IT website for a wealth of information and advice (assist-it.org.uk/assets/content/ switch_access.htm).
You can try out their Interactive Scanning Tool at switchscanning.org.uk.

If you would like to get stuck in then you can create scanning activities yourself using packages such as SwitchIt! Maker 2 which includes sample pictures, videos, music and Picture Communication Symbols.

Overlay keyboards

Overlay keyboards such as the Concept, Intellikeys, Enterpad and XKeys can provide for easier access because not only can the 'keys' be made much larger, the overlays can be whole words, pictures and symbols. Concept also allows teachers to design their own overlays to suit the particular needs of their children.

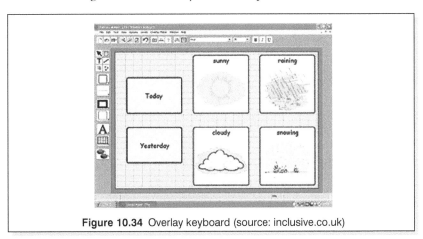

Figure 10.34 Overlay keyboard (source: inclusive.co.uk)

Touch screens

A touch screen allows data to be input by touching it with a finger or stylus. Touch screens can also provide SEN pupils with easier access than keyboard or mouse though they tend to be quite expensive. Touch screens are available as dedicated screens (for use with a computer), tablet PCs, Smartphones and other mobile devices.

English as an additional language (EAL)

There are many children in mainstream schools for whom English is an additional language. They may already speak a native tongue or they may be learning their native language and English together. It is challenging for teachers to accommodate these children because no two children will be at the same stage of language development and, as they are developing a mastery of a second language, they may fall behind in terms of progressing through the curriculum. In addition, teachers are expected to plan their lessons so that all children can take part. This may mean that some children will need to use their first language at times.

ICT can help with EAL learners because it not only offers a range of useful resources, it also offers a common medium through which learning can be effected. Children who are struggling to learn another language may not struggle with the basic computing skills required to give them access to language tools.

Here are some of the ways in which ICT might enhance the provision for EAL pupils.

Word processors

Word processors provide a number of support features which are advantageous to EAL pupils. Spelling and grammar checking highlights mistakes in a non-threatening way and this reduces anxiety and encourages experimentation. Dictionaries and thesauruses aid and extend the learning of vocabulary. Text manipulation tools such as cut, copy and paste allow writing to be redrafted without the need to rewrite lengthy passages. Some word processors, including MS Word, offer this support in a range of languages and can perform limited language translation too.

Alternatively, specialist individual language software can be used (usually to augment MS Office) which may provide better script quality and additional support.

If you need to type in a foreign language then a special keyboard may be required though you can buy keyboard gloves for English keyboards and a number of virtual keyboards are available too.

Overlay keyboards

An overlay keyboard may be used in place of or alongside a standard keyboard. The preferred option would be a keyboard that allows teachers to design their own overlays (e.g. the concept keyboard). The keyboard can then be divided into areas in order to create any number of 'buttons' (usually from 1 to 255). Words, sentences, pictures and sounds can be assigned to each button. Words can be associated with pictures, English and first language can be used side by side and words can be spoken as they are typed.

Cross-curricular software

First, it should be noted that one of the main advantages of ICT is that it typically combines textual, audio and visual representations in learning materials. This lends itself well to a range of learning styles (including those of EAL pupils) and therefore the general incorporation of ICT resources across the curriculum will have benefits for language learning too. Multimedia authoring software is particularly effective because it enables text, images, animation, video and sound to be combined and this is useful for teachers when creating learning materials and for pupils when completing activities and projects. Simple packages include MS PowerPoint, HyperStudio, Mediator, Opus Pro, Story Maker and Kids Animation Maker. The more ambitious author might try Adobe Authorware.

Visual aids

Visual aids play an essential role and ICT can be used to generate a wide range of materials including: signs, drawings, diagrams, charts, tables, flash cards, posters, labels, picture dictionaries, matching games and worksheets. Competence in one or two basic multimedia authoring or DTP packages will go a long way here. MS Word, MS PowerPoint and MS Publisher may be all a teacher needs in this respect. As ever, the interactive whiteboard excels here.

Pictorial and audio software

ICT is particularly effective in providing pictorial support. Many software packages include pictorial support for learning basic vocabulary such as food, clothing, travel, the body, colours, home, family, pets, numbers, shapes, time, weather, animals and familiar places. Examples include: Picture This, Junior World of Words, Games Box, Windows Box, Play and Learn, Living Books, Oxford Literacy Web – Sound Stories, Wordshark, Lexia, Smart Talk, Flash!Pro 2, MatchWord, Colour Magic, My World, Listen and Learn English, Talk Now, World Talk and Rosetta Stone.

Any software with visual and audio representations, signs, symbols, word banks, grids and speech will be beneficial. Talking word processors like TextEase, Clicker 6, Writing with Symbols 2000, Communicate in Print and Talking First Word are obvious choices.

Audio recordings made with simple recording software can provide useful revision aids which speak native words and their English equivalents. Windows Sound Recorder, Audacity and Podium are good creation tools. Children will need audio players (e.g. Windows Media Player, Real Player and Quicktime) or a mobile mp3 player to play them back.

Mind mapping

Graphic organisers, mind mapping and concept maps are powerful tools which help children to organise, plan and present ideas in pictorial form and they help children to understand and remember. They are particularly useful for pupils with EAL. Examples include Inspiration, IdeasMap, Kidspiration, Visual Mind and 2Connect.

Reading schemes on CD-ROM

Reading schemes on CD-ROM provide practice at learning to read, listening and pronunciation in a second language. Animations, sound cues and other interactive features enhance the process. Examples include: Oxford Reading Tree, Wellington Square, Rainbow Stories, Listen and Learn English and Planet Wobble.

Digital story telling

Following traditional storytelling, children can capture the main points in a story board (perhaps using simple multimedia authoring software) or using simple Duplo models. They can then record or animate their stories using video cameras, visualisers or other devices which can capture still or moving pictures. Their own versions of the stories can then be replayed and narrated. Group interaction such as this immerses the EAL learner in the English language, language structure and vocabulary in an informal way.

Email and chat rooms

A school's learning platform will provide controlled email and chat room features which provide great opportunities for learners to communicate with first language speakers.

Web-based resources

There's plenty of stuff on the web that's worth considering too (some free). See Appendix 3 for details.

What else can you do?

Given the resources and a little creativity there are many things that you could create for EAL pupils. For example, when considering what to do with new arrivals you might try a buddy system, introductory booklets, a dictionary, bilingual school word lists, phrase books and other support materials. You could develop much of this yourself using ICT. You might design a pack of resources which are published to CD-ROM or the school learning platform (and shared across other schools perhaps?).

 Activity

Link to the Primary ICT site at primaryict.org.uk/icthandbookv2.htm and look at the pdf document 'Using ICT to Support EAL Pupils' which should give you some further ideas.
     You will also find plenty of useful documents on the Community & Cohesion site at communitycohesionncc. org.uk/resources/eal.asp.

Gifted and talented (G&T) children

Gifted and talented (G&T) refers to pupils that demonstrate, or have the potential to demonstrate, an outstanding level of ability in one or more fields of activity and whose needs may not be served by the normal curriculum (e.g. Key Stage 3 pupils who are comfortable meeting the demands of the Key Stage 4 curriculum). It is important to remember that they may not be gifted in all subjects or in all aspects of any one subject.

Research has shown that that there does not appear to be any evidence to support claims that any single strategy is more effective for this heterogeneous group of pupils. The diversity means that personalised, differentiated provision is needed. What works for gifted and talented pupils in the classroom depends on the student, the teacher, the curriculum and the classroom context.

Pupils may benefit from the use of ICT to support their learning and may also be able to use more advanced features and techniques of ICT itself. They will also benefit from a wider degree of freedom and flexibility in order to enhance their own learning and meet their own individual needs.

There are some specific ICT resources for G&T though it is more about the way in which pupils are encouraged, how their learning is facilitated and how the uses of resources (ICT and other) are extended to provide challenging enrichment activities. Schools might audit their existing ICT provision (in all subjects) in order to ensure that they do have resources which are capable of extending G&T pupils.

In terms of ICT as a subject, pupils who are gifted in ICT are likely to:

- demonstrate ICT capability significantly above that expected for their age. For example, Key Stage 2 pupils may be comfortable meeting the demands of the Key Stage 3 curriculum;

- learn and apply new ICT techniques quickly. For example, pupils use shortcut keys for routine tasks effectively and appropriately; they quickly apply techniques for integrating applications such as mail merge and databases;

- use initiative to exploit the potential of more advanced features of ICT tools. For example, pupils investigate the HTML source code of a website and apply features such as counters or frames to their own web designs;

- transfer and apply ICT skills and techniques confidently in new contexts. For example, having learned about spreadsheet modelling in a mathematical context, they recognise the potential of applying a similar model in a science investigation;

- explore independently beyond the given breadth of an ICT topic. For example, they decide independently to validate information they have found from a website; having learned control procedures for a simple traffic light model, they extend their procedure to include control of a pedestrian crossing;
- initiate ideas and solve problems, use ICT effectively and creatively, and develop systems that meet personal needs and interests. For example, they create an interactive fan club website that sends out a monthly newsletter to electronic subscribers (either working on their own, or collaboratively with peers).

When using ICT in other subjects, teachers should:

- have high expectations of pupils and make this known;
- encourage pupils to make more use of packages, exploring and utilising advanced features;
- introduce pupils to a wider range of resources and technologies;
- encourage pupils to be critical about, and to explain and justify, their approach to tasks, and to evaluate the resources and methods used;
- extend tasks in order that pupils attain a deeper understanding;
- expect pupils to transfer skills to differing contexts;
- provide pupils with tasks that involve the higher order skills of analysis, synthesis and evaluation;
- expect pupils to use a wider range of source materials;
- encourage pupils to build knowledge and skills through collaboration with others;
- promote a greater degree of independent working whilst affording opportunities for formative appraisal;
- provide increased access to ICT (timetable constraints permitting);
- provide opportunities for extended learning including homework and out-of-hours use of school resources (including ICT) by way of breakfast clubs, lunchtime clubs and after school sessions;
- consider facilitating some of their learning alongside older pupils;
- challenge underachievement (not all G&T pupils are eager to enhance their education).

 Activity

If you want more guidance on teaching G&T pupils using ICT, link to the Primary ICT Website at primaryict. org.uk/icthandbookv2.htm and read the document 'Gifted'.

Enrichment activities

You will find a number of useful websites which offer free enrichment activities and ideas in Appendix 3. Here are just a few possibilities:

- Simon Tatham's Portable Puzzle Collection comprises 27 different abstract puzzles and neat re-packaging of some well-known (and some not so well-known) puzzles in a portable format (executable files). They are challenging and an ideal extension for the gifted and talented. Find it at chiark.greenend. org.uk/~sgtatham/puzzles.
- An intriguing online resource, Escher Web Sketch, allows pupils to experiment with symmetry by drawing repeating patterns. This is just one of a number of cross-curricular resources available from the Brightonline website: brightonline.org.uk.
- The School Run: theschoolrun.com/what-enrichment.

- Gift: giftltd.co.uk/node/15.
- Metagifted: metagifted.org/products/enrichmentProjectList.
- National Society for the Gifted & Talented: nsgt.org.

Commercial software

From the limited offerings from commercial retailers you might try the following:

- From r-e-m: Activities for Able Mathematicians, Brain Academy (series), Maths Challenges for Able Pupils, MissionMaker, Power Maths and PredICTion.
- From the Chalkface Project: Extension Activities for More Able Students, Thinking Skills for G&T students, and more.
- From Rising Stars: Maths for the More Able, Wonderwall.

 Activity

Visit the Primary ICT Website at primaryict.org.uk/icthandbookv2.htm and view the 'SEN Resources' video. There are other videos about SEN and ICT on the TES Connect website and on the Teacher's TV section of the GOV.UK site at gov.uk/government/publications/teachers-tv. *Teachers TV closed in 2011.*

Music technology for SEN

As you will have seen in Chapter 8, technology lends itself well to supporting teaching and learning in music. There are also a number of music technologies that are particularly useful for pupils with special needs and, in particular, for providing better access for pupils with physical disabilities.

Soundbeam

Soundbeam® is a system that detects the distance, direction and velocity of body movements in a defined space, and translates these body gestures into control signals for creating electronic music or manipulating multimedia. Ultrasonic detectors and various contact switches connect to the Soundbeam unit, which provides MIDI connections to synthesizers, sound modules, keyboard instruments and other MIDI compatible musical and multimedia equipment.

> Soundbeam can allow instruments to be played simply by detecting movement of the hand (or other part of the body). It narrows for everyone the gap between what can be imagined and what can be physically achieved. Soundbeam is intuitive, engaging, and encourages collaboration.
>
> Soundtree (2014)

Brainfingers

Brainfingers transforms brain and body electrical potentials from the forehead into hands-free computer controls which can be customized to each individual's needs. It can control most Advanced Audio Coding (AAC) software, educational software and video games.

A headband fitted with sensors detects electrical signals from facial muscles, eye movements and brainwaves. Software converts forehead signals into computer controls or 'Brainfingers'. Controls are tailored to the individual's needs and can range from a simple left mouse click to a complex combination of cursor control, mouse buttons and keyboard keys.

Brainfingers can give a voice to people who are non-verbal or who have limited expressive language, and may be appropriate for individuals with severe and multiple disabilities such as Cerebral Palsy (CP), Lou Gehrig's Disease (ALS/MND), Spinal Muscular Atrophy (SMA), Muscular Dystrophy (MD), Traumatic Brain Injury (TBI) and Spinal Cord Injury (SCI).

Brainfingers (2014)

Skoog

Roughly hand-sized, the Skoog is a tactile cube that simply plugs into a home computer or laptop via a USB connection. By touching, pressing, squashing, twisting or tapping the Skoog's five colour-coded sides, users can play a wide range of physically modelled instruments, MIDI, or sounds they have recorded themselves. With the Skoog's accompanying software, users can easily create unique musical compositions using its sampling, looping and layering features.

The Skoog's technology mimics the behaviour of conventional musical instruments and creates a direct correlation between the gestures a player makes and the sound that is produced. Playing sensitivity can be adjusted to respond to an individual user's movements, delivering a powerful and adaptable platform for creating and controlling sound.

PRWeb (2013)

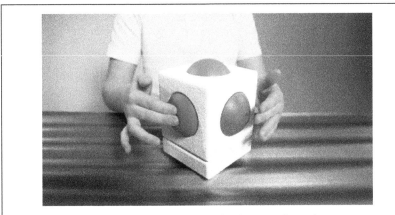

Figure 10.35 The Skoog (by skoogmusic.com)

 Activity

Visit the Primary ICT website at primaryict.org.uk/icthandbookv2.htm and watch the two videos, Orchestral Piece and Skoog.

The former is a news bulletin showing how three disabled musicians were able to take centre stage in an orchestral piece to celebrate the 2012 Olympics. The latter introduces the Skoog.

Apps for SEN

For a long list of iPad/iPhone apps, visit the Educational Technology site at educatorstechnology.com/2012/10/top-200-special-education-apps.html.

Environmental health and safety

ICT health and safety is extremely important for children with SEN and this should perhaps be your first consideration. Prior to deciding on access methods and appropriate resources it is important to remember good basic practice when working with children in the ICT room. Just a few points:

- Is the room tidy? Adequate space, free from clutter, no trailing cables, no dangerous objects, adequate well-labelled storage for computer equipment, books, software etc?

- Is the seating appropriate and comfortable? Legs, back and arms should all be at right angles with feet flat on the floor, chairs should be adjustable.

- Is the screen positioned correctly and at the right height for the child? The top of the monitor should be level with the eyes, monitors should tilt and swivel.

- Is the screen clean and free from glare? Back to the window, use non-reflective screens, use window blinds if necessary.

- Is the ambient lighting correct to provide good contrast? Adjust lighting, turn the brightness of the screen as low as possible and the contrast as high as possible.

- Can the child comfortably reach the access device? No sharp edges on the computer table, use keyboard and mouse rests.

- Is there adequate space at the computer? Space for reading/writing materials, space for more than one child in order to facilitate pair work.

- Would the child benefit from working in a quieter area?

- Can all children see a demonstration clearly? Room layout should provide adequate view of teacher/ IWB.

- Are children supervised when using the IWB? Keep backs to the projector beam, never stare at the projector.

- Is the room at the correct working temperature? 18–24°C, well ventilated, low humidity.

The SENCO

The requirement

Governing bodies of maintained mainstream schools and the proprietors of mainstream academy schools (including free schools) must ensure that there is a qualified teacher designated as SENCO for the school and they must achieve a National Award in Special Educational Needs Coordination within three years of appointment.

DfE (2015)

Responsibility

The SENCO has day-to-day responsibility for the operation of SEN policy and coordination of specific provision made to support individual pupils with SEN, including those who have Education Health and Care (EHC) plans. The SENCO will have responsibility for advising on special needs provision across the school (though responsibility for SEN pupils within each class lies with the class teacher who should liaise closely with the SENCO and ICT coordinator).

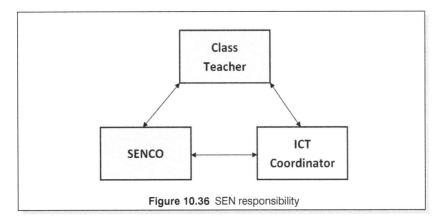

Figure 10.36 SEN responsibility

The key responsibilities of the SENCO may include:

- overseeing the day-to-day operation of the school's SEN policy;
- coordinating provision for children with SEN;
- liaising with the relevant designated teacher where a looked after pupil has SEN;
- advising on the graduated approach to providing SEN support;
- advising on the deployment of the school's delegated budget and other resources to meet pupils' needs effectively;
- liaising with parents of pupils with SEN;
- liaising with early years providers, other schools, educational psychologists, health and social care professionals, and independent or voluntary bodies;
- being a key point of contact with external agencies, especially the local authority and its support services;
- liaising with potential next providers of education to ensure a pupil and their parents are informed about options and a smooth transition is planned;
- working with the head teacher and school governors to ensure that the school meets its responsibilities under the Equality Act (2010) with regard to reasonable adjustments and access arrangements;
- ensuring that the school keeps the records of all pupils with SEN up-to-date.

ICT could be used as a tool for the following:

- assessing pupils' abilities;
- assisting in the administration of the SEN Code;
- providing direct support for pupils with special educational needs;
- accessing information;
- advice and support.

Assessing pupils' abilities

Periodic assessment of pupils provides up-to-date information to measure progress and inform the teaching and learning process.

Assessment software is available to help assess and analyse pupils in basic skills (literacy and numeracy and short-term memory) and learning styles. There are several recognised tests covering a range of needs. Some can be taken online or they can be administered in school using CD-ROMs. One example is Lucid Baseline by Lucid Research Ltd. (formerly known as CoPS Baseline).

Pupils who are not making satisfactory progress may require their own individual education plan (IEP) or personal learning plan (PLP). IEPs document targets, level of support, parental input and evidence of achievement between reviews.

There are a number of IEP software packages available including IEP Writer and IEP Manager.

*It must be stressed that, whilst some pupils will have IEPs, **all** pupils will have their own individual needs.*

Assisting in the administration of the SEN Code

The majority of management information systems (MIS) used in schools facilitate the collection and sharing of information on special educational needs. This can be a real time saver for SENCOs and it also means that all staff can be actively involved and have some ownership. Some include special features to help schools meet the requirement of the SEN Code of Practice (2014). MIS software includes SIMS, CMIS and RM Integris (Cloud based).

When choosing a package it should be understood that there is no 'one size fits all' and the system must fit the school's own requirements. Some of the features to be considered are:

- Can the system be customised to suit the school's needs?
- Can the system bring together assessment, IEPs and monitoring?
- Is it easy to produce data and tables for reports?
- Can you compare data easily?
- Can information be presented in different forms for letters to parents and so on?
- Is data transferable from existing school management systems?
- Can graphs and data analysis be produced?

Providing direct support for pupils with SEN

Having established the individual needs of all pupils, the SENCO will need to work in conjunction with the ICT coordinator and other key staff in order to identify and make appropriate provision of ICT resources. Previous sections have outlined resources which can be used for a wide range of special needs.

Accessing information, advice and support

There are many websites which offer useful information and guidance on the entire spectrum of SEN. These are listed in Appendix 3.

Managing ICT

CHAPTER

11

ICT management and leadership

Introduction

This book has presented a range of ideas for using ICT resources in primary schools. However, it is only when such resources are used within a sound strategic framework that schools will achieve and sustain maximum benefit in terms of enhancing learning and teaching and supporting management and administration.

This chapter examines the requirements for successfully managing ICT processes and links closely with the Naace Self-Review Framework (SRF). Each primary school will differ in its current practice, provision and level of ICT experience. The guidance offered here should therefore be treated as general rather than specific (though examples of best practice will be offered throughout).

The approach taken will be simplistic and 'top-down' – firstly identifying the basic components and then gradually breaking them down into more detail. It will work on the principle of bridging the 'strategic gap' between 'where you are now' and 'where you would like to be in the future'.

The Naace Self-Review Framework

The purpose of the Self-Review Framework is to support school improvement through a reflective practice that allows schools to measure and improve their provision against a well-researched and evidenced set of criteria. In doing so, pupils will become digitally literate and are able to use and express themselves and develop their ideas through information and communications technology.

The Self-Review Framework is based around a set of descriptors. These are statements that summarise different stages of maturity in the way your school might be using technology. By comparing your development against these statements you can identify where you need to improve to achieve best practice.

The framework is divided into six elements which will support and challenge your school:

1. **Leadership and management:** Do staff feel encouraged and supported, by colleagues at all levels, in developing and sharing new practices with technology?

2. **Use of ICT in the curriculum:** To what extent is the development of technology capability systematically mapped across the whole curriculum?

3. **Teaching and Learning:** Does the use of technology in and beyond school help pupils become more effective and confident learners?

4. **Assessment of digital capability:** Is there effective assessment of progress in technology capability, of all groups of pupils?

5. **Professional Development:** Can staff explain why and how they use technology in lessons and to support other aspects of their work?

6. **Resources:** Are the right technology resources, including hardware and software for digital learning and school management, accessible in the right place at the right time?

Each element has a number of detailed strands each of which will be examined in this chapter.

Naace offer the 'ICT Mark' award to schools that are assessed as successfully attaining level 2 in each of the elements where:

- Level 4 = Made a start
- Level 3 = Strategy in place
- Level 2 = Coherence
- Level 1 = Aspirational

 Activity

Visit the Primary ICT website at primaryict.org.uk/icthandbookv2.htm where you'll find a copy the Naace Self-Review Framework.
Skim through each of the elements to get a 'flavour' for what is required.
The framework (dated January 2014) is updated regularly and, for an up to date copy, you should visit the Naace website at naace.co.uk.

Even if you are not applying for the Naace award, the Self-Review Framework is a useful guide to help you improve your school's position. You will note from the level descriptors that, whilst employing good ICT resources has merit, focussing on resources alone will not raise you to level 2.

Leadership and management

There is no specific order in which to tackle each of the six elements. However, since the development of ICT will follow a pre-determined strategic plan, then leadership and management should be the first port of call.

ICT team

With the exception of very small schools, managing ICT is too big a prospect for just one person. Most schools will appoint an ICT leader (e-learning manager) to lead a small team.

 Activity

Who do you think should be in your school ICT Team and who would lead it?
Your team needs to include those people who are able to effect the necessary changes which you will ultimately agree to implement. A member of the headship, the ICT coordinator and subject representatives are likely candidates. In many schools, the deputy head leads the team – in others, it is recognised that, whilst the head and/or deputy should be a member, he/she is already extremely busy and responsibility for leading the team is better invested in the ICT coordinator. The composition of the team can vary enormously but should adhere to sound management principles. If the team is too small you will deny yourself vital expertise but if the team is too large it will prove difficult to manage. A compromise is to form a small core team and perhaps an 'extended' team.

For example, the core team might comprise:

- ICT leader (deputy head)
- ICT coordinator
- subject leaders
- technical representative.

In a small school the leader and coordinator might be the same person.

An extended team might include one or more of: teachers, teaching assistants, SENCO, pupil representative(s), parents, governors, LEA representative, commercial partner(s).

It is important that you represent all key stakeholders in one way or another and that, in order to obtain maximum 'buy in' to your policies, you consult with members and make them feel included. This is absolutely essential for teachers, particularly those who are not ICT 'enthusiasts' and those who are technophobes.

It will be helpful to the team if:

- its task is clearly defined;
- the roles and responsibilities of the individual members are agreed;
- it is clear who the team will report to and what will happen to its recommendations.

Sharing responsibility for the management of ICT is known as *distributed leadership*, a concept that has become increasingly popular over the last decade or so – particularly in UK primary schools. It is based on the premise that leadership is uncoupled from positional authority and brings about benefits that would not occur with singular leadership.

For a better insight you might examine the work of Professor Alma Harris, a leading researcher on this topic: *Distributed Leadership Matters* (2014, Corwin).

Choice of the ICT coordinator

The traditional role of the ICT coordinator in primary schools has changed enormously over the last decade because of the widening impact of ICT on the whole school and beyond. The choice of ICT coordinator used to be quite straightforward – choose someone with good ICT skills. However, the role is now becoming increasingly complex and it may require someone with a goodly amount of teaching experience and good people skills.

 Activity

Take a look at the video from St Thomas's C.E. Primary School (copy on the Primary ICT website at primaryict.org.uk/icthandbookv2.htm). It shows how the ICT position of a school changed with the appointment of a new ICT Coordinator.

In the video the ICT Coordinator has a middle management role. Part of her role is to encourage teachers to integrate ICT into all subject areas and to provide training for staff.

Team roles and responsibilities

When deciding on team responsibilities it may be a good idea to carry out the exercise of listing (brainstorming) all the things that the school will be required to do with regard to ICT. These will range from the simple to the complex. Here are some examples (the list is in no particular order and is not exhaustive):

- Writing policies and procedures
- Audits
- Planning
- Purchasing hardware
- Purchasing ICT consumables
- Repair and maintenance of hardware
- Evaluating software
- Purchasing software (and licensing)
- Using ICT for administration and management
- Network issues

- Sourcing of funding
- Using ICT in each subject area
- Using ICT for assessment
- Replacing printer cartridges
- Managing information
- Staff training
- Review and evaluation
- Health and safety
- Data protection
- Extended learning

This exercise can be carried out over a period of time and you would be wise to consult school-wide as a first step toward involving everyone. Indeed, now may be a good time to benchmark yourself against other schools, particularly one or two that have already achieved the ICT Mark.

Once you've decided who should do what, duties can be further delegated. For example, it may be a good idea to involve the pupils – they could replace printer cartridges and keep the paper topped up. Sharing responsibility in this way also reduces the dependency and the burden on the ICT coordinator.

Roles, responsibilities, duties and so on should eventually be documented in an ICT handbook.

The vision

The starting point for a school is to express its vision for ICT, not in terms of assets or resources, but in terms of measurable benefits. Such a vision might be summarised in a 'vision statement' which is written in quite general terms, owned by all key personnel and shared with all stakeholders. An effective vision should support and enhance the school's aims in terms of learning, teaching, management and administration (i.e. all aspects of the school). It would need to be periodically updated as part of the normal management cycle.

In this respect an ICT vision is no different from an organisation's vision.

 Activity

Do you know the ICT vision for your school?
   Hopefully the answer is yes. Ideally it will be properly communicated and prominently displayed in easily accessible places. At the very least, you should be aware that there is a vision and know where to find it.

If you are starting from scratch then it would be wise to keep your vision simple and achievable. Some of the issues that might be included are: pupil entitlement, the value of ICT as a teaching and learning tool, cross-curriculum use, improving attainment, promoting learning styles and extended learning. Here is one example.

ICT will be used safely and effectively to raise awareness of the benefits and uses of technology, to enhance learning and teaching in all subjects, to improve school management and administration processes, to promote home–school links and, overall, to improve the attainment of all pupils.

 Activity

Visit the Primary ICT website at primaryict.org.uk/icthandbookv2.htm where you'll find some sample vision statements from primary schools in the UK. These may give you a few ideas about your own statement.

ICT audits

Once you know where you want to be (the vision), you need to know where you are now. This may seem obvious but you should do it systematically in order that you don't miss something important. To establish your current position you should carry out an audit. The audit is effectively a quantitative and qualitative analysis of all aspects of ICT.

 Activity

How would you carry out an ICT audit in your school – what aspects would you need to consider?
    Essentially you will need to find out what resources you have, where they are, how they fit together, how they are being used, who is using them and how often. You will need to break each of these down into as much detail as you think you will need. You may need to break your audit into several chunks. Some will require physical inspection in order to draw up inventories and others will take the form of interviews, observations, discussions, document inspection etc.

The questions you need to ask, and the evidence you will expect to find, will become evident as you proceed through the subsequent sections of this chapter. However, sources of evidence will include:

- schemes of work (all subjects);
- individual lesson plans;
- classroom observations;
- teaching and learning policy;
- INSET and staff development planning;
- discussions with pupils, teachers and support staff;
- IEPs and other learning programmes for pupils with special needs;
- documents relating to individual self-evaluations;
- personal development plans/action logs/learning logs/pupil diaries;
- cross-curricular ICT planning, including minutes of meetings;
- student peer review and evaluation documentation;
- inventories of ICT resources.

These are certainly the sources of evidence which will be examined by a Naace assessor if you have applied for the ICT Mark!

 Activity

Visit the Primary ICT website at primaryict.org.uk/icthandbookv2.htm where you'll find an audit form for leadership and management.

It has been compiled by summarising the key components of the leadership and management element of the Naace SRF and mapping these to possible sources of evidence. Where possible, more than one source of evidence has been included in order to provide triangulation.

The form is deliberately incomplete – some of the strands and possible sources of evidence are missing. You are invited to complete the design of the form by referring to the Naace SRF (copy on website), identifying the missing strands and mapping them to possible sources of evidence.

Development plan

Having collated the information collected you can compare what you have in place now with your vision for the future (if you haven't yet done so then you need to break the vision down into more detailed elements).

This difference is the 'strategic gap' and, to bridge it, you need to compile a development plan. The plan will set targets in terms of: what needs to be done; how it will be achieved; who will be responsible for it (and who will provide support); and the timescale for completion. You might also include possible performance indicators which will help you to monitor progress along the way.

A few words of caution. DON'T be too ambitious with your plan – it could easily take on unmanageable proportions and become ineffective. Prioritise what needs to be done and do it in phases. You can periodically modify the plan as part of a continuous cycle of improvement. DON'T give everything to the ICT coordinator; involve other staff too – it helps to include people. DON'T try to convert everyone into an ICT enthusiast – there will be those who are 'technophobes' and those who are resistant to change. They may need to be nurtured, their skills and enthusiasm growing organically as they are gradually influenced by the actions of others.

School ICT policy

A school's ICT policy will describe the school's approach to achieving the vision for ICT (over a specified period of time). It will cover all important aspects including: strategy, leadership and management, use of ICT in the curriculum, teaching and learning, assessment of digital capability, professional development and resources.

It is the first step in communicating the aims to the whole school and should therefore be easily accessible to everyone. The first draft need only be an outline of intentions and will be reviewed and modified as part of the management cycle. The sections to be found in the policy could be:

Introduction

The introduction should outline what you want the policy to achieve:

- To ensure all staff understand and agree on the approach to using ICT.
- To assist planning.
- To explain the school's position to outsiders.
- To assist the governors in the allocation of funds.
- etc…

For example:

> This policy document sets out the school's aims, principles and strategies for the delivery of Information and Communication Technology. It will form the basis for the development of ICT in the school over the next five years...

It should define the meaning of ICT. For example:

> We interpret the term 'information and communication technology' to include ...

and make clear the significance of ICT. For example:

> Information and communication technology (ICT) prepares pupils to participate in a rapidly changing world in which work and other activities are increasingly transformed by access to varied and developing technology. Pupils use ICT tools to find, explore, analyse, exchange and present information responsibly, creatively ...

Vision statement

A summary of the school's ICT vision.

Managing ICT

Outline the duties of the ICT Management Team and other staff and stakeholders.

The remainder of the policy will cover the expectations for the remaining elements of the SRF.

 Activity

If you wish to compare and evaluate existing school policies, you will find four on the Primary ICT website at primaryict.org.uk/icthandbookv2.htm. There are plenty more to be found on the Internet.
Some of these are quite basic whilst others are far more comprehensive. They may give you some ideas about the composition of your own policy.

ICT handbook

The school policy outlines the principles behind the use of ICT in the school. Procedures, guidance, rules and other operational matters should be placed in a handbook. The handbook might include:

- role of the ICT team;
- duties of the ICT coordinator;
- duties of all those with specific responsibilities (see previous section);
- detailed procedures required in order to fulfil duties;
- acceptable use of the Internet;
- e-safeguarding;
- data protection and security;
- health and safety.

Case study: An example development plan

A school has used a questionnaire, a number of observations and some informal discussions to audit the competence of staff in using ICT. The results reveal that:

- There is no formal process for identifying staff training needs – staff sometimes receive training if they request it or if a new resource is installed (e.g. an interactive whiteboard).
- There is no allocated budget specifically for ICT and staff suggest that ICT takes on a lower priority than other areas.
- Only a few staff feel comfortable with using common ICT resources and know when it is appropriate to use them in learning and teaching.
- Most staff feel that they are not best prepared for using ICT, they are unsure of the resources available for each subject area and they don't know how and when to use them.
- There doesn't appear to be anyone with responsibility for staff development in ICT.
- and so on ...

Needless to say, this school has yet to achieve its ICT Mark!

Part of the vision for this school is that all staff will feel comfortable using a range of ICT resources to aid their teaching and to enhance children's learning. The ensuing CPD section of the development plan therefore includes the following:

What/How	Who	By when
Nominate someone to take responsibility for identifying staff development needs	ICT leader	Now
Develop a simple procedure for identifying staff development needs.	The nominated person	End of current term
Add a section on ICT development into the ICT Handbook.	The nominated person	End of current term
Provide basic training for those who need it. A number of options are available including: in-house training (e.g. a devoted INSET day); team teaching/observation; external training course – cascaded to other members of staff; etc.	ICT coordinator, competent staff	Progressively and within 1 year
Familiarise staff with available ICT resources and how they can be used in each subject area.	ICT coordinator, subject leaders	End of current term

and so on ...

The plan is not exhaustive and could, of course, be broken down into more detail if required.

Management cycle (evaluation)

And finally, each part of the ICT management process needs to be regularly monitored, evaluated and updated as required. Evidence needs to be collected to determine how effective the process is. The periodicity of review will depend on a number of factors.

- First, the rate of development of technology and its application to schools means that review must be carried out on a frequent basis.
- Second, there are many elements to the implementation of ICT and schools are unlikely to think of everything at the outset.
- Third, the curriculum itself is forever changing.

■ Finally, the notion of short, medium and long-term planning has itself changed significantly over the last twenty years. What used to be 2 years, 5 years and 10 years is now more likely to be 6 months, 1 year and 2 years.

It may also be that each element of ICT demands its own cycle. To begin with you might review some aspects on a termly basis until the cycle settles down.

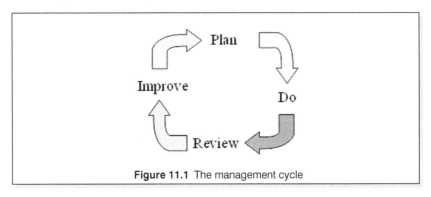

Figure 11.1 The management cycle

ICT curriculum

Pupils should be given opportunities to apply and develop their ICT capability through the use of ICT tools to support their learning in all subjects. In the old (pre-2014) curriculum there were statutory requirements for the teaching and the use of ICT. Whilst this no longer applies in the new curriculum (2014), schools, and teachers, should use their own judgement to decide where it is appropriate to teach the use of ICT and to use it to enhance teaching and learning across all subjects.

The main justification for having an ICT curriculum is that it is a tool to aid teaching and learning and a set of key skills which permeate through many aspects of life. In order to allow pupils to develop their ICT skills in interesting and challenging ways, the ICT curriculum needs to be well planned by implementing both discrete and cross-curricular opportunities which include a wide range of up to date software applications and other resources.

The balance between discrete and cross-curricular approaches will depend upon a number of factors including: the skills of all staff, ICT resources available, deployment of resources, current level of pupil skill etc. In general, curriculum planning should seek to achieve a balance between developing pupils' ICT skills and applying them to the learning that takes place in all subjects.

The Naace Self-Review Framework does not recommend any particular approach (although where ICT is taught as a discrete subject there is an assumption that ICT capability will be applied subsequently in a variety of contexts across the curriculum).

Discrete courses have their own schedule, aims and objectives and are therefore easier to plan and assess. Planning can be centralised. However, the danger of centralising discrete courses is that skills and knowledge may be divorced from application and the contexts chosen may be inauthentic or inappropriate owing to ICT teachers having insufficient depth of knowledge of other subjects. This has perhaps been the case with functional skills teaching in colleges. For example, copying text from a book is an unsatisfactory way to develop word processing skills, whereas analytical writing in the context of History may be a more appropriate use.

It may be that some skills are taught in discrete ICT sessions, some are taught during other curriculum subjects whilst others are developed by pupils themselves (inside and outside school). Skills may need to be taught by subject teachers and some by ICT teachers.

Teachers themselves may need to acquire these skills and a nominated staff member should identify needs and decide how these are best satisfied.

Skills may be split into a number of 'components':

- **Basic skills** (routines) – such as using a mouse or double clicking an icon;
- **Techniques** – such as adjusting margins on a page;
- **Processes** – such as developing a presentation for English, researching a project for geography or analysing the results of a survey in maths;
- **Higher order skills** – such as recognising when the use of ICT may be appropriate, planning how to approach a problem, deciding where to source information, testing a hypothesis, reflecting on the effectiveness of ICT in a task.

Each component is typically developed in a different way:

- **Basic skills** – are primarily learned through practice;
- **Techniques** – are developed slowly through trial and error, and copying others;
- **Processes** and **Higher order skills** – are developed through examples, exploration, experience and reflection. The teacher's role may be one of support and guidance – taught sessions need not be overly elaborate.

Learning and teaching

ICT can be used in a variety of ways to enhance both learning and teaching. It won't happen by accident – it needs to be planned. There should be a consistent approach to the use of ICT and this should be communicated in the school ICT Policy.

Once staff are familiar with the statutory requirements for using ICT across the curriculum, they are aware of the available resources, they have an appreciation of the uses to which ICT can be put, and they are competent users of ICT themselves, they will be in a position to decide when it is appropriate to use ICT and how best they can use it. In particular, teachers will readily identify when ICT is preferable to more traditional methods.

There is no strict model – it will depend to some extent on the creativity and ingenuity of teachers and how they are able to share their practice with others.

The same will apply to pupils. Not only should they be able to use ICT resources in planned ways, they should also be increasingly able to decide when and how to make use of ICT to help themselves (particularly in Key Stage 2). After all, they will have their own expectations too. For example, when finding things out, Year 1 children will require guidance and direction in order to find information from books, CD-ROMs, the Internet etc. However, Year 6 children will be more independent and, to some extent, can decide for themselves how they will access information. In fact, these pupils may be able to independently and safely select and use the most appropriate resources for a variety of tasks and explain why they have done so.

Not all pupils will be at the same level and each should expect to build upon previous experiences. This includes pupils with individual learning needs whether it be learning difficulties, physical impairment or gifted and talented.

The impact of using ICT should be measurable and should be part and parcel of the school's routine evaluation process. Ideally, the quality of work should improve over a period of time, children become more motivated and involved (particularly those who might otherwise be disengaged or disruptive), the variety of learning activities expands, lessons are deemed more effective and interactive and, children's attainment improves! The process will also identify weak areas which can be developed over time.

Responsibility for developing ICT in each subject area or in each year should be devolved to subject/ year leaders (with advice from the ICT coordinator). Such development would be part of the overall development plan.

ICT will also play a pivotal role in the development of children with special educational needs – see Chapter 10 for more details.

Staff should make full use of ICT in their planning and recording. Word processors and other office applications can be used to create templates for schemes of work, lesson plans and so on. The school website and/or learning platform will provide ways to communicate with learners (e.g. timetables, learning activities etc.) and to share ideas and materials with other staff. The school management information system (MIS) will provide a number of features for recording data and producing reports. These, and more, will provide a handy set of tools which are well worth investing in.

Impact on pupil outcomes

If the implementation of ICT is to be effective then it must improve teaching and, more importantly, have a significant impact on pupils' overall attainment, acquisition of skills and overall enjoyment of their learning experience. What's more, the impact must also be measurable.

The assessment process should measure year-on-year progress in terms of 'value added'. That is to say, each pupil, whatever their starting point, will show an improvement over time. This offers a significant advantage both to weaker (and disadvantaged) pupils and also to the gifted and talented because they are being measured in relative terms rather than against a norm.

This improvement is not only in academic achievement but also in motivation, attitude, behaviour, confidence, self-esteem, creative ability and learner independence. In particular, pupils will eventually have mastered the generic skills which apply to all subjects. Namely to:

- access, select and interpret information;
- recognise patterns, relationships and behaviours;
- model, predict and hypothesise;
- test reliability and accuracy;
- review and modify their work to improve its quality;
- communicate with others and present information;
- evaluate their work;
- improve efficiency;
- be creative and take risks;
- gain confidence and independence.

Assessment

Assessment can become a very broad and complex issue. For the purposes of this chapter however, it will be constrained to:

1. assessing the achievement of ICT skills;
2. making effective use of ICT during the assessment of all subjects.

Assessing ICT skills

One of the advantages of teaching ICT as a discrete subject is that it can easily be assessed in isolation from the rest of the curriculum – particularly when measuring attainment of basic skills and techniques.

However, let's assume that you have decided to 'fully' embed ICT into the curriculum. How then do you go about assessing it? Well, you could allow your pupils to assess themselves on basic skills and techniques (self and peer assessment) leaving teachers to assess processes and higher order skills. The problem then is 'which teacher assesses which skill?'

This requires coordination in order to produce an agreed assessment schema such that all teachers know what they are assessing and when. This will ensure that pupils are assessed consistently across the curriculum and over time. This is one of the key duties of the ICT coordinator (in cooperation with the assessment coordinator if you have one).

A moderation process should be implemented whereby assessment methods and results are checked for consistency (i.e. teachers are administering and grading their assessments in a comparable way and in accordance with any established procedures and standards). Benchmarking between departments, and perhaps between schools, is useful. This allows schools to adopt 'best practice'.

The idea of formative self and peer assessment isn't new though often it isn't implemented in primary schools. It does have benefits because, as a result, pupils are able to gain an understanding of what constitutes good quality and, eventually, they will begin to develop their own criteria against which they are able to judge their own work and that of others. One way in which they can do this is to discuss their work in pairs or small groups.

Using ICT to support assessment

ICT can be an effective tool in the assessment process itself – both for the creation of assessment instruments and for the subsequent recording and processing of results. Here are some examples.

Reception class ICT assessment

MS Word (or Publisher) is used to create a simple self-assessment sheet. The parts of the teddy are labelled as shown in the diagram below.

Each child has a printed copy and is allowed to colour in each part when they show that they can do what it says.

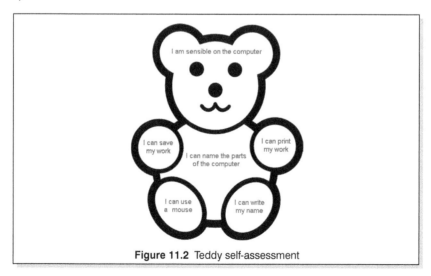

Figure 11.2 Teddy self-assessment

Computer diary

Year 2 children keep computer diaries. The teacher has created a diary template in MS Word for each pupil. It contains sections for them to type in:

- their task;
- who they worked with;
- what they did;
- how they feel about their work.

They use a new template each time they complete a new task. When the task is complete, they save the diary to their own area of the school learning platform. Their parents can then view them.

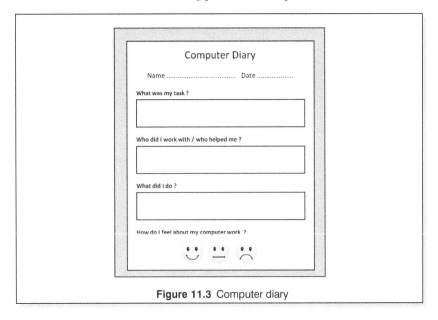

Figure 11.3 Computer diary

Profile

Year 3 children use a profile of ICT skills. They have created this themselves using a spreadsheet. For each skill they tick a box:

- Green: I can do this.
- Amber: I can do this with help.
- Red: I can't do this yet.

	Yes	Partly	Not yet
I can cut and paste paragraphs			
I can insert tabs and indents			
I can use formatting features			
I can use tables			
I can resize and crop images			
I can number and bullet			

Figure 11.4 Pupil profile

Software with built-in assessment

Some software includes built-in assessment which offers formative feedback as pupils progress through the learning content. Other titles are designed specifically to assess components of the National Curriculum. For example, Rising Stars Mathematics and English.

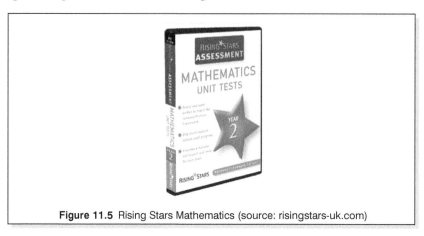

Figure 11.5 Rising Stars Mathematics (source: risingstars-uk.com)

Software for creating assessments

Free and commercial packages are available for teachers to design simple assessments. For example, Hot Potatoes is a free package used for creating interactive exercises including multiple-choice, jumbled-sentence, short-answer, matching/ordering, crossword and gap-fill.

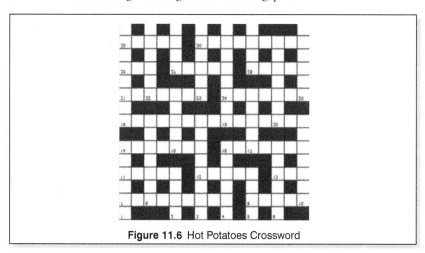

Figure 11.6 Hot Potatoes Crossword

Wimba Create easily converts MS Word documents into linked web-based learning content and assessments at the touch of a button. Questionmark Perception manages the whole process from creating assessments to delivery to grading to recording.

Learning platforms

Most learning platforms include their own set of content and assessment creation tools. Results can be managed, analysed and stored if the platform is connected to the school's MIS. Pupils can also use this medium to submit projects and assignments electronically and to store their work, making it accessible to teachers and parents.

E-portfolios

E-portfolios, blogs and wikis can be used as assessment tools (students can use these as records of their own achievement).

Interactive voting systems

Interactive voting systems actively involve pupils in quizzes, evaluations etc. in a fun and motivating way. They encourage full participation and can be used for formative and summative assessment. Feedback is instant and results can be stored and analysed. There are several offerings on the market.

Computer-mediated communication (CMC)

CMC, in the form of discussion forums, can be used to perform collaborative constructive learning (CCL). Used widely in higher education, the claim is that collaborative learning can accomplish far more than individuals could hope to achieve on their own. This principle, if applied well, can be equally useful in the primary classroom where children often share and compare ideas following a variety of activities. With the advent of learning platforms, this has now become a serious option for children and is not only a means of learning, it is also a convenient method of assessment.

Recording achievement

There are several ways in which teachers and schools can record, manipulate, analyse, store, present and communicate assessment results in a way that paper-based systems could never match. Contenders include: tabulated data in word processed documents, spreadsheets, simple database, specific assessment software and management information systems. In addition, work can now be handed in (and results shared with parents) via the learning platform or email.

Continual professional development (CPD)

The right to CPD

Teachers, like employees in other vocations, have a right to expect opportunities to develop their knowledge and skills throughout their career. This is known as continual professional development (CPD). This is especially true when related to technology which is advancing so quickly that it is often difficult to keep pace. Not only are teachers having to come to terms with new resources and ICT initiatives, they also need to keep abreast of the accompanying changes in curriculum, policy and pedagogy. For example, the recent introduction of a Computing curriculum requires teachers to get to grips with the principles of computing and the resources associated with teaching the subject.

Staff need development so they can:

- improve their knowledge of teaching and learning – including the use of ICT (pedagogy);
- improve their knowledge of management and administration – including the use of ICT;
- keep pace with developments in ICT curriculum and legislation;
- work effectively in a teaching team;
- extend their subject knowledge of ICT;
- extend their technical skills and knowledge.

It has become evident that the ICT skills of teachers vary enormously between the 'enthusiasts' on one extreme and the 'technophobes' on the other. Many teachers feel intimidated by technically superior colleagues and shy away from ICT as a result. Even with the best will in the world it is difficult to keep pace with change and it may be that we need to slow down and take better stock of what we already have in place before slavishly transiting from one phase of policy to another and from one generation of technology to the next. However, that doesn't mitigate schools from undertaking CPD.

So, when should CPD start? Well newly qualified teachers, as part of Initial Teacher Training (ITT) will have passed an ICT skills test and should have the ability to teach Computing and ICT. They may also have used a range of ICT tools such as software, interactive whiteboards, discussion forums, video conferencing and e-portfolios as a component part of their own training. As a result, they are more likely to accept ICT as an integral part of their professional life. However, this is only the starting point and, even for them, CPD should commence on their first day as a newly qualified teacher in school.

As a school, the first step is to delegate responsibility for CPD to a member of staff. In a small school this will likely be the ICT coordinator though it need not be so. The agreed duties should be documented and included in the ICT handbook alongside other ICT policies.

The CPD process, like any other, is cyclical and begins with an audit of both staff and whole-school needs. This will require an assessment of competence in using ICT and the ability to incorporate it effectively into learning.

 Activity

If you were responsible for CPD in your school, how would you go about auditing staff ICT needs?

If you've already carried out a 'resources' audit then you will know what resources you hold and what you are likely to hold in the short to medium term (in order to fulfil your vision). Using this inventory as a checklist you can use a questionnaire, forum or other suitable survey instrument to gather the information you need (perhaps an informal approach would be more acceptable to your colleagues). Split the survey questions into categories such as:

- computer basics (file management, loading software etc.);
- common office applications (e.g. word processing, presentations, spreadsheets, database, email, Internet etc.);
- generic resources (e.g. IWB, digital camera, software toolkit etc.);
- subject specific resources (e.g. maths software, floor robots etc.);
- network;
- learning platform;
- understanding how these resources can be used in curriculum subjects. You might ask for examples of how they are being used and how frequently;
- teaching ICT as a discrete subject;
- teaching the Computing curriculum.

You will find plenty of sample audit forms on the Internet. Try the grids for learning listed in Appendix 2. There's also a sample ICT Skills Audit Form on the Primary ICT website at primaryict.org.uk/icthandbookv2.htm.

You should endeavour to keep the audit as simple as possible otherwise you may not get the response you require and the subsequent task of collating and analysing the data may become unmanageable. You can carry out the audit in phases, tackling the most important issues first.

The ICT coordinator will have additional responsibility for keeping abreast of developments in technology and updating staff.

Methods of CPD

Once the needs of staff are established you will want to find ways of satisfying them. Budgetary constraints will come into play here so try to identify the most cost-effective solutions.

- Low-cost solutions include: self-reflection; mentoring; team teaching; observing colleagues (and inviting critique of your own performance); informal chats; discussion forums (face-to-face and CMC); INSET days; utilising the services of advanced skills teachers; liaison with other schools; and self-help (there's plenty of help to be found: tutorials on the Internet, help menus within software packages, ICT books etc.). Don't forget also that your own pupils are a source of knowledge – they often know more than the teacher about some aspects of ICT and this should be harnessed! Don't forget, discussion forums, sharing ideas and resources and perhaps online learning opportunities can all be facilitated via your learning platform.

- Medium-cost solutions include: courses provided by local authorities; online learning (e.g. primaryict. org.uk); books, and cascaded training by individual teachers that have attended external courses, seminars, exhibitions (e.g. BETT), conferences etc.

An incentive might be to sponsor staff for courses which lead to recognised qualifications such as the ICT Mark course offered by Naace.

Training in whatever form should be 'just in time'. This simply means that staff must be in a position to put their training to immediate use or they will quickly forget what they have learned.

Evaluating CPD

The quality and effectiveness of staff development should be measured to ensure that it is effective and good value for money. This can be done in a number of ways including:

- immediate reactive feedback from individual teachers to the ICT Coordinator (e.g. completion of an evaluation form);

- feedback from individual teachers to the ICT Coordinator once they have had sufficient opportunity to practise new skills;

- observation of subsequent lessons;

- perceived improvement in pupil achievement;

- interview during annual appraisals (which leads to setting future CPD targets).

Extended learning

Extended learning is about creating opportunities for pupils and their families outside normal school hours and/or away from the school itself (at home and in the community). It not only helps children on the wrong side of the digital divide but it also supports the notion that children in the twenty-first century should be able to learn whenever and wherever is best for them. If this in some way includes their parents then evidence suggests that they are likely to achieve better results (whilst helping some parents and families too).

Uses of extended learning

Extended learning should be used by all teachers, and with all pupils, for homework, revision, consolidation and voluntary additional work. It can also be used to provide opportunities for pupils who are absent through illness and those who are disengaged from mainstream learning.

Home–school links allow the promotion of a number of e-assessment methods including online tests, e-portfolios and blogs. It is also possible for electronic submission of work.

Parents are able to take an active interest in their children's work and to access their children's records, reports and attendance. Indeed, parents themselves might be offered classes in ICT in order that they can better help their children.

Facilitating extended learning

Extended learning can be facilitated using a variety of media and methods including:

- school learning platform/website/VLE (including discussion boards);
- email;
- third-party websites (including those associated with Extended Schools);
- CD-ROMs;
- podcasts/vidcasts;
- radio;
- television;
- tablet PCs, Smartphones and other mobile devices;
- making ICT resources/facilities available to families outside normal working hours (including breakfast clubs, after school clubs, loan of laptops/mobile devices and other initiatives);
- ICT facilities offered by the wider community (libraries, colleges etc.).

Involvement of governors may prove useful here because they will have interests and connections outside the school.

Resources

Schools need to hold a good range of ICT resources to consistently support learning, teaching and administration. This means that resources must be both appropriate and accessible. A walkaround audit of the school would show evidence of ICT in use in all classrooms, other learning spaces and offices. If you are doing this formally, the audit should record what resources your school holds and where they are located.

For each piece of hardware, determine how old it is, what warranties it carries and how much life you think it has left (this will in part be determined by the currency of its specification, i.e. is it still up to the job in terms of its speed of operation, storage capacity, whether it can support the latest generation of software etc.). Look also at how hardware is networked and whether it is efficient.

For each software title you need to decide whether it is still giving you adequate support for the subject(s) it is used in and whether an upgrade or switch to an alternative title would be better.

Procedures are also necessary for the identification and procurement of resources which meet the current and future needs of the school. Deciding what to spend your money on is a difficult task – Chapter 12 discusses this in more detail.

Technical support

Adequate technical support will ensure that equipment is largely serviceable with procedures of preventive maintenance and timely repair in place.

It is important that schools can keep a high rate of operability of their technology with the minimum disruption to learning and teaching. Technical support will normally be provided on a contract basis, either via the local authority, link-secondary school or commercial contract. Large schools may have a permanent, on-site, technician(s), but smaller schools will have to rely on either periodic visits (e.g. fortnightly half-day visit) or on an as required basis. For the latter, it would be prudent to train one or more members of staff in the basics of looking after ICT environments.

Before staff wade in too deep, do bear in mind that staff may cost more per hour than a technician!

The bottom line here will be cost. Consider tapping into your local authority if it has a service level agreement or share support with other local schools.

It is often the case that technical and pedagogical matters are kept distinctly separate. The technician is not interested in teaching and teachers don't want to be technicians. Whilst this is quite natural it is not healthy and you need to find ways of 'dovetailing' these two aspects together if you are to get the best out of your ICT system.

Whatever your decision you should have a procedure which deals with what to do when technology breaks down and the preventive maintenance to be carried out to minimise such eventualities.

Self-Review Framework (SRF) software

Naace provide an online tool which helps schools to assess and improve their use of ICT and to achieve the ICT Mark. There are also some comprehensive SRF software packages available from commercial providers. For example, the bluewave.SWIFT all in one school improvement system (bluewaveswift. co.uk).

Finding the funding for ICT

It started with news that Becta was to lose its funding and hence would close in the spring of 2011. And from then the changes came thick and fast.

The Home Access programme was concluded and not extended; the BSF programme, which contained extensive ICT investment, was cancelled; Harnessing Technology funds disappeared; ICT advisers in local authorities started their redundancy "consultation" and schools no longer had to operate a learning platform (VLE) or offer online home-school links.

And just to make life interesting for schools, overall capital spending looks about to take a major hit, making it hard for schools to both maintain their existing infra-structure and acquire new technology based resources.

So where do schools stand with the use of ICT in education? And if they wish to maintain and grow their investment in technology based resources, how will they finance and manage them?

Growth in adoption

Over the last 20 years schools have progressively adopted technology not just for back office functions and basic communications but increasingly for curriculum delivery. Sceptics claim the case has not been made for the role of ICT for learners, but the benefits have become much clearer over the past five years and increasingly hard to deny. Pupils are more motivated, attention spans increase (especially amongst boys), teachers can tailor a pupil's programme to their specific abilities and needs, learners can be supported outside the classroom as well as during lessons, and pupils are leaving schools with a set of ICT skills that are absolutely vital to the world of work in the 21st century.

And yes, these are skills more important than tidy handwriting and knowing a bit of Latin!

The adoption continues; most schools now offer a wireless environment across the school allowing portable devices to be used as and when they are required rather than having to troop 30 pupils into the ICT Suite. More and more school learning resources are accessed through the VLE with pupils drawing on resources out of school hours and posting their completed assignments online. And children who have difficulties attending school (traveller children, excluded pupils, children with caring responsibilities, sick children, etc) can now participate in their education and school life in a way that would have been thought impossible in the past.

Where will we find the funds?

The government has been very clear that their policy is one of delegation of responsibility to schools. Whether all the funds will also be delegated remains unclear until all the budgets have been announced. In principle though, it will be down to schools to decide whether ICT remains a major area for investment in the curriculum, and at the heart of the school improvement plan.

Our contact with schools suggests that many have already decided that they will remain on the path they embarked on some time ago and are already planning new programmes for September, involving exciting new technologies and 1:1 provision for pupils.

Inconsistent local authority policies on leasing finance have been a barrier to some schools in the past, but with growing independence comes a new generation of savvy business managers who are more comfortable negotiating the lease finance they need to cover assets that will depreciate over the next three years.

In the past, asking parents to help schools provide the pupils with more resources has been an uncomfortable area for many teachers and governors. Yet when those resources are allocated to an individual child, and allowed home, then the case for parental financial involvement becomes stronger.

The e-Learning Foundation (e-learningfoundation.com) helps schools engage with parents in this way, but on a voluntary basis so that no child is excluded because of their family circumstances. The approach also has the advantages of attracting Gift Aid and grants from the Foundation. This "equity model" is in use with over 500 schools and has allowed schools to stretch limited IT budgets up to 6-fold and move from the ICT suite approach to every child having their own device.

Donations from parents vary from £7 to £20 a month depending on the device in use and the period of time the programme runs. Schools are providing laptops, netbooks, and handheld devices like the iPod touch, Smartphones and increasingly the new generation of tablet devices. Pupils respond positively to them and teachers are finding better and better ways of deploying the technology to support learners.

Pressure on headcount

With the new budgets comes pressure to keep headcount numbers down. So any new programme that involves large amounts of administration is inevitably going to raise concerns over who will do the work. The Foundation is able to provide a service called the Donation Management Service that handles all the donation collection work, responds to queries from parents, provides the reports on donations that schools need via a web portal and liaises with the Inland Revenue over the Gift Aid.

Nearly 200 schools now use this service and in a recent survey carried out by the Foundation, nearly half said it had made a "significant difference" to the workload involved in collecting regular donations from parents.

New opportunities

Most children now have good access to a computer and broadband at home. So the concerns that used to be voiced by teachers about deploying technology to complete homework and independent learning are abating. However, the problem has not entirely gone away. About 1 million school-age children still cannot go online at home and whilst that number is steadily reducing it remains an area of concern due to the growing assumptions that all children are now connected to the Internet.

In our survey we asked teachers how they felt pupils were affected by having no access to a computer and the Internet at home. From 486 responses, 43 per cent "agreed strongly" that children were seriously advantaged, and 42 per cent "agreed". The government has expressed concerns about the attainment gap, yet it is being left to schools to address this particular area of educational disadvantage.

The new generation of low-cost portable devices can be purchased by schools, part funded by parents and used by all children for when and where they want to learn i.e. at home, in the classroom, in the after school club and at the child-minders'. The huge total cost of providing and maintaining ICT suites (i.e. the total cost of ownership) becomes more and more difficult to financially justify when compared to 1:1 provision of a device that can be utilised 24/7.

Pupil Premium

As well as the increased delegation of decision-making and budgets to the school level there is the matter of the Pupil Premium. Intended to help schools address the attainment gap amongst children from low income families, some of this funding could be used to address the digital divide and ensure pupils who have poor home access are equipped with the resources they need.

In the survey carried out by the e-Learning Foundation, 29 per cent of the 500 respondents who do not run any form of home access programme said they planned to use some of their Pupil Premium funds to address 1:1 access, whilst that number increased to 51 per cent amongst schools already running a programme.

So is ICT history? The answer has got to be absolutely not, but in the absence of any enthusiasm from the Department for Education, the loss of Becta and a major reduction in local authority advisory services, schools will need to develop their own strategies, learn from the best schools, re-visit policies on leasing and parental contributions and find new sources of expertise, inspiration and support.

Education Business (2014)

Funding

Since the election of the coalition government in May 2010, the role of ICT in education, and the associated funding, has changed dramatically. The extract from *Education Business* explains it in more detail.

E-safeguarding

The Internet is creating new and exciting opportunities for children's learning and creativity. However, whilst there may be significant benefits, schools have a duty of care to safeguard children against the potential risks involved.

E-safeguarding is therefore a major priority for schools. As schools' connectivity to the outside world steadily improves, and the number of sites and systems that can be accessed increases, so does the chance that children may encounter inappropriate materials, meet undesirable people and become subject to cyber-bullying or intimidation.

E-safeguarding covers a number of issues but is essentially about staying safe whilst online and keeping personal information secure. It is an important element of 'digital citizenship' where pupils and teachers are proactive in preventing anti-social behaviour and helping those who might be affected by these issues.

 Activity

The National Education Network (NEN) provide comprehensive guidance on e-safeguarding.
The purpose of the guidance is to highlight procedural areas of importance in e-safeguarding as part of a schools' Safeguarding Policy and to inform individual school's development of a working Acceptable Use Policy (AUP).
You will find a copy of the National Education Network guidance on the Primary ICT website at primaryict. org.uk/icthandbookv2.htm. You will also find two older but nevertheless useful documents 'AUPs in Context' and 'Signposts to Safety'.
The NEN provide a range of e-safety info at nen.gov.uk/esafety.

E-safety audit tools

The National Education Network (NEN) provide a free online tool that can help you with the adoption of good e-safety practice: northerngrid.org/nen/esg_audit.

Useful Internet safety websites

You can't have too much advice on e-safety so here are a few useful links:

- WMnet: wmnet.org.uk/21.cfm?p=293,index&zz=20081117193128939.
- Childnet International: childnet.com (includes their '5 smart rules' plus links to other e-safety websites).
- Childnet knowITall: childnet-int.org/kia (also available on CD-ROM).
- Kidsmart: kidsmart.org.uk.
- Get Safe Online: getsafeonline.org.
- Grid Club Cybercafe: gridclub.com.
- Smart Surfers: smartsurfers.co.uk.
- CEOP: ceop.police.uk (Child Exploitation and Online Protection Centre).
- HGfL: thegrid.org.uk/eservices/safety (Hertfordshire Grid for Learning – e-safety).

- UKCCIS: gov.uk/government/groups/uk-council-for-child-internet-safety-ukccis (The UK Council for Child Internet Safety).

Summary

In summary, here are the key things you need to do to successfully implement ICT in your school:

1. Establish the ICT team and define its task – led by a member of the senior management team and driven by an ICT coordinator.

2. Express your vision for ICT in general terms.

3. Agree roles and responsibilities – delegate to the extended team.

4. Carry out an audit – break it into chunks which cover the key elements – leadership and management, learning and teaching, curriculum, CPD, assessment and resources. Use prepared audit forms.

5. Draw up an ICT Development Plan to bridge the strategic gap. Split it into two or more phases based on priorities and available funding.

6. Document your overall intentions (including the vision) in a school ICT policy – share it with everyone.

7. Create an ICT handbook with helpful guides, policies and procedures (including e-safeguarding).

8. Put your plan into action – continually monitor and review.

The whole process could be achieved in two to three years.

If you wish to gain the Naace ICT Mark then you will need to subscribe to the Self-Review Framework. This could be part of your development plan and should be started during phase 1.

ICT resources

Choosing resources

Technology advances at an ever increasing pace as does the range of available ICT software and hardware. Equipping schools with effective ICT resources can therefore be a daunting prospect and, as part of the ICT strategy for a school, it requires a plan.

Fortunately, most suppliers of ICT equipment are 'in tune' with education and utilise the skills of teachers and other professionals in the design process such that equipment and software is child-friendly and very much meets the needs of the current national curriculum.

With careful evaluation, schools will find a plentiful and ever increasing supply of appropriate and cost-effective resources. In fact, there are now so many options to choose from it can be difficult to know where to begin!

The degree of control over the purchase of resources seems to vary widely between schools. Some are governed by the contracts formed by their local authority whilst others have complete freedom of choice. Most schools will indeed relish the freedom to exercise independent control over their finances. However, it is always worth considering 'aggregate' purchasing by a group of schools or through the local authority (if such systems are in place). Aggregate purchasing does potentially offer a discount and may also provide schools with reassurance when it comes to trickier matters such as network infrastructure and Internet connectivity. On the down side however, it may also mean that schools don't get exactly the resources they want and therefore there may need to be a trade-off between bulk buying and individual purchases.

Assuming that you do have a say in the matter then how would you choose your core ICT resources? Here's one possible approach:

1. Establish an all-round staff awareness of the 'types' of resources available and their possible benefits. This is primarily the responsibility of the ICT coordinator. Remember, it isn't just about software, there are many other resources. Note that specific products and software titles should not be considered at this stage.

    This is often a gradual process and can be done in a number of ways: exhibitions, training, team teaching, observations, liaison with other schools and leading by example. The ICT coordinator and subject leaders must be key to this process and NQTs will undoubtedly have an awareness of a range of contemporary products. The list of common resources (below) may help.

2. Draw up a shortlist of your general requirements. You might ask staff to place bids with a stated level of importance for each item (e.g. essential, important and desirable). Involving staff in this way promotes ownership and you are less likely to overlook something.

3. Prioritise the shortlist. Essential items will take precedence as will the most cost-effective items and items that serve more than one function (learning, teaching and administration) or more than one curriculum subject.

4. Allocate your ICT budget. If it won't stretch far enough you may need to further filter your shortlist. In doing so you might give special consideration to:

    ■ resources that benefit whole class teaching (for example, interactive whiteboards, content free software, digital cameras and office applications);

    ■ whether core subjects should be allocated more funding;

    ■ whether funding is weighted or spread evenly across the year groups;

    ■ giving priority to versatile resources (for example, resources that can be used across the curriculum, resources that can be shared between classes etc.).

5. Now look at specific products and cost them. Again, revise the list to suit your budget if necessary. You can spread the cost over time and phase in resources in accordance with your ICT development plan and budgeting cycle. Don't forget that there are many free resources to be found (see the list of useful websites in Appendix 3) and open source software (see the section on Open Source Software).

6. Evaluate each item to assure its suitability (see the section on Evaluating resources).

Common resources used in schools

Table 12.1 Common resources in schools

2D/3D plotter	Language software
A4 scanner	Laptop computer
A3 scanner	Large screen display
Apps	Learning platform
Assessment creation software	Microphone
Atlas/Maps on CD	Management Information System (MIS)
Audio CDs	Multimedia authoring software
Augmentative communication aid	Multi-sensory equipment
Automatic weather station	Musical keyboard
Braille Notetaker	Netbook
Branching database	Network (cable/wireless/hybrid)
Browser	Online resources
Calculator	OCR software
CD-ROM	Overlay keyboard
Clipart	Painting/retouching software
Cloze software	Palmtop (PDA)
Computer	Pattern sequencing software
Computer game	Phonics software
Concept keyboard	Photocopier
Concept mapping software	Podcasting/vidcasting software
Content free software	Presentation software
Content rich software	Printer
Control software	Programming software
Course authoring software	Programmable toy

Data–logging system

Data projector (and loudspeakers)

Database

Desktop publishing software

Dictionary software

Digital book

Digital camera

Digital effects unit

Digital microscope

Digital notetaker

Digital pen

Digital recorder/player (mp3/mp4)

Digital video camera

Document camera

Drawing packages (inc CAD)

DVD/CD writer

Dyscalculia software

Dyslexia software

Email program

eBook

Encyclopaedia software

E-portfolio

Ergonomic keyboard/mouse

Floor robot

Gaming console

Gifted and talented software

Global positioning system (GPS)

Graphic calculator

Graphics tablet

Handheld PC for blind pupils

Heart rate monitor

Image production and editing

Integrated learning system

Interactive voting system

Interactive whiteboard

iPad (inc iPad Mini)/iPhone/iPod

Keyboard

Keyboard glove

Reading pen

Reading ruler

Role play equipment

Rollerball mouse

Scanner

Screen reading software

Self-evaluation framework (SEF) software

Signing software

Simulation package

Social/life skills software

Software toolkit (suite of programs)

Sound production/editing software

Smartphone

Sound system

Specialist keyboards

Spreadsheet

Stopwatch/digital timer

Subscription website

Switch

Symbol software

Tablet PC

Talking word processor

Tape recorder

Television

Timing mat

Touch screen

Touch typing software

Turtle software

Video conferencing system

Video editing software

Visualiser

Virtual learning environment (VLE)

Voice output communication aid (VOCA)

Voice recognition software

Web authoring software

Webcam

Word processing software

Your final decision about the actual products to be purchased will be influenced by the particular needs of your school and, above all, the school's vision for ICT. There should be a clear link between the purchase of resources and learning benefits for pupils. If your staff have a choice in the selection of resources then they will be more likely to use them.

This chapter does not recommend specific products because there are so many to choose from. It is better that schools familiarise themselves with the resources on offer and select resources which best match their own needs.

Evaluating resources

Evaluating resources before committing to buy is a sensible thing to do. It may seem tedious yet it could save you a good deal of money and lots of frustration too. If you buy something that's unsuitable you'll need to go through the procurement process again!

The easiest approach to evaluation is to get someone else to do it for you. You might for example get a good recommendation from a colleague or consult with other schools to see if any of them are using your intended resources to good effect. They may be willing to loan resources to you or agree to share the cost of purchase whilst you jointly carry out trials (lending libraries may well loan software too).

Commercial suppliers will provide overviews of their products and, whilst they will have an obvious bias, you can still learn much about the product from them. They may be willing to provide you with evaluation copies of software, particularly if you become a regular customer. However, don't put all your eggs in one basket; there are many suppliers and lots of products to choose from.

You should always pay a visit to the TEEM website (Teachers Evaluating Educational Multimedia) at teemeducation.org.uk. This will certainly help you to choose suitable software, CD-ROMs and Internet-based resources. There are a number of other sites which also provide evaluation including Schoolzone (schoolzone.co.uk/evaluations).

Whatever else you do, you should always perform your own evaluation if possible. Draw up a set of criteria which your resources must satisfy. There will be several general criteria and some which are peculiar to your own school. The criteria will include pedagogical and design principles:

- **Pedagogic principles**: those that underpin effective learning and teaching, drawing from learning theory and commonly accepted best practice. They include: Match to the Curriculum, Inclusion and Access, Learner Engagement, Effective Learning, Assessment, Ease of Use and Innovation.

- **Design principles**: covering issues such as resource design, accessibility and interoperability. They include: good design, robustness, interaction, quality of assets, accessibility, interoperability, effective communication and pre-testing.

 Activity

Link to the Primary ICT website at primaryict.org.uk/icthandbookv2.htm and read the Becta documents entitled 'Choosing Digital Resources' and 'Quality principle for digital learning resources'.
These are excellent documents which provide thorough and detailed guidance in choosing all types of digital resource.

To help you there are some simple evaluation templates in Appendix 5 which you can modify to your own requirements if you wish.

Suppliers

BETT

There are hundreds of suppliers of ICT resources to choose from and, if you've ever visited the BETT exhibition, you'll already have an idea who the big players are. For a full list of the exhibitors to their most recent show, visit bettshow.com.

BESA

BESA is a trade association (they currently sponsor BETT). They don't sell resources themselves but they provide information about their 300+ member companies who provide ICT resources across the curriculum at all levels from early years upwards. BESA members adhere to a code of practice which ensures that they are reputable providers of quality products. To find members and products, visit BESA at besa.org.uk.

Regular suppliers

Appendix 4 lists many of the regular suppliers.

Managing resources

Total cost of ownership (TCO)

As with all other elements of management, the purchasing, review and updating of ICT resources should be part and parcel of the management cycle. You will need to keep a record of the costs of your current assets and those you intend purchasing in the future (in accordance with your ICT development plan). These costs will include the cost to acquire resources (including software licensing fees), running and maintenance costs (including technical support), Internet connection charges and consumables. This is referred to as the total cost of ownership (TCO) and it is something you will be required to do if you wish to obtain the Naace ICT Mark.

If you haven't already done so then you should carry out an audit to determine your current holdings and draw up an inventory. A spreadsheet would be ideal because you will need to perform some simple calculations.

Forecasting costs over a period of several years (known as long-term costing) will provide a good illustration of the future ICT needs of the school. It will allow you to build in depreciation (in terms of cost, changes to the curriculum, and developments in technology) so that you can see when each of the resources will need to be replaced or upgraded. It will also give you some indication as to how meaningful your medium- and long-term development plans are.

Software licensing

Software licensing is quite simple but it can easily catch you out if you are not particularly careful and the penalties if you are prosecuted for being under-licensed can be quite harsh. In general terms you need to be licensed for each machine onto which your software title is installed. You can buy single, multiple or site licences.

The licence will contain a set of rules governing the usage of the software. This is called the end user licence agreement (EULA). The EULA will vary from one manufacturer to another. Some will allow a backup copy of the CD-ROM to be made and some will allow software to be installed on staff machines in their office and/or at home without paying for additional licences. You need to read the EULA carefully.

Store the licences safely and document the number of licences you hold and which of your machines the software is loaded on (this information could be part of your software inventory). You are allowed to uninstall from one machine and re-install onto another but ensure that you update your paperwork if you do. If you hold site licences then make sure you are adhering to the definition of site. It may be that your school has a hybrid network which serves more than one building and perhaps in more than one location. Make sure that you are covered. Site licensing is probably the safest bet but you may not need, or be able to afford, this option for all the titles you require.

Some software is paid for by annual subscription. You need to ensure that you renew your subscription each year. If your subscription is paid automatically (perhaps by your budget holder or bursar) then make sure that you still use it. If not, cancel the subscription and save yourself a pile of money.

Finally, an obvious statement perhaps, but don't use illegal software – and if you happen to download what you believe to be free software then copy or print the copyright information and store it with your licensing records.

You may have placed the management of your ICT infrastructure in the hands of an ICT service provider, in which case licensing, and other issues will be their responsibility.

Open source software

There are many thousands of free software programs available for download. The term 'free' can be quite misleading. Some free packages may come with strings attached. For example, you are offered a basic package for free but need to spend money if you elect to buy the 'premium' version or if you wish to upgrade to the next version when it comes along. The only truly free software is 'open source' because it not only comes free of charge, it also gives you complete freedom to do with it what you wish.

What is open source software?

An open source software (OSS) program is a free package which allows its users not only to run the program but also to modify it and to redistribute copies without having to pay royalties to its developers.

For some time now we have become conditioned to using proprietary software, particularly the very familiar packages like MS Office. For many they provide a comfort zone – they have always used them (as does everyone else), there's plenty of training available and lots of books written about them. With many commercial packages you also buy into valuable support. Many large organisations, including schools, will automatically upgrade to the latest version of Microsoft (and other products) without a second thought and staff, particularly administrators, may be reluctant to make a change. But is it time to start thinking outside the box?

Why use open source software?

The most obvious answer to this question is 'because it's free' and, unlike other 'free' products, it comes with no strings attached. In addition you can access the source code. This means that, unlike commercial packages which allow you only to run the compiled code, you can get into the original instructions and make modifications in order to adapt the software to your own needs. The sceptic in most of us will naturally question why anyone would want to spend time developing programs in order to provide us with free software! Well that's a debate in itself and you may wish to research it in more detail yourself.

Suffice to say, however, that OSS software is on the rise and certainly here to stay. A very good example is MOODLE, a free OSS virtual learning environment (VLE) which has been around for several years and is now used as the VLE of choice by many universities, colleges and schools.

Obtaining a free software package is all well and good but this amounts to little unless it is comparable (or better) than its commercial counterparts. There are now many claims that, for some OSS packages, this is indeed the case and, whilst there are obviously many sceptics, here are some of the advantages together with answers to some of the concerns.

Advantages

- **Lower software costs**. Open source solutions generally require no licensing fees. The logical extension is no maintenance fees. The only expenditures are for media, documentation and support, if required.

- **Simplified license management**. Obtain the software once and install it as many times and in as many locations as you need. There's no need to count, track, or monitor for license compliance.

- **Lower hardware costs**. In general, Linux and open source solutions are elegantly compact and portable, and as a result require less hardware power to accomplish the same tasks as on conventional servers (e.g. Windows or Solaris) or workstations. The result is you can get by with less expensive or older hardware.

- **Total cost of ownership**. Some schools argue that using OSS software brings down the total cost of ownership (TCO) for ICT.

- **Scaling/consolidation potential**. Again, Linux and open source applications and services can often scale considerably. Multiple options for load balancing, clustering, and open source applications, such as database and email, give organisations the ability to scale up for new growth or consolidate to do more with less.

- **Ample support**. Support is available for most open source software and is often superior to proprietary solutions. It is freely available and accessible through online communities via the Internet and conventional user groups. These communities can be an important part of the education process because they promote a sense of ownership and participation and tie in closely with the philosophy of social constructivism/social constructionism.

- **Escape vendor lock-in**. Frustration with vendor lock-in is a reality for all IT managers. In addition to ongoing license fees, there is lack of portability and the inability to customise software to meet specific needs. Open source exists as a declaration of freedom of choice.

- **Quality software**. Evidence and research indicate that open source software is good stuff. The peer review process and community standards, plus the fact that source code is out there for the world to see, tend to drive excellence in design and efficiency in coding. The freedom to modify source code results in more frequent updates.

- **Adaptability**. The code can be modified such that the program will do exactly what you want it to and will look exactly how you want it to look (the code can also be re-distributed and shared with the community which uses it).

- **Security**. OSS is less vulnerable to viruses because attacks are primarily aimed at large commercial companies (e.g. Microsoft).

Concerns

- **Open source isn't really free**. 'Free, as in a free puppy' is the adage meaning no up-front costs, but plenty (often unseen or unanticipated) afterward. However, implementation, administration, and support costs can be minimised and if you choose to pay for such services then, on balance, you are still likely to make significant savings.

- **There's no service and support**. Newer OSS packages may need time for support services to grow but for many OSS packages, support is equal to that available for proprietary software and is available for the same price or less.

- **Development resources are scarce.** Linux and open source resources are actually abundant; the developers can use the same tools, languages, and code management processes. In reality, the universe of developers is the largest of any segment. And, with the evolution of Mono (the open source equivalent to .NET), all of those Windows/.NET developers become an added development resource for Linux.

- **Open source is not secure**. It might seem to be a simple deduction of logic to think that the code is available, so anyone can figure out how to break it. That's not quite true with the momentum of the community (especially Linux). Also, the modularity required for distributed development of Linux and open source also contributes to security with tight, function-specific and isolated code segments.

- **Training is not available**. This used to be true, but not anymore. Available Linux training, for example, has ballooned with certification courses coming from every major training vendor. Training businesses have grown around OSS software, particularly the longer established products such as MOODLE.

- **All open source is a work-in-progress**. True for some, but not for all. Many of the available products are stable, secure, and well developed. Some open source offerings are still maturing, but they are nevertheless workable, and for the companies that use them (with access to source code), the software is good enough.

There are already plenty of schools that are using (or trialling) OSS software and, in particular, the Linux (operating system), Open Office (a complete suite of office packages), Firefox (web browser), Apache (web server), PHP (scripting language), MySQL (database) and several curriculum-based packages too.

Open source packages

This section outlines some of the open source software already available for free download. Many of these are tried and tested packages with a good reputation and adequate support.

- *Apache* – An HTTP web server which can be used as a local server when testing websites that incorporate scripts and MySQL databases.

- *Audacity* – Cross-platform software for creating and editing sound. Great for podcast!

- *Blender* – 3D computer graphics software for creating animated films, visual effects, interactive 3D applications and video games.

- *Blueberry Flashback* – Can record all computer screen activity, webcam activity and sound.

- *CamStudio* – Can record all computer screen and sound audio activity on your computer and create industry standard AVI video files and streaming flash videos. Use it to create demonstration videos for teaching and for training.

- *CarMetal* – Cool mathematical modelling tool.

- *Celestia* – A real time 3D space simulation featuring a database of over 100,000 stars and nearly 100 solar system objects.

- *Celtx* – Media pre-production software for creating and organising media projects such as videos, films, comics, games and podcasts.

- *Dia* – Can be used to draw many different kinds of diagrams including flowcharts, network diagrams and many others.

- *Drupal* – A content management system that offers blogs, forums and social networking. Other packages include Elgg, Pligg, NewsCloud, Mugshot and AroundMe.

- *Edubuntu* – A more user-friendly derivative of Linux.

- *Firefox* – Commonly used open source web browser.

- *FreeCiv* – An empire-building strategy game. Lead your tribe from the Stone Age to the space age.

- *FreeMind* – A mind-mapping application allowing the user to create a hierarchical set of ideas around a central concept.

- *GanttProject* – Fully fledged project management software.

- *GCompris* – An educational software suite with over 100 activities for children aged 2–10.

- *Geogebra* – Interactive graphics, algebra and spreadsheet for primary school to university level.

- *Gimp* – An image editing program that compares favourably with commercial products such as Photoshop and PaintShop Pro.

- *GnuCash* – An accounting software program that implements a double-entry book keeping system.

- *GraphCalc* – An all-in-one solution to everything from everyday arithmetic to statistics.

- *InkScape* – A vector graphics editor similar to Illustrator or CorelDraw.

- *Joomla* – A content management system that puts non-technical users in charge of content.

- *KompoZer* – A WYSIWYG HTML editor similar to Dreamweaver.

- *LibreOffice* – An office/productivity suite containing Writer, Calc, Impress, Draw, Math and Base.

- *Linux* – An operating system. Most commonly used on servers but can be used on PCs and local area networks.

- *Mahara* – An e-portfolio system.

- *Marble* – A virtual globe and world atlas.

- *Moodle* – A very widely used virtual learning environment.

- *MuseScore* – Create, play back and print beautiful sheet music.

- *MySQL* – The world's most popular SQL database.

- *NASA Worldwind* – Discover the earth and other planets.

- *Numpty Physics* – A cross-platform application that supports problem solving and understanding the nature of forces.

- *Ooo4Kids* – Office software suite for kids aged 7–12.

- *Open Office* – An office suite that's every bit as good as MS Office.

- *Pencil*– 2D graphical animation software.

- *PHP* – A widely used server side scripting language.

- *Piano Booster* – Plays standard Midi files and allows you to change the speed of playback, transpose the music etc.

- *RSSOwl* – Allows you to organise, search and read all your RSS feeds in a comfortable way.

- *Scratch* – A graphical programming tool for young children.

- *Scribus* – A desktop publishing application. Competes well with commercial applications such as Abobe Pagemaker and QuarkXPress.

- *Stellarium* – A planetarium for your computer.

- *TCExam* – TCExam is an open source computer-based assessment (CBA) software system that enables educators to author, schedule, deliver and report on surveys, quizzes, tests and exams.

- *TuxGuitar* – A multi-track guitar tablature to practise and record music.

- *TuxMath* – An arcade style video game for learning arithmetic.

- *TuxPaint* – Helps children learn how to draw.

- *TuxTyping* – A touch typing program to help improve skill and speed on a computer keyboard.

- **VLC Media Player** – A cross-platform multimedia player that plays most file types including DVD, Audio CD, VCD and various streaming protocols.
- **Wordpress** – A blogging environment.
- **Xerte** – A suite of powerful tools for the rapid creation of e-learning content. Developed by Nottingham University, it provides a visual, icon-based authoring environment.

Creative commons

Creative Commons is a non-profit organisation that enables the sharing and use of creativity and knowledge through free legal tools. There are many instances of images, website code (HTML, css, JavaScript etc.) and other items that you can use free of charge. They usually require some form of acknowledgement but otherwise there is no cost.

Resource guides

If you are the ICT coordinator or you have an interest in technology then you may well know exactly what ICT resources the school holds, where to find them and how they can be used. However, this will not hold true for all staff, particularly new teachers or supply teachers.

It's a good idea therefore to produce ICT resource guides for each subject. These will list the resources you hold for the subject together with a brief overview/evaluation of each.

Appendix 1
Answers to programming activities

Activity (p. 23)

Can you list the logo instructions to trace out:

1. An equilateral triangle
2. A hexagon
3. A circle?

Answer:

1. FD 100, RT 120, FD 100, RT 120, FD 100.
2. FD 100, RT 60, FD 100, RT 60, FD 100, RT 60, FD 100, RT 60, FD 100, RT 60, FD 100
3. This one is a little tricky. A circle can be traced by moving a very short distance and then turning through a small angle. For example:
   FD 1, RT 1 repeated 360 times
   This would take time to type into the computer but you can save time by using the repeat command:
   REPEAT 360 [FD 1, RT 1]

Activity (p. 26)

What do you think the following instructions achieve?
    REPEAT 36 [LT 5, FD 50, RT 10, FD 50, RT 170, FD 50, RT 10, FD 50, RT 10]

Answer:

You can split the instructions into chunks:

1. LT 5 FD 50, RT 10, FD 50, RT 170, FD 50, RT 10, FD 50.
   If you trace this out with a pencil it creates a vertical petal shape.
2. *RT 10*. This turns the turtle 10° to the right.
3. REPEAT 36 [ ]. This repeats steps 1 and 2 to create a flower shape.

Activity (p. 28)

Can you find the Logo commands that will perform each of the following?

1. Clear the screen
2. Change the pen colour
3. Lift the pen up
4. Put the pen down

Answer:

1. clearscreen
2. setpencolour x (where x is a number between 0 and 15)
3. penup
4. pendown

Activity (p. 31)

Try this out on your pupils.

1. Place the following instructions for making toast into the correct order.
   - Remove toast from toaster
   - Wait 2 minutes
   - Start
   - Put bread into toaster
   - Stop
   - Push down handle
2. Convert the result into a flowchart.
3. Add a 'decision' to the flowchart to check whether the toast is ready at regular intervals.

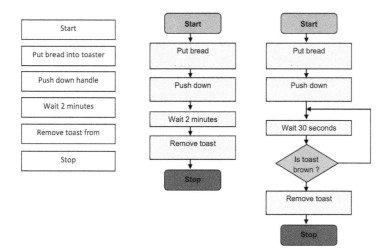

Appendix 2
Logo challenges

First, a reminder of some of the commands:

- **FD** forward
- **BK** backward
- **LT** left
- **RT** right
- **PU** pen up
- **PD** pen down
- **HT** hide turtle
- **ST** show turtle
- **CS** clear screen
- **CT** clear text

Challenge 1

1. What does the following program achieve?
   REPEAT 5 [FD 100 RT 72]   (Try it out in FMSLogo)

2. Now write programs to create:

   - A pentagon
   - An isosoles triangle
   - A rectangle
   - Your initials   (Try them out in FMSLogo)

Challenge 2

Can you write a Logo program to draw the 5-square below?

Challenge 3

Now that you have seen how easy it is to draw squares, triangles, pentagons, hexagon, heptagons etc., let us use these shapes as basic units of a pattern.

Why not repeat what you have already repeated!

Imagine:

Drawing a square (Say, REPEAT 4 [FD 50 RT 90])

Now turn 30° left.

Draw another square.

Now turn another 30°.

Draw another square.

Now turn another 30°.

Draw another square.

Now turn another 30° and so on until you get back to where you started.

Now this is really: REPEAT 12 [REPEAT 4 [FD 50 RT 90] LT 30] (hint: 12 x 30 is 360)

Why not experiment with other turns, other sizes, other shapes etc?

You might also want to experiment with changing the colour of your pen:

SET PENCOLOUR (abbreviation SETPC). You need to tell this primitive how much

[Red, Green, Blue] to mix to make your pencolour.

Try SETPC[255 0 0] – and start drawing. Was it what you expected?

N.B. 255 is the largest amount of any colour you can use.

SHOW PC tells you what pencolour you are using.

Challenge 4

This challenge introduces the idea of a procedure (function). Procedures allow you to save instructions in LOGO, creating procedures of your own, which you can use elsewhere. Programs can be built from a sequence of procedures. Once you have "taught" LOGO what the word "PATTERN" means – it will remember what to do whenever you type in "PATTERN". Providing you save your procedure at the end of your session you can call it up again the next time you wish to use it, perhaps as just part of a larger program.

Consider the following procedure:

```
TO PATTERN
REPEAT 12 [PU FD 60 PD REPEAT 4 [FD 45 RT 90] PU BK 60 LT 30]
END
```

What do you think is happening?

The command PU means Pen Up and PD means Pen Down.

Try tracing out the instructions step by step:

- You have something to do – 12 times!

- In doing that something you have to repeat something else 4 times!

Type in the procedure and run it. Were you right? Now, try changing different parts of the procedure. Can you anticipate what is going to happen to your diagram?

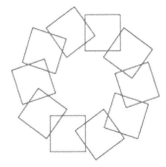

Challenge 5

You have already created a circle using the instructions:

    REPEAT 360 [FD 1 RT 1]

Now experiment with:

- a different number of REPEATS

- going BACKWARD instead of FORWARD

- increasing/decreasing the amount moved

- going LEFT instead of RIGHT

- increasing/decreasing the amount turned.

You might then like to try to replicate the patterns below.

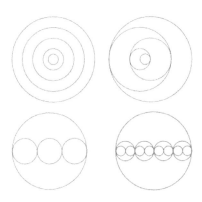

Challenge 6

Consider the following procedure:

```
TO PATTERN: SIZE
REPEAT 5 [FD: SIZE RT 144]
END
```

What is different about this procedure?
Yes, it has a name (PATTERN) but it also has :SIZE
SIZE is called a VARIABLE.
What does the word variable suggest to you?
Now create the procedure and then type the following on the command line:

1. PATTERN 30

2. PATTERN 60

3. PATTERN 120

Experiment with different numbers for yourself and see what patterns you can produce.
Are you feeling happier with the idea of a variable? If so, why not explore further this idea of using a variable in those procedures you have met previously.

```
TO SQUARE: SIZE
REPEAT 4 [FD: SIZE RT 90]
END      (create the procedure then type SQUARE:10 on the command line)
TO HEXAGON: S
REPEAT 6 [FD: S RT 60]
END      (create the procedure then type HEXAGON:100 on the command line)
```

Challenge 7

You created a circle using REPEAT 360 [FD 1, RT 1]
You may find the following procedure a quicker way of drawing circles and circular patterns.

```
TO CIRCLE: STEP
REPEAT 360 [FD: STEP RT 1]
END
```

N.B. you could name the variable STEP with any letter or letters that you wish!
Now experiment with the procedure:

CIRCLE 3
CIRCLE 6
CIRCLE –3
CIRCLE 9

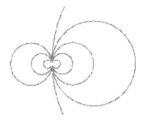

Building on this idea of a procedure we could have written:

TO CIRC: STEP: ANG
REPEAT 360 [FD :STEP RT :ANG]
END

This is a procedure with two variables! (If your procedure doesn't work it may be that you have missed a space or you have a space where there shouldn't be one)
Can you anticipate what will change and what will happen now?
Can you see what is now possible?
Go on experiment!
Try:

CIRC 3 3
CIRC 3 6
CIRC 3 30

What is happening?
Why not be bolder and try:

CIRC 30 90
CIRC 30 45
CIRC 30 18 etc., etc.,

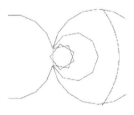

What do you notice?
What conclusions can you come to?

Challenge 8

In challenge 7 you considered and explored the following procedures:

TO CIRCLE: STEP
REPEAT 360 [FD: STEP RT 1]
END
TO CIRC: STEP: ANG
REPEAT 360 [FD: STEP RT: ANG]
END

As a consequence, different sized circles and some polygons may have resulted. Did you manage to draw a heptagon (7-sided)? A nonagon (9-sided)? A hendecagon (11-sided) etc?

Imagine walking around the outside of a pentagon, as you: go forward then turn, go forward then turn, go forward then turn, go forward then turn, ... finally go forward then turn. You should be back where you started ... go on try it, convince yourself. In your journey you should have turned through 360°.

Five times you turned through 72°. N.B. 5 x 72 = 360.

Hence:

For a pentagon – REPEAT 5 [FD 45 RT 360/5]

For a heptagon – REPEAT 7 [FD 45 RT 360/7]

For a nonagon – REPEAT 9 [FD 45 RT 360/9]

See the pattern?

POLY 7 25
POLY 9 45
POLY 11 35
POLY 13 25

So why not experiment?
Go on try:

TO POLY: N
REPEAT: N [FD 45 RT 360/:N]
END

Then try:

TO POLY:N :M
REPEAT:N [FD :M RT 360/:N]
END

Challenge 9

In challenge 8 you looked at the following procedures and were invited to alter them at your leisure:

```
TO POLY:N
REPEAT:N [FD 45 RT 360/:N]
END
```

```
TO POLY:N :M
REPEAT:N [FD :M RT 360/:N]
END
```

Now … two activities:

 Activity one:

Consider REPEAT 5 [FD 100 RT 144] … what do you think this means? Try to imagine what is happening before entering the procedure into the computer. Imagine being the 'turtle' that creates the graphic … how many times does it turn? Through how many degrees has it turned when it has finished the procedure?

 Activity two:

Consider the procedure below. What do you think is happening? Talk through with your friends what you think the procedure is all about. Only then enter it into the computer and experiment with it.

```
TO GAZE: M: N
REPEAT: N [FD:M LT 720/:N]
END
```

Try GAZE 100 5;
GAZE 120 7;
GAZE 200 9;
GAZE 50 8 (Beware maybe not what you think!)
Okay then what about GAZE 150 12?
GAZE 250 16?

Alternatively, you might like to write a procedure for any of these shapes. Walk them first – either in your mind, using paper and pencil or in the playground.

You might also be interested in how the shapes were filled with colour.

This needs two new commands:

SETFLOODCOLOUR [:red :green :blue].

This works in a similar way to SETPC described in challenge 3.

FILL

This is the command that you use to fill your shape with the "Flood Colour".

One word of warning – you have to be inside the shape to fill it!

Challenge 10

Count Up – Count Down

WARNING – You may need to click "Halt" to stop some of these procedures! The WAIT command simply pauses the program so that you have time to see the output.

You might like to begin by thinking about two procedures:

```
TO COUNTUP: X
PR: X
WAIT 50
COUNTUP: X + 3
END
```

Try COUNTUP 2

```
TO COUNTDOWN: X
PR: X
WAIT 50
COUNTDOWN: X – 2
END
```

Try COUNTDOWN 189

As before, discuss with others and try evaluating the procedures BEFORE copying them out and experimenting further.

Now, here are two more procedures you might like to think about:

```
TO FAC: X: A
PR: A
WAIT 50
FAC: X + 1 :X ★ :A
END
```

Try FAC 11

```
TO MULTI: X: A
PR: A
WAIT 50
MULTI:X: X + :A
END
```

Try MULTI 2 0; MULTI 2 1 … etc.

Try programming some sequences of numbers for yourself.

Appendix 3
Useful ICT websites

This appendix offers some useful web links on a range of ICT issues.

There is no guarantee that these links will remain stable though you can usually find your way from the root of the site if the full path doesn't work.

Curriculum resources and activities

For subject specific websites refer also to the relevant section(s) of Chapters 6–8.

Alice: alice.org. Computer programming software.

ARKive: arkive.org At School: atschool.co.uk.

BBC Education: bbc.co.uk/education. BBC resources for students and teachers.

BBC Inter-faith Calendar: bbc.co.uk/religion/tools/calendar.

BBC Languages: bbc.co.uk/languages.

BBC Schools: bbc.co.uk/schools.

British Association of Advisers and Lecturers in PE: baalpe.org.

CBeebies: bbc.co.uk/Cbeebies.

CBeebies Stories: bbc.co.uk/cbeebies/stories.

Channel 4 Learning: channel4learning.com.

Classroom Video: classroomvideo.co.uk/free-resources/free-ict-resources.html.

Code Academy: codecademy.com. Learn to code interactively for free.

Count On: counton.org. Games and resources.

Crickweb: crickweb.co.uk. Free educational resources and games.

Dictionaries: dictionary.com, yourdictionary.com, pdictionary.com Eco Schools: eco-schools.org.uk.

Digimap for Schools: digimapforschools.edina.ac.uk.

Edublogs: edublogs.org. Educational blogging service.

Elica: elica.net. Logo implementation.

Fact Monster: factmonster.com.

First School Years: firstschoolyears.com.

Free Teaching Resources: free-teaching-resources.co.uk.

Funbrain: funbrain.com.

Geographical Association: geography.org.uk/eyprimary.

Good Night Stories: goodnightstories.com.

Google Earth: earth.google.co.uk.

Happy Fun Coding: happyfuncoding.com (open using Firefox or Chrome, *not* I.E.).

History on the Net: historyonthenet.com.

Horrible Histories: horrible-histories.co.uk.

Hubbard's Cupboard: hubbardscupboard.org.

I Can Teach: icanteach.co.uk. Teaching resources.

ICT Games: ictgames.com.

ICT Skills Workshop: www.skillsworkshop.org/ict.

Institute of Historical Research: history.ac.uk.

Just Basic Programming: justbasic.com.

Kizclub: kizclub.com. Learning resources for kids.

Kodu Programming: research.microsoft.com/en-us/projects/kodu.

Learn English Kids: learnenglishkids.britishcouncil.org. Lots of free online games, songs, stories and activities for children to have fun and learn English too.

Learn ICT: learn-ict.org.uk.

Learn Spanish: studyspanish.com/travel.

Learning Alive: eduweb.co.uk.

Learnwise: learnwiseesolcentre.co.uk.

Lego Education: education.lego.com.

Lifelong Kindergarten: llk.media.mit.edu.

Lingu@net Worldwide: linguanet-europa.org.

Maths Zone: mathszone.co.uk.

MathSphere: mathsphere.co.uk.

Method Behind the Music: method-behind-the-music.com/piano.

Microworlds: microworlds.com. Create science simulations, mathematical experiments etc.

Musescore: musescore.org.

MyMaths: mymaths.co.uk.

Naace Primary: primary.naace.co.uk.

National Association for Pastoral Care in Education: napce.org.uk.

National Geographic (Education): education.nationalgeographic.com/education.

National Geographic (Kids.): kids.nationalgeographic.com.

Natural England: naturalareas.naturalengland.org.uk/Science/natural/NA_search.asp.

Notepad++: notepad-plus-plus.org.

Nrich Maths: nrich.maths.org.uk.

Nuffield Primary History: primaryhistory.org.

Numeracy World: numeracyworld.com.

Parapal Online: parapal-online.co.uk.

Pearson Primary: pearsonschoolsandfecolleges.co.uk/Primary.

Planet Science: planet-science.com.

Primary Blogger: primaryblogger.co.uk.

Primary Classroom Resources: primaryclassroomresources.co.uk.

Primary Games: primarygames.co.uk.

Primary Homework Help: primaryhomeworkhelp.co.uk.

Primary Interactive: primaryinteractive.co.uk.

Primary Resources: primaryresources.co.uk.

Primary Stuff: primarystuff.co.uk.

Primary Worksheets: primaryworksheets.co.uk.

Raspberry pi: raspberrypi.org. Credit-card sized computer.

RE Today: retoday.org.uk.

REonline: reonline.org.uk.

Revisionstation: revisionstation.co.uk.

RM Learning Alive: eduweb.co.uk

Ruby Programming: kidsruby.com.

Scholastic Interactive Stories: teacher.scholastic.com/clifford1.

School Express: schoolexpress.com.

School History: schoolhistory.co.uk.

School Zone: schoolzone.co.uk.

SchoolsNet: schoolsnet.com.

Science Clips: bbc.co.uk/schools/scienceclips.

Science Learning Centres: https://www.sciencelearningcentres.org.uk.

Science Made Simple: sciencemadesimple.com.

Scratch programming: scratch.mit.edu.

Sebastian Swan Stories: sebastianswan.org.uk.

Shapes of Time: shapesoftime.net.

Simple Codeworks: simplecodeworks.com Simple Modular Programming.

Skillswise: bbc.co.uk/skillswise/maths. English and Maths.

Sport England: https://www.sportengland.org.

Starfall Learn to Read: starfall.com/n/level-a/learn-to-read/play.htm.

Teachfind: http://webarchive.nationalarchives.gov.uk/20131216163513/http://www.teachfind.com.

Teach ICT: teach-ict.com.

Teachers Media: teachersmedia.co.uk. CPD provider and access to Teacher's TV videos.

Teaching and Learning Resources: teachingandlearningresources.co.uk/funscience.shtml.

Teaching Ideas: teachingideas.co.uk

TeachingPets: teachingpets.co.uk.

Terrapin Logo: terrapinlogo.com.Logo programming.

TES Connect: tes.co.uk/teaching-resources.

The Association for Teaching Citizenship: teachingcitizenship.org.uk.

The Guardian Teacher Network: theguardian.com/teacher-network.

The Historical Association: history.org.uk/resources/resources.html.

The Music Land: themusicland.co.uk.

Time to Teach: timetoteach.co.uk.

Wellbourne Primary: welbourneprimary.com/links/ict/ict_links.htm

World Book Day: www.worldbookday.com.

World E-Citizens: worldecitizens.net.

World Religions: uri.org/kids/world.htm.

Youth Sports Trust: http://www.youthsporttrust.org.

★ *See also: icanteach.co.uk/resources/a-to-z-listing for a list of links to resources.*

Information (including lead bodies)

Ask Kids: sp.askkids.com/docs/askkids. Search engine tailored to find child-friendly sites.

Association for Citizenship Teaching: teachingcitizenship.org.uk.

Awesome Library: awesomelibrary.org. Over 14,000 librarian-reviewed resources for kids.

Barefoot Computing: barefootcas.org.uk. The Barefoot Computing project is helping primary school teachers get ready for the computer science element of the new computing curriculum.

BBC Schools: bbc.co.uk/schools.

BESA: (British Educational Suppliers Association) besa.org.uk.

BETT: bettshow.com.

British Council – Teaching English: teachingenglish.org.uk.

Collins Education: collinseducation.com.

Computing at School: computingatschool.org.uk. Promoting excellence in computing education.

Curriculum (EYFS, post-2014): gov.uk/government/publications/early-years-foundation-stage-framework--2.

Curriculum (EYFS, pre-2014): webarchive.nationalarchives.gov.uk/20110809091832/http://teachingandlearningresources.org.uk/early-years.

Curriculum (National, post-2014): www.gov.uk/government/collections/national-curriculum.

Curriculum (National, pre-2014): webarchive.nationalarchives.gov.uk/20131202172639/http://www.education.gov.uk/schools/teachingandlearning/curriculum/primary.

Dep. for Education: gov.uk/government/organisations/department-for-education.

Design and Technology Association: data.org.uk/for-education/primary.

Dictionaries: dictionary.com, yourdictionary.com, bigiqkids.com/spellingwords/onlinedictionary.shtml, pdictionary.com, wordsmyth.net.

DirectGov: direct.gov.uk.

E2BN ICT in the Early Years: ictearlyyears.e2bn.org.

Family Education: familyeducation.com.

Futurelab: futurelab.org.uk.

GOV.UK: gov.uk.

ICT Coordinator: ictcoordinator.co.uk.

ICT in Education: ictineducation.org.

ICT Teachers: icteachers.co.uk.

Ictopus: ictopus.org.uk.

KidSMART: kidsmart.org.uk. Keeping kids safe online.

Literacy Trust: literacytrust.org.uk.

Logo Programming: mckoss.com/logo.

MathsNet: mathsnet.net.

MoLeNET: molenet.org.uk.

My Primary: heinemann.co.uk/Primary/Primary.aspx.

Naace: naace.co.uk.

NAPE: nape.org.uk. National Association for Primary Education Information available for birth to thirteen years.

National College for Teaching and Leadership: nationalcollege.org.uk.

NEN Education Network: nen.gov.uk.

Nursery World: nurseryworld.co.uk.

OFSTED: ofsted.gov.uk.

Physical Education Update: physicaleducationupdate.com.

Poptropica: poptropica.com.

Primary ICT: primaryict.org.uk.

Qualifications and Curriculum Authority (QCA): qca.org.uk.

Schemes of work: webarchive.nationalarchives.gov.uk/20090608182316/standards.dfes.gov.uk/schemes3.

Schoolsworld TV: schoolsworld.tv.

Schoolzone: http://www.schoolzone.co.uk.

Smart Web Searching: commonsensemedia.org/blog/teach-your-kids-the-secrets-of-smart-web-searching.

Spartacus Educational: spartacus-educational.com.

STEM Centre: nationalstemcentre.org.uk

Swimming: www.swimming.org.

TDA Teacher: tda.co.uk.

Teach ICT: www.teachict.co.uk.

Teacher Vision: teachervision.com.

Teaching Expertise: teachingexpertise.com.

Teaching Ideas: teachingideas.co.uk/ict/contents.htm.

Teaching Times: teachingtimes.com.

TEEM: teemeducation.org.uk/primary.

The Educational Technology Site: ictineducation.org.

Times Educational Supplement (TES Connect): tes.co.uk.

Virtual Teacher: virtual-teacher.co.uk.

Wikipedia: en.wikipedia.org.

Subscription websites

At School: atschool.co.uk.

Brain POP: brainpop.co.uk.

Busy Things: busythings.co.uk.

Charanga Musical School: charanga.com/site/musical-school.

Education City: educationcity.com.

Espresso: espresso.co.uk.

MyMaths: mymaths.co.uk.

Sing Up: singup.org.

Spark Island: sparkisland.com.

What2Learn: what2learn.com.

Interactive whiteboards

Clasus Interactive Smart Board: clasus.com.

Hitachi StarBoard: eu.hitachi-solutions.com.

Mimio Teach: mimio.com

Promethean: prometheanworld.com.

RM Classboard: rmeducation.com.

Smart Tech: smarttech.com.

Interactive whiteboard resources

ABC Teach: abcteach.com/directory/interactive-smart-notebook-files-9606-2-1.

ACCE: cardiffschools.net/~roelmann/whiteboard/smart2.html.

BGFL: bgfl.org/bgfl/15.cfm.

ClassTools: classtools.net.

Crickweb: crickweb.co.uk.

Active Maths: active-maths.co.uk/whiteboard/index.html.

Have Fun Teaching: havefunteaching.com/activities/smartboard-lessons.

Interactive Resources: interactive-resources.co.uk.

Interactive Teaching Resources: iwb.org.uk.

Internet4Classrooms: internet4classrooms.com/smart_board.htm.

Promethean Planet: prometheanplanet.com.

RM Easiteach: easiteach.co.uk.

Scholastic: scholastic.com/Smarttech.

Smart Exchange: exchange.smarttech.com.

Super Teacher Worksheets: superteacherworksheets.com/smartboard.html.

Teachers Love SMART Boards: teacherslovesmartboards.com.

Teachit: teachit.co.uk/notebook.

Teq: teq.com/erc-categories.

The Teacher's Guide: theteachersguide.com/SmartBoards.htm.

Top Marks: topmarks.co.uk/Interactive.aspx.

Apps and iPad resources

Apps4PrimarySchools: apps4primaryschools.co.uk.

Blippit: blippit.co.uk.

Educational Technology & Mobile Learning: educatorstechnology.com.

Innovate my School: innovatemyschool.com/industry-expert-articles/item/166-107-favourite-ipad-apps-for-learning.html.

iPad Apps for School: ipadapps4school.com.

iPad Educators: ipadeducators.com.

Mr Andrews Online: mrandrewsonline.blogspot.co.uk/2012/03/apps-for-primary-education-apps-for.html.

Teach Hub: teachhub.com/20-amazing-ipad-apps-educators.

Teach with your iPad: teachwithyouripad.wikispaces.com.

Learning platforms

Blackboard: blackboard.com.

DB Primary: getprimary.com.

Eschools: eschools.co.uk.

FrogLearn: frogeducation.com.

its Learning: itslearning.com.

Learn Anywhere: learnanywhere.co.uk.

MOODLE: moodle.org, moodle.com and demo.moodle.net.

RM Learning Platform: klp.rm.com.

Studywiz: studywiz.com.
Talk 2 Learn: com.fronter.info.
UniServity: uniservity.com.
Viglen: viglen.co.uk.

Mobile learning

M-Learning: m-learning.org/knowledge-centre/whatismlearning.

Course authoring tools

Centre for Learning & Performance Technologies: c4lpt.co.uk/directory-of-learning-performance-tools.
Wimba Create: wimba.com/products/wimba_create.

Podcasting

Audacity: audacity.sourceforge.net.
BBC Podcasts: bbc.co.uk/podcasts.
iTunes Podcast Resources: apple.com/itunes/podcasts.
Podbean: podbean.com.
Podcasting Tools: podcasting-tools.com.

Social networking

Netmums: netmums.com/teenagers/safe-surfing-on-the-internet/your-children-and-the-internet-social-networking-s.
Social Bookmarking: delicious.com.
SuperClubs: superclubsplus.com.

E-safety

CBBC Stay Safe: bbc.co.uk/cbbc/topics/stay-safe.
CEOP: ceop.police.uk.
Childnet: childnet.com (including Know-It-All: childnet-int.org/kia).
Get Safe Online: getsafeonline.org.
Grid Club: gridclub.com.
HGfL E-Safety: thegrid.org.uk/eservices/safety.
Internet Matters: internetmatters.org.
Kidsmart: kidsmart.org.uk.
NEN E-Safeguarding Audit Tool: northerngrid.org/nen/esg_audit.
Smart Surfers: digitalbirmingham.co.uk/smartsurfers.
Teachers TV: gov.uk/government/publications/teachers-tv.
Thinkuknow: thinkuknow.co.uk.
UKCCIS: gov.uk/government/groups/uk-council-for-child-internet-safety-ukccis.
UK Safer Internet Centre: saferinternet.org.uk.

Video conferencing

British Council – SchoolsOnline: schoolsonline.britishcouncil.org.

HGfL: thegrid.org.uk/learning/ict/technologies/videoconferencing.

LGfL: lgfl.net/services/pages/video-conferencing-teaching-resources.aspx.

Janet: http://www.ed.ac.uk/schools-departments/information-services/computing/comms-and-collab/videoconferencing/recordingservice.

Special educational needs

General

AbilityNet: abilitynet.co.uk. Charity providing advice on adaptive technology.

Ace Centre: ace-centre.org.uk. Help and support for parents and carers.

Adapted Learning: adaptedlearning.com. Free sharing of Boardmaker and other resources.

Advisory Unit: advisory-unit.org.uk. Provides advice, training and technical support for pupils with a range of difficulties.

ASBAH: asbah.org. Information about spina bifida.

Assist – IT: assist-it.org.uk.

Better Living Through Technology: bltt.org. Promotes the use of technology to help people with a range of disabilities.

British Dyslexia Association: bdadyslexia.org.uk.

Claro Training: clarotraining.com. High quality training for people using educational and assistive software.

Communication Matters: communicationmatters.org.uk. Charitable organisation concerned with augmentative and alternative communication.

Equals: equals.co.uk. Promotes, shares and reflects best practice in learning and teaching through collaborative working with practitioners and professionals.

Experia: experia-innovations.co.uk.

First School Years: firstschoolyears.com/sen.

GIFT: giftltd.co.uk. provision for the Exceptionally Able, Gifted and Talented

KidNeeds: kidneeds.com.

Makaton: makaton.org. Communication using signs and symbols.

Mencap: mencap.org.uk. UK charity for people with a learning disability.

Nasen: nasen.org.uk. The national association for special educational needs. Nasen is the leading organisation in the UK which aims to promote the education, training, advancement and development of all those with special and additional support needs.

National Association for SEN: nasen.org.uk.

NCTE: ncte.ie/SpecialNeedsICT. Advice and resources for teachers.

NSGT: nsgt.org. Supporting Gifted Education

Osborne Technologies: osbornetechnologies.co.uk. Sensory classrooms.

Scientific Learning: scilearnglobal.com.

SEN Bookshop: senbooks.co.uk.

SEN Magazine: senmagazine.co.uk. The journal for special needs.

SEN Teacher: senteacher.org. Free SEN teaching resources.

SwitchScanning: switchscanning.org.uk.

Teaching Ideas: teachingideas.co.uk/more/specialneeds/contents.htm.

The School Run: theschoolrun.com/what-enrichment. Enrichment.

Widgit: widgit.com.

Communication

Afasic: afasic.org.uk. Unlocking speech and languages – range of services and information.

Ebooks: ebooks.com. Books in electronic format.

I Can: ican.org.uk. Supports the development of speech, language and communication skills.

Phonics for parents: phonics4parents.co.uk.

Project Gutenberg: gutenberg.org. Free e-books.

Talking Point: talkingpoint.org.uk. All the stages of language development.

The Call Centre: callcentre.education.ed.ac.uk. Expertise in technology for children who have speech, communication and/or writing difficulties.

Dyslexia

British Dyslexia Association: bdadyslexia.org.uk.

Dyslexia: dyslexia.com/library/classroom.htm.

Dyslexia Action: dyslexiaaction.org.uk. Services and support for people with dyslexia and literacy difficulties.

Dyslexic.com: dyslexic.com. Assistive technology website.

Graded book list: dyslexia-inst.org.uk/graded.htm.

Helen Arkell Dyslexia Centre: arkellcentre.org.uk. A registered charity helping those with dyslexia.

SLD Institute of Child Education and Psychology: icepe.eu/dyslexia.html.

Word finding difficulties: wordfinding.com.

Autism

Autism Independent UK: autismuk.com.

Autism Speaks: autismspeaks.org.

Autism Today: autismtoday.com.

National Autistic Society: autism.org.uk.

NHS: nhs.uk/conditions/autistic-spectrum-disorder/Pages/Introduction.aspx.

Open Autism Software: openautismsoftware.org.

Research Autism: researchautism.net.

Scottish Autism: scottishautism.org.

Teach Town: web.teachtown.com.

The National Autistic Society: nas.org.uk. Help, support and services for autistic individuals and families.

Zac Browser Gold: zacbrowser.com.

Behavioural, emotional and social development (BESD)

Adders: adders.org. Promotes awareness of ADD/ADHD.

ADDinSchool: addinschool.com/elementary/socialskills.htm.

Anti-Bullying Network: antibullying.net. Information for parents, pupils and others.

Bullying UK: bullying.co.uk. Registered charity offering advice. Includes mobile phone bullying.

LD Online: ldonline.org . The world's leading website on learning disability and ADHD.

The Good Schools Guide: goodschoolsguide.co.uk.

Down's syndrome

Downsed: dseinternational.org/en-us. Down Syndrome Education International works around the world to improve education for young people with Down syndrome.

Dyscalculia

About Dyscalculia: aboutdyscalculia.org.

BBC Skillswise: bbc.co.uk/skillswise. For information, number fact sheets, work sheets, quizzes and games.

Brain: brainhe.com/staff/types/dyscalculiatext.html.

English as an additional language (EAL)

A4ESL: a4esl.org . For ESL activities.

British Council – Learn English: learnenglish.org.uk . For help, advice and resources.

Discovery Educational Software: discoveryeducationalsoftware.co.uk. Free worksheets.

English Club: englishclub.com/esl-games/index.htm. For ESL games.

ESL Cyber Listening Lab: esl-lab.com. for EAL listening quizzes.

I love languages: ilovelanguages.com. For a guide to languages on the web.

NALDIC: naldic.org.uk. National Association for Language development in the curriculum.

Primary Classroom Resources: primaryclassroomresources.co.uk. For general vocabulary support.

Puzzles: sites such as teach-nology.com and puzzlemaker.com. Allow you to enter word lists and create your own word searches, word puzzles and worksheets.

Teachers–Direct: teachers-direct.co.uk. For lots of SEN resources.

Your Dictionary.com: yourdictionary.com. For online dictionaries in 260 languages.

Gifted and talented

BrightonOnline: (G&T) brightonline.org.uk. G&T resources.

CSIE: csie.org.uk. Centre for Studies on Inclusive Education.

Mensa: mensa.org.uk/gifted-talented. British Mensa Ltd (Junior Branch).

Metagifted: metagifted.org.

NACE: nace.co.uk. National Association for Able Children in Education.

NAGC: nagcbritain.org.uk. National Association for Gifted Children.

Nrich: nrich.maths.org.uk/public/index.php. Problem-solving puzzles for gifted pupils.

Simon Tatham's puzzle collection: chiark.greenend.org.uk/~sgtatham/puzzles.

Visual impairment

RNIB: rnib.org.uk. Royal National Institute of Blind people.

Sight & Sound: sightandsound.co.uk. Solutions for the visually impaired.

Hearing impairment

Action on hearing loss: actiononhearingloss.org.uk.

BATOD: batod.org.uk. The British Association of Teachers of the Deaf.

British Sign Language: british-sign.co.uk.

Dame Hannah and the Magic Carpet: damehannah.com. Dame Hannah Rogers Trust provides education, therapy, care and respite for children and young people with profound physical disabilities.

Deaf Books: deafbooks.co.uk.

NDCS: ndcs.org.uk. National Deaf Children's Society.

Appendix 4
ICT suppliers

You'll find a comprehensive listing on the BETT Show website at bettshow.com.

2Simple Software: 2simple.com. Simple, powerful and creative software.

4Mation: 4mation.co.uk. Motivating, fun and engaging educational software.

AbleNet (SEN): ablenetinc.com. Assistive technology products.

Accelerations Educational Software: dttrainer.com. Autism and other Learning Disabilities.

Assistive Technology (SEN): assistive.co.uk.

Assistiveware (SEN): assistiveware.com. Access and language products.

AVP: avp.co.uk. Supplier of educational resources to schools.

Barry Bennett (SEN): barrybennett.co.uk. Specialist supplier for people with disabilities of all ages.

BESA: besa.org.uk. British Educational Suppliers Association.

BETT: bettshow.com. Largest exhibitor of educational and training technology.

Blazie (SEN): blazie.co.uk. Access technology for blind and partially sighted people.

Blissymbol Communications (SEN): blissymbols.co.uk. A system of meaning-based symbols for people with severe difficulties in speaking.

Blooming Kids (SEN): bloomingkids.com. Teaching software for children with special needs.

Blue Hills (SEN): bluehills.co.uk. Management software for teachers and Local Authorities.

Bluewave Swift: bluewaveswift.co.uk. The ultimate school improvement planning system.

Clasus: clasus.pt. Educational solutions.

Commotion: commotiongroup.co.uk. High quality educational resources.

Cricksoft (SEN): cricksoft.com. Educational software (inc. Clicker 6 and ClozePro).

Data Harvest: data-harvest.co.uk. Data logging and control systems.

DB Primary: dbprimary.com. Learning Platform for primary education.

DCP Microdevelopments: dcpmicro.com. Datalogging and control (inc. LogIT).

Deaf Books (SEN): deafbooks.co.uk. Educational resources from DEAFSIGN.

Deltronics: deltronics.co.uk. Computer control and data logging interfaces.

Digital Blue: digitalblue.org.uk. Cameras, microscopes and other resources.

Dolphin (SEN): dolphinuk.co.uk. Improving the lives of people with vision and print impairments.

Don Johnston (SEN): donjohnston.com. For pupils with physical, cognitive or learning difficulties.

Dynavox (SEN): dynavoxtech.com. Augmentative and alternative communication (AAC) products.

Economatics: economatics-education.co.uk. Effective teaching resources across the curriculum.

Education City: educationcity.com. Leading subscription website used by over 1.5 million pupils.

ESP: espmusic.co.uk. A range of music and computer resources.

Espresso Education: espresso.co.uk. Popular subscription website for Foundation, Key Stage 1 and Key Stage 2.

FineReader (SEN): finereader.abbyy.com. Linguistic and artificial intelligence (AI) software.

Fisher Marriot Software: fishermarriott.com. StarSpell, StarFrench, StarStories and more.

Flexible Software: flexible.co.uk. Software programs for primary schools.

Focus Educational Software: focuseducational.com. Software (inc. Bee-Bot) and Learning Platforms.

Freedom Scientific (SEN): freedomscientific.com. For people with visual impairments (inc. JAWS).

Fronter: com.fronter.info. Learning platform.

FUZE: fuze.co.uk. A programmable computer and electronics workstation.

GL Assessment: gl-assessment.co.uk. A range of online assessments.

Griffin Education: griffin-education.co.uk. Scientific equipment.

Halliday James Ltd (SEN): hallidayjames.com. Cognitive and physical support.

Hope Education: hope-education.co.uk. Teaching resources for Pre-School & Primary.

Horrible Histories: horrible-histories.co.uk.

Humanware (SEN): humanware.com. Assistive technologies for visual impairment and learning difficulties.

iANSYST (SEN): iansyst.co.uk. Assistive Technology and disability services.

TES iBoard: iboard.co.uk. Resources for interactive whiteboards.

IEP Writer: iepwriter.co.uk. Software for producing Individual Education Plans.

Immersive Education: immersiveeducation.eu. A number of resources including Kar2ouche.

Inclusive (SEN): inclusive.co.uk. Provider of some of the best special educational needs software.

Indigo Learning: indigolearning.com. Educational software that is designed to inspire creativity.

iTeddy: iteddy.com. The cuddly way to watch, learn and play.

Jolly Learning: jollylearning.co.uk.

Keen 2 Learn: keen2learn.co.uk. ICT resources for the whole curriculum.

Key Notes: keynoteseducation.com. Resources for the whole curriculum.

Key Tools (SEN): keytools.co.uk. Helping people to use computers without risking their health.

Kurtzweil (SEN): kurzweiledu.com. Complete reading, writing, and study solutions.

LCP: lcp.co.uk/ict-resource-files. Teaching resources.

LD Online (SEN): ldonline.org. The world's leading website on learning disability and ADHD.

Leap Frog: leapfrog.co.uk. Innovative, technology-based educational products.

Learn 2 Soar: learn2soar.co.uk. Helping children to soar to new heights of musical excellence.

Lexion (SEN): lexion.co.uk. A computer-based system for stimulating and training people with language related learning disorders, dyslexia or aphasia.

Liberator (SEN): liberator.co.uk. A wide range of products, training and support for communication, inclusion and independence.

Listening books (SEN): listening-books.org.uk. The national listening library.

Logotron: logotron.co.uk. A leading supplier of educational software to schools.

Lucid Research (SEN): lucid-research.com. Software for SEN assessment and training.

Maltron PDC (SEN): maltron.com. Enabling keyboard access to computers.

Mayer-Johnson (SEN): mayer-johnson.com. Enhancing learning and human expression for individuals with special needs through symbol-based products, training and services.

Microlink Education (SEN): microlinkpc.com. Technology to help with learning difficulties.

Mike Ayres (SEN): mikeayresdesign.co.uk. Multi-sensory and soft play provision.

MOODLE: moodle.org, moodle.com. Moodle is an open source learning platform.

Mouse Trial (SEN): mousetrial.com. Fun animated online exercises to help kids with autism.

Netop: netop.com. Classroom management software.

NVDA (SEN): nvda-project.org. A free and open source screen reader.

Optelec (SEN): optelec.co.uk. Solutions for people with a visual impairment.

Orb Education: orbeducation.co.uk. A variety of digital teaching resources.

Page One: Mobile technology and text messaging service.

Pearson: pearsonschool.com. Technology products, solutions and support (inc. SuccessMaker).

Penfriend (SEN): penfriend.ltd.uk. Literacy aid for those with dyslexia, physical disabilities, visual impairment and anyone learning another language.

Philip Harris: philipharris.co.uk. Science equipment for schools.

Phrogram: phrogram.com. Programming for children.

Possum (SEN): possum.co.uk. A range of products to enhance the independence and quality of life for people with special needs.

Professional Vision (SEN): Services professional-vision-services.co.uk. Visual aids for the blind and visually impaired.

Promethean: prometheanworld.com. Leading interactive whiteboard provider.

Raising Horizons (SEN): raisinghorizons.com. Training materials for people with learning difficulties.

REM: r-e-m.co.uk. A well-established company offering resources and services.

Resource (SEN): resourcekt.co.uk. Software resources across the curriculum and key stages.

Rising Stars: risingstars-uk.com. An independent publishing company.

RM: rm.com Wide range of popular ICT resources plus the RM Classboard interactive whiteboard.

Schoolzone: schoolzone.co.uk. Teacher support and evaluation of educational multimedia.

ScienceScope: sciencescope.co.uk. Sensing and data logging for science education.

ScreenReader (SEN): screenreader.co.uk. Assistive technology for the blind and visually impaired.

SEMERC: semerc.com. Software and tools for inclusion.

Sensory Company (SEN): thesensorycompany.co.uk. A wide range of sensory products.

Sensory Software (SEN): sensorysoftware.com. Augmentative and Alternative Communication.

Sensory Technology (SEN): senteq.co.uk. Multi-sensory technology.

Serotec (SEN): serotek.com. Accessibility products that help those who are blind or low vision.

Sherston Software: sherston.com. Leading provider of educational software for primary schools.

Sight and Sound (SEN): sightandsound.co.uk. Solutions for the blind and visually impaired.

Sirius: siriusit.co.uk. Provider of free and open source software services to schools.

Skoog Music: skoogmusic.com. Provider of the Skoog musical instrument.

Smartkids: smartkids.co.uk. Educational games and resources.

SmartLearning: smart-learning.co.uk.

Smarttech: smarttech.com. Producers of the Smartboard and related products.

Social Skill Builder: socialskillbuilder.com. Social skills software & curriculum.

Soundbeam (SEN): www.soundbeam.co.uk. For special needs and music therapy.

Soundlinks (SEN): soundlinks.com. Sound solutions for music and speech.

Spark Space (SEN): spark-space.com. Software products for education.

Studywiz: studywiz.com. Learning environment for schools.

Sparklebox: sparklebox.co.uk.co.uk. Computing/ICT teaching resources.

Synapse (SEN): synapseadaptive.com. A range of SEN products.

TAG (SEN): taglearning.com. Educational software for schools.

Teachable: teachable.net. Teaching resources.

Teach IT Primary: teachitprimary.co.uk. Online library of learning resources.

Team Asperger (SEN): ccoder.com/GainingFace. Software to help people with Asperger's syndrome.

TEEM: teemeducation.org.uk. Teachers Evaluating Educational Multimedia.

TextHelp (SEN): texthelp.com. Worldwide leader of literacy software solutions.

The Keyboard Company (SEN): keyboardco.com. Keyboard and mouse specialists in the UK.

Thomson Software Solutions: thomson-software-solutions.com. Leading supplier of software for vision testing and screening in the UK.

Toby Churchill (SEN): toby-churchill.com. Communication aids and environmental control.

Topologika: topologika.co.uk. Educational software for school and home.

TTS: tts-group.co.uk. Educational supplies.

Twinkl: twinkl.co.uk. Primary resources.

UniServity: uniservity.com. A learning platform providing learners with social learning tools.

Valiant Technology: valiant-technology.com. Educational robots.

Viglen: viglen.co.uk. Total ICT teaching and learning solutions.

Visual Learning for Life (SEN): skillsforlearning.net. Stimulating visual perceptual skills.

White Space (SEN): wordshark.co.uk. Literacy and numeracy software for pupils and dyslexics.

Widgit (SEN): widgit.com. Symbol based software.

Worksheet Factory: worksheetfactory.com. Printable worksheets.

Zig Zag Education: zigzageducation.co.uk.

Appendix 5
Evaluation sheets

Software evaluation sheet

Software Title: _____

Supplier: _____

Summary of resource: give a brief overview of how the resource works and the things it can do.

National Curriculum: what curriculum area/topic does it cover; can it help to satisfy the specific curriculum aims and objectives which you might include in your lesson plans?

Content: is information accurate and factual; is there any unnecessary cultural or moral bias; is the content acceptable in terms of the quantity and the balance of text, images and sound?

Currency: is it up to date; is it the most recent version available; when was it published?

Reading age: is vocabulary, structure and sentence length suitable for the intended age range; does it have a built-in dictionary; are there differentiated versions of text, is text supported with images or audio?

User interface: is it easy for the user to interact with the software; is it clear what to press or click; is there any on-screen help available; what is the quality of illustrations; can you alter colours and sizes of text or images?

Indexing: is there a menu or table of contents; is there an index; is it easy to navigate; is the program easy to enter and exit?

Presentation: is the information structured in a logical order; is it visually stimulating?

Facilities: is the software easy to install with clear instructions; are there print/save options; is there a bookmark facility; does the package keep records of a child's progress; are there any additional motivating features (e.g. hidden cues)?

Differentiation: are different levels/options available for use with children with different abilities; does the software automatically adjust to the level of the child or does an adult have to alter the settings; how easy is it to alter the settings; does it support SEN?

Assessment: does it have built-in assessment instruments?

Diversity: does it enable creativity, collaboration and flexibility; can it be used in more than one topic area?

Any other comments:

Hardware evaluation sheet

Hardware Title: _____

Supplier: _____

Summary of resource: give a brief overview of how the resource works and the things it can do.

National Curriculum: what curriculum area/topics does it potentially cover; can it help to satisfy the specific curriculum aims and objectives which you might include in some of your lesson plans?

Currency: is it the most up-to-date version; is it a contemporary resource?

Reading age: is vocabulary, structure and sentence length of supporting children's materials suitable for the intended age range/ability of the child?

User interface: is it easy for the user (teacher and children) to use the resource; are there any instructions; are these comprehensive?

Visual effect: does the appearance of the resource provide motivation/stimulation?

Differentiation: are different levels/options available for use with children with different abilities and SEN?

Assessment: does it have built-in assessment instruments?

Diversity: does it enable creativity, collaboration and flexibility; can it be used in more than one topic area?

Any other comments:

Website evaluation sheet

Name of website (include address) _____

Activity: _____

Summary of website: give a brief overview of what the website provides.

National Curriculum: what curriculum area/topic does it cover; can it help to satisfy the specific curriculum aims and objectives which you might include in your lesson plans?

Content: is information accurate and factual; is there any unnecessary cultural or moral bias; is the content acceptable in terms of the quantity and the balance of text, images and sound?

Currency: is it up to date; is it the most recent version available; when was it published?

Reading age: is vocabulary, structure and sentence length suitable for the intended age range; does it have a built-in dictionary; are there differentiated versions of text; is text supported with images or audio?

Differentiation: are different levels/options available for use with children with different abilities; does the software automatically adjust to the level of the child or does an adult have to alter the settings; how easy is it to alter the settings; does it support SEN?

Assessment: does it have built-in assessment instruments?

Indexing: is there a menu or table of contents; is it easy to navigate; are there useful hyperlinks?

Presentation: is the information structured in a logical order; is it visually stimulating; is good use made of web page layout; are frames used effectively?

Authority: reputation of publisher; author's identity, qualifications; source.

Stability: how often does web page content change; will the site still be there next week?

Any other comments

References

BBC (2013) *Swansea tablet computer project boosts pupils' reading* available from the Internet at bbc.co.uk/news/uk-wales-22806246 [accessed 22/6/14].

Berry, M. (2013) *Computing in the national curriculum: A guide for primary teachers* available from the Internet at http://www.computingatschool.org.uk/data/uploads/CASPrimaryComputing.pdf.

Brainfingers (2014) *Brainfingers: Hands free computer control* available from the Internet at brainfingers.com [accessed 6/7/14].

Brunton, P. and Thornton, L. (2005) *Understanding the Reggio Approach* London: David Fulton.

Cairns, G. (2008) *Brain boxes: How digital technology can improve maths scores* available from the Internet at independent.co.uk/news/education/schools/brain-boxes-how- digital-technology-can-improve-maths-scores-993741.html [accessed 24/11/08].

Clements, R. and Fiorentina, L. (2004) *The Child's Right to Play* Portsmouth, NH: Greenwood Press.

DfE (2013) *English programmes of study: key stages 1 and 2* available from the Internet at gov.uk/government/publications/national-curriculum-in-england-english-programmes-of-study [accessed 26/5/14].

DfE (2014a) *Computing programmes of study: key stages 1 and 2* DFE-00171-2013.

DfE (2014b) *Statutory Framework for the Early Years Foundation Stage* DFE-00337-2014.

DfE (2015) *Special Educational Needs Code of Practice: 0 to 25 years* DFE-00205-2013

Education Business (2014) *Finding the funds for ICT* available from the Internet at educationbusinessuk. net/index.php/features/5-/2463-finding-the-funds-for-ict [accessed 14/6/14].

Garagouni-Areou, F. and Solomonidou, C. (2004) Towards the design of educational environments suitable to the needs of pupils with attention deficit hyperactivity disorder (ADHD) symptoms in Cantoni, L. and McLoughlin, C. (eds), *Proceedings of World Conference on Educational Multimedia, Hypermedia and Telecommunications 2004* (pp. 4446–4451), Wainesville, NC: AACE.

Harris, A. (2014) *Distributed Leadership Matters* Thousand Oaks, CA: Corwin.

McLeish, J. (2008) 'Virtual boost for literacy skills' *Times Education Supplement*, 25 April.

Montessori, M. (2007) *The Montessori Method* New York: BN Publishing.

National Autistic Society (2006) *Computers: applications for people with autism* available from the Internet at http://www.nas.org.uk [accessed 7/5/15].

National Curriculum (2014) *National curriculum in England: computing programmes of study* available from the Internet at gov.uk/government/publications/national-curriculum-in-england-computing-programmes-of-study/national-curriculum-in-england-computing-programmes-of-study [accessed 20/5/14].

NCCA (2004) *Information and Communications Technology (ICT) in the Primary School Curriculum: Guidelines for Teachers* Dublin: NCCA.

NHS (2007) *Autistic Spectrum Disorder* available from the Internet at http://www.nhs.uk/Conditions/Autistic-spectrum-disorder/Pages/ Introduction.aspx?url=Pages/What-is-it.aspx&r=1&rtitle=Autistic+ spectrum+disorder+-+Introduction [accessed 7/5/15].

NEN (2014) *The History of NEN* available from the Internet at nen.gov.uk/aboutus/6/the-history-of-nen.html [accessed 21/5/14].

Politics.co.uk (2013) *Michael Gove's 'anti-Mr Men' speech* available from the Internet at politics.co.uk/comment-analysis/2013/05/09/michael-gove-s-anti-mr-men-speech-in-full [accessed 20/6/14].

PRWeb (2013) *Free the musician inside: The Skoog launches on the Apple Store* available from the Internet at uk.prweb.com/releases/2013/11/prweb11362531.htm [accessed 11/7/14].

Rose, J. (2009) *Independent Review of the Primary Curriculum* available from the Internet at http://www.educationengland.org.uk/documents/pdfs/2009-IRPC-final-report.pdf [accessed 20/5/14].

Scholastic (2014) *100 things to do with a digital camera* available from the Internet at scholastic.com/teachers/lesson-plan/100-ways-use-digital-cameras [accessed 30/5/14].

SEN Code of Practice (2014) *Special educational needs and disability code of practice: 0 to 25 years* available from the Internet at https://www.gov.uk/government/uploads/system/uploads/attachment_data/file/398815/SEND_Code_of_Practice_January_2015.pdf [accessed 7/5/15].

Sparrowhawk, A. and Heald, Y. (2007) *How to Use ICT to Support Children with Special Educational Needs* Cambridge: LDA.

Soundtree (2014) *Soundbeam 5* available from the Internet at soundtree.com/Soundbeam [accessed 6/7/14].

Vygotsky, L.S. (1978) *Mind in Society: Development of Psychological Processes* Cambridge, MA: Harvard University Press.

Index

eBooks
from Taylor & Francis

Helping you to choose the right eBooks for your Library

Add to your library's digital collection today with Taylor & Francis eBooks. We have over 50,000 eBooks in the Humanities, Social Sciences, Behavioural Sciences, Built Environment and Law, from leading imprints, including Routledge, Focal Press and Psychology Press.

Choose from a range of subject packages or create your own!

Benefits for you

- Free MARC records
- COUNTER-compliant usage statistics
- Flexible purchase and pricing options
- All titles DRM-free.

Benefits for your user

- Off-site, anytime access via Athens or referring URL
- Print or copy pages or chapters
- Full content search
- Bookmark, highlight and annotate text
- Access to thousands of pages of quality research at the click of a button.

Free Trials Available
We offer free trials to qualifying academic, corporate and government customers.

eCollections

Choose from over 30 subject eCollections, including:

Archaeology	Language Learning
Architecture	Law
Asian Studies	Literature
Business & Management	Media & Communication
Classical Studies	Middle East Studies
Construction	Music
Creative & Media Arts	Philosophy
Criminology & Criminal Justice	Planning
Economics	Politics
Education	Psychology & Mental Health
Energy	Religion
Engineering	Security
English Language & Linguistics	Social Work
Environment & Sustainability	Sociology
Geography	Sport
Health Studies	Theatre & Performance
History	Tourism, Hospitality & Events

For more information, pricing enquiries or to order a free trial, please contact your local sales team:
www.tandfebooks.com/page/sales

www.tandfebooks.com